The Soldier and the State in South America

Latin American Studies Series

General Editors: **Philip O'Brien** and **Peter Flynn**

The series is an initiative designed to give a comprehensive analysis of some of the many complex problems facing contemporary Latin America and individual Latin American countries.

Titles include:

Rob Aitken, Nikki Craske, Gareth A. Jones and David E. Stansfield (*editors*)
DISMANTLING THE MEXICAN STATE?

Miguel A. Centeno and Patricio Silva (*editors*)
THE POLITICS OF EXPERTISE IN LATIN AMERICA

David E. Hojman (*editor*)
NEO-LIBERAL AGRICULTURE IN RURAL CHILE

Dermot Keogh (*editor*)
CHURCH AND STATE IN LATIN AMERICA

Peter Lambert and Andrew Nickson (*editors*)
THE TRANSITION TO DEMOCRACY IN PARAGUAY

Patricio Silva (*editor*)
THE SOLDIER AND THE STATE IN SOUTH AMERICA
Essays in Civil–Military Relations

David Slater
TERRITORY AND STATE POWER IN LATIN AMERICA
The Peruvian Case

Latin American Studies Series
Series Standing Order ISBN 0–333–71483–0
(*outside North America only*)

You can receive future titles in this series as they are published by placing a standing order. Please contact your bookseller or, in case of difficulty, write to us at the address below with your name and address, the title of the series and the ISBN quoted above.

Customer Services Department, Macmillan Distribution Ltd, Houndmills, Basingstoke, Hampshire RG21 6XS, England

The Soldier and the State in South America

Essays in Civil–Military Relations

Edited by

Patricio Silva
Lecturer in Political Sociology
Leiden University
The Netherlands

First published 2001 by
PALGRAVE
Houndmills, Basingstoke, Hampshire RG21 6XS and
175 Fifth Avenue, New York, N.Y. 10010
Companies and representatives throughout the world

PALGRAVE is the new global academic imprint of
St. Martin's Press LLC Scholarly and Reference Division and
Palgrave Publishers Ltd (formerly Macmillan Press Ltd).

ISBN 0–333–93093–2

This book is printed on paper suitable for recycling and
made from fully managed and sustained forest sources.

A catalogue record for this book is available
from the British Library.

Library of Congress Cataloging-in-Publication Data
The soldier and the state in South America : essays in civil–military
relations / edited by Patricio Silva.
       p. cm. — (Latin American studies series)
    Includes bibliographical references and index.
    ISBN 0–333–93093–2
    1. Civil–military relations—South America. I. Silva, Patricio. II. Latin
    American studies series (New York, N.Y.)
    JL1856.C58 S65 2000
    322'.5'098—dc21
                                                              00–048354

10   9   8   7   6   5   4   3   2   1
10   09 08 07 06 05 04 03 02 01

Printed and bound in Great Britain by
Antony Rowe Ltd, Chippenham, Wiltshire

Contents

Preface

After a long era of military rule, the South American nations have initiated the paramount task of constructing a new democratic order. Since then several institutional and legal transformations have taken place in an attempt to eradicate the authoritarian legacy left by former military regimes. Over the past years a broad consensus has arisen about the need to thoroughly reformulate the traditional patterns of civil–military relations in order to prevent future authoritarian regressions. This requires, among other things, the realization of a long-term historical assessment about what have been the main features of civil–military relations from Independence until the current process of democratic consolidation.

This volume is the outcome of the international conference 'The Soldier and the State in South America', held in Leiden, The Netherlands, on 24–25 October 1997. During that academic event, a group of scholars from Europe, Latin America and the United States came together to discuss from a long-term perspective on some key aspects of civil–military relations in South America, with special emphasis on the cases of Argentina, Brazil, Chile and Peru.

I am especially indebted to Hans Vogel from Leiden University who co-organized the conference and with whom I very much enjoyed all the facets of this common academic project. Special thanks go also to Phil O'Brien for his constant encouragement and useful comments during the entire editing process. I also want to acknowledge the generous financial support provided to this event by the Leiden University Fund (LUF), the Dutch Royal Academy of Sciences (KNAW), and the Centre for Non-Western Studies (CNWS) in Leiden. The production of the book went smoothly thanks to Alison Howson and her staff at the publishers. I also thank Keith Povey who meticulously copy-edited the book. Finally, I want to express my gratitude to the Netherlands Institute for Advanced Study (NIAS) at Wassenaar which provided me an excellent working place during the 1998–99 academic year, and particularly to Anne Simpson who revised the entire manuscript in search of linguistic errors.

Notes on the Contributors

Paul Cammack is Professor of Political Science at the Department of Government, University of Manchester. He is the author of numerous articles and contributions to books on South American politics. He is also the author of *Capitalism and Democracy in the Third World* (1997) and co-editor of *Generals in Retreat: The Crisis of Military Rule in Latin America* (1985) and *Third World Politics* (1993).

Celso Castro is researcher at the Fundação Getulio Vargas/CPDOC, Rio de Janeiro, Brazil. He is author of several books on the military in Brazilian history and society, including *O Espírito Militar* (1990) and *Os Militares e a Republica* (1995) and co-editor of the trilogy on the military regime (1964–85) in Brazil *Visões do Golpe, Os Anos de Chumbo* and *A Volta aos Quartéis* (1994 and 1995) and the interview *Ernesto Geisel* (1997).

Kees Koonings is Lecturer in Development Studies at the Department of Anthropology, Utrecht University. His research has dealt with the politics of (regional) industrial development, and the political role of the military, especially in Brazil. He is the author of *Industrialization, Industrialists and Regional Development in Brazil* (1994) and co-editor of *Societies of Fear: The Legacy of Civil War, Violence and Terror in Latin America* (1999).

Frederick M. Nunn is Professor of History and International Studies, and Vice Provost for International Affairs at Portland State University, USA. He has published a number of books and articles on comparative civil–military relations, including *The Time of the Generals: Latin American Professional Militarism in World Perspective* (1992). He is the editor of the English translation of José Victorino Lastarria's *Literary Memoirs* (2000).

George Philip is Reader in Comparative and Latin American Politics and Director of the Argentina Programme at the London School of Economics and Political Science. He has written recent articles on populism, presidentialism and democracy in Latin America, and has published many articles and contributed to several books. He is also the author of *The Rise and Fall of the Peruvian Military Radicals* (1978) and *The Military in South American Politics* (1986).

Antonius C.G.M. Robben is Professor of Anthropology at the Department of Cultural Anthropology at Utrecht University, the Netherlands. He is the author of *Sons of the Sea Goddess: Economic Practice and Discursive Conflict in Brazil* (1989) and co-editor of *Fieldwork under Fire: Contemporary Studies in Violence and Survival* (1995) and *Cultures under Siege: Collective Violence and Trauma in Interdisciplinary Perspectives* (1999).

Francisco Rojas Aravena is Director of FLACSO-Chile and co-Director of the Program Peace and Security in the Americas. He is also Professor at the Instituto de Estudios Internacionales of the Universidad de Chile and at the University of Stanford in Santiago. He is author and editor of several books, including *Balance Estratégico y Medidas de Confianza Mutua* (1996); *Gasto Militar en América Latina: Procesos de Decisiones y Actores Claves* (1994).

Patricio Silva is Lecturer in Political Sociology at the Institute of Social and Cultural Studies, Leiden University, The Netherlands. His recent research has focused on democratization processes in the Southern Cone and the technocratization of the political arena in several countries in the region. He is the author of *Estado, neoliberalismo y política agraria en Chile, 1973–1981* (1987) and co-editor of *Designers of Development: Intellectuals and Technocrats in the Third World* (1995) and *The Politics of Expertise in Latin America* (1998).

Hans Vogel is Lecturer in Latin American History at the Department of Latin American Studies and the Department of History, Leiden University, The Netherlands. His research has been mainly focused on the nineteenth-century history of the La Plata region and the military history of South America. He is the author of *Een wereld in oorlog: militaire geschiedenis in hoofdstukken* (*A World in War: Main Episodes of Military History*, 1995) and *Geschiedenis van Latijns-Amerika* (*A History of Latin America*, 1997).

1
The Soldier and the State in South America: Introduction

Patricio Silva

The detention of General Pinochet in London in October 1998 and its political consequences has dramatically illustrated the fragile nature of current civil–military relations in many South American nations. This event generated a veritable political earthquake in Chile as it forcefully brought the painful authoritarian past to the center of the national political debate. As was almost inevitable, in other South American countries the 'Pinochet affair' also revived the discussion about their own recent authoritarian past and the still very sensitive question of human rights abuses committed by the military during the 1970s and early 1980s. Needless to say, this has resulted in increasing tensions between the armed institutions, the political authorities and the civil population.

In the 1980s many had expected that the re-establishment of civilian rule would gradually lead towards increasing normalization of civil–military relations. The idea was that with the passing of time urgent issues about the present and the future of these countries would help people to forget the deep cleavages of the past. The fact is that today these deep divisions between the military and the civilian world still remain. The clearest expression of this lies in the existence of two conflicting and mutually excluding readings about the recent authoritarian past. On the one hand, the military and their civilian supporters in countries like Argentina, Uruguay and Chile argue that the armed forces actually saved their nations from complete chaos and disintegration. On the other, the left and human rights organizations blame the armed forces for having destroyed the old democratic system and for the systematic use of state terrorism against their opponents. The passing of time has definitely not reduced the enormous breach existing between these two interpretations. On the contrary, they seem to have become virtually petrified as neither of the contending sectors are willing to change a single word in their versions of their countries' recent political history.

Despite the existence of these tensions, the probabilities of an authoritarian regression in the region have been substantially reduced during the 1990s. The reasons for this, however, have not always been a direct accomplishment of the new democracies themselves. So, for instance, the almost complete disappearance of the revolutionary left has eliminated one of the main grounds on which the armed forces attempted to legitimize their military coups in the past. While a large part of the left has adopted social-democratic positions and showed a strong commitment to the preservation of democratic rule, in some countries the military has consciously chosen to remain outside contingent politics and to concentrate their attention on the further modernization of their institutions (cf. Millet and Gold-Biss, 1996). In addition, following the end of the cold war, the United States seems no longer disposed to support military coups in the region, as they made clear to the military which deposed President Jean-Bertrand Aristide in Haiti in September 1991 and to seditious officers threatening Paraguay's fragile democracy in April 1996. Since the late 1980s, US foreign policy towards Latin America has begun to give importance to the countries' human rights performances, the achievement of good government, and the consolidation of democratic rule (cf. Wiarda, 1990).

Nevertheless, it is still too early to say that the South American armed forces have fully accepted their institutional subordination *vis-à-vis* the civilian authorities in their countries. It has been said, for instance, that today the Peruvian army co-governs the country. In Chile, the armed forces still maintain a strong presence in strategic political institutions such as the state security council and even in the Senate where they have even constituted their own 'bench' (the so-called *bancada militar*). Also in countries like Paraguay the armies continue to have a strong influence in national political events, while in Venezuela a possible intervention by the military in political events has not yet been completely dissipated. In short, most of the new democracies have so far been unable to fully eliminate the 'authoritarian enclaves' left by the former authoritarian regimes in the form of non-democratic legislation and special attributions for the armed forces (cf. Goodman, Mendelson and Rial, 1990; Fitch, 1998).

In the coming years, poor management of the country's affairs (*desgobierno*) and conspicuous corruption will remain serious threats to the new democracies, as the destitution of president Abdala Bucaram in Ecuador in February 1997 eloquently demonstrated. That situation gave an opportunity for the army to play a decisive role in forcing him to abandon power and, at that critical moment, a coup d'état was clearly among the possible outcomes of the crisis. The legitimacy provided by democratic procedures towards elected authorities is certainly not enough to guarantee the support of the people under any circumstance. What many democracies still have to prove to the citizenry is that this form of government is more efficient and successful in economic terms, and more sensible from the perspective of social justice than had been the case during the previous authoritarian regimes. The cases of Bolivia and Venezuela indicate that the population is even disposed to elect ex-putschist military leaders such as the former General Hugo Banzer and the former Lieutenant Colonel Hugo Chávez as presidents. The people have put their hopes on a 'strong man' who is expected to eliminate criminality and corruption and to provide the economic prosperity that traditional democratic forces have so far been unable to achieve.

The beginning of the twenty-first century is an excellent moment to look back in time and to have some long-term reflections about what has been the nature of the civil–military relations in the region since its independence from Spain in the early nineteenth century. This will allow us to escape from the high degree of historical fragmentation which until now has characterized the study of civil–military relations in South America. Most of the existing studies are generally circumscribed to one of the following five periods; the process of nation-building in the early nineteenth century; the so-called liberal reforms of the 1870s; the socioeconomic and political turmoil during the 1930 depression; the military regimes of the 1960s and 1970s; and, finally, the contemporary democratic era. In this book an attempt is made to transcend these historic subdivisions by trying to identify some main historical continuities and changes, as well as regional commonalties and differences in the patterns of civil–military relations.

Frederick M. Nunn, in Chapter 2, examines the important role played by the professionalization of the armed forces in shaping the type of relations between the military and civilians in Latin America since the late nineteenth century. The political role of the Latin American armies during most of the nineteenth century was not an exclusive feature of this region. Also in Europe at that time, the French and German armies in particular displayed a clear disposition to participate in major political events in one way or another. In addition, the subsequent professionalization of Western European armies also became models for several programs of modernization of South American armies. Nunn argues that in order to fully understand the current political role of the army, much attention has to be paid to the past where the roots of these actions lie. Although he recognizes the existence of some similar patterns in the political orientation of the military in the continent, he stresses the need to look at the marked differences also to be found among the armies' histories in the different countries. These differences are not only internally configured, but external influences in the process of military professionalization have also been critical. The professionalization of many South American armies at the beginning of the twentieth century helped the military institutions to elaborate the idea that they constituted not only the main defence of national territorial integrity, but were the main protectors of inalienable national values. So, from this perspective, the active political role adopted by the military in several South American countries during the 1960s and early 1970s cannot be seen solely as the product of the cold war and the Cuban revolution. It, in fact, primarily represents the culmination of numerous decades of lessons in the self-assigned roles in internal affairs. Looking at the future, Nunn foresees that the South American armies will continue to show their interest in national politics and developments as they have always done in the recent past. The same element of continuity is expected in relation to foreign military influences, as they are not a thing of the past and hence they will continue to play a role in the technical and doctrinaire orientation of South American armies in the years ahead.

Historical continuities in the nature of civil–military relations can also be found between the late colonial period and the post-independence era. Hans Vogel, for instance, in Chapter 3, stresses the distinct legacy of the late colonial period (like the Ordenanzas of Charles III of 1768) in the organization and training of the South American armies following Independence. In their turn, during the late colonial period Spanish military doctrines were strongly influenced by Prussia and France.

The war of independence and subsequent wars during the nineteenth century were of immense importance for the organization of society and the shaping of a sense of nation in several South American societies. In the case of Chile, for example, the unbroken military struggle between the Spanish army and the Araucano Indians almost completely dominated the national institutional and administrative scene for more than three centuries. Independence did not significally change this situation. The military conquest of the Araucanía region – which became a major national objective for the new Chilean army – was only accomplished in the late nineteenth century.

The weakness of the South American national states during most of the nineteenth century was evident, as the authority of the central state could not be effectively imposed within their entire national territories. So the army became the instrument par excellence used by the oligarchic regimes to crush separatist movements of the interior and to defend the national boundaries. But wars were also crucial for the South American armies in the subsequent construction of their own 'glorias militares', heroes and myths. The *hazañas* and victories during the War of Independence and following wars (such as the Paraguayan War of 1864–70 and the War of the Pacific in the early 1880s) provided the raw materials for the shaping of their own image and for the formulation of their self-imposed 'mission' in society.

Celso Castro, in Chapter 4, focuses on what has been another important function of most South American armies in society: the socialization of the young and the poor and the dissemination among them of modern practices and values. He describes in full detail the state of affairs in the Military Academy of Rio de Janeiro in the final years of the Empire and the beginning of the Republican era, portraying the Military Academy as an 'isle of modernity' amid a very traditional society. So while Brazilian society was still impregnated by the aristocratic spirit of the old monarchic system, the professionalizing Brazilian army embraced the ethos of personal merit.

The Military Academy of Rio de Janeiro was organized following modern forms of bureaucracy, in which a meritocratic system determined promotion by rewarding talent and dedication. The *mocidade militar*, the military youngsters, were the direct product of this new way of looking at Brazil and its position in the broader world. The aims of change and progress brought many among them to embrace the republican cause and to actively participate in the 1889 coup that put an end to monarchy. Making use of several archives Castro reconstructs the lives, hopes and frustrations of the youngsters in the Military Academy of Rio de Janeiro, who were united by a strong *esprit de corps*. The modernity of the Brazilian army was reflected in its strong defence of 'scientificism', which was seen as a method to obtain solutions for military and societal problems by technical and scientific means. So the Academy was literally seen by the youngsters as a 'Tabernacle of Science'.

The military's emphasis on the modernizing potential of mathematics and science was also directed against the legal profession that controlled the traditional political class. Following the establishment of the Republic, many military youngsters experienced an astonishing career occupying important positions in society. In the first decades of the twentieth century the army continued its process of modernization marked, as in other South American countries, by strong European influences. Many of the former youngsters of the Military Academy were later members of the *Tenentismo* movement and participated in the 1930 revolution. According to Castro, both the fall of the monarchy and the revolution of 1930 represent two decisive experiences for the later evolution of the Brazilian army, which also played a role in their involvement in politics following the fall of João Goulart in 1964.

But when the military enters into politics, politics also penetrate the military institutions. As George Philip argues in Chapter 5, the political role of the army represented a distinctive feature of the political system in South America in the period 1925–82. The interrelation between the military and civilian political forces during this period was such that Philip does not hesitate to talk about the existence of a civil–military system. Critical for the functioning of this system was the alternation in power between civilian governments and military regimes, marking a pendulum movement between authoritarianism and democratic rule. In addition, most of the political interventions of the South American armies has been accompanied by the demand of certain civilian sectors to bring down the government or even the entire existing political order.

Until the early 1970s the inability of civilian governments to control inflation or deal successfully with serious social and economic crises were often sufficient reasons for the army to take power. The interesting question is then why, since the latest restoration of democracy in the 1980s, the military have not retaken the old path of open political interventionism despite the deep financial and political crisis many countries have been experiencing ever since. According to Philip, both the overall social modernization experienced by South American societies during the past decades – expressed among other aspects in expanded levels of urbanization – and international factors such as the ending of the cold war have produced a decisive shift in the political consciousness of the population. Today there exists a general awareness that big national problems cannot be solved by simply changing the nature of the political system but require the achievement of broad consensus among the major social and political actors.

In Chapter 6, Patricio Silva explores a common feature of most of the South American military governments of the 1960s and 1970s – the ample presence of civilian technocrats in charge of economic decision-making. The question is how to explain the chemistry or 'elected affinity' existing between the military men and civilian technocrats? For this purpose, Silva explores a series of commonalties which can be found in the 'world vision' of both actors, such as the possession of a meritocratic ethos, an admiration for modernity and technological change, and a strong aversion towards party politics and mass participation. Nevertheless, the existence of these common features is certainly not sufficient to explain the actual constitutions of techno-military alliances. He particularly stresses the decisive role played by very specific political and economic circumstances in facilitating the 'marriage' between the army and these technocrats. So, according to Silva, the existence of severe economic and political crises in the past not only provoked the military to take power, but it often also produced a general 'anti-politics mood' among the population which facilitated the ascendancy of technocrats who were expected to be able to adopt technical and apolitical policies. Silva also argues that this elected affinity between the military and civilian technocrats already existed in the early decades of the twentieth century and hence represents a continuous feature in the way the military view technicians and civilians with scientific knowledge. For this purpose he compares the military government of Colonel Ibáñez (1927–31) with the Pinochet regime (1973–89) in Chile, showing a series of striking resemblances in the ways both military leaders established an alliance with civilian technocrats.

But what is certainly one of the most salient and painful characteristics of the military interventions during the 1970s were the severe and systematic human rights abuses committed by the military institutions against the civil population. In this respect, the Argentine 'dirty war' symbolizes the state terror imposed by the military in the Southern Cone countries that resulted in the disappearance of thousands of political opponents. In Chapter 7, Antonius Robben examines how the attempt by the Argentine army to silence the political opposition through the weapon of disappearance produced a powerful moral reaction from the victims' relatives. The weekly protests of the mothers of the Plaza de Mayo in front of the Casa Colorada presidential palace invigorated a moral indignation among important sectors of Argentine society demanding the right of parents to know the whereabouts of their children. The human need of parents to bury their dead offspring powered their struggle to at least obtain their bodies from the military authorities. As Robben points out, the practice of disappearance followed by the Argentine juntas has deeply affected civil–military relations until today. The same can be said for Chile and Uruguay, where the continuous refusal of the military to provide full information about the final location of their victims' remains continues to be a major obstacle in the achievement of a sustainable national reconciliation.

The fact that most of the arrests took place in the victims' own homes violated the sanctity of those homes. With this action, the military transgressed a very important social, material and symbolic barrier common to all Latin societies. The violation of the most intimate and private domain profoundly damaged the trust of the citizens in the state which, after many years of democratic restoration, has not yet been completely repaired.

The mothers' protest placed the military in serious trouble as the latter had always publicly prized the role of motherhood and family values in society. By placing motherhood at the center of their struggle, the mothers of the Plaza de Mayo successfully managed to reveal to the entire Argentine public the repressive and patriarchal nature of the state. This study makes clear that the question of the military's human rights abuses has created very profound wounds in the soul of society which will require a very long period of time to heal.

Kees Koonings, in Chapter 8, analyses the constitution of the army as a political actor in Brazil and the specific ways factionalism within the armed forces influenced the general orientation adopted in its different stages by the military government inaugurated in 1964. As in other South American military regimes, the quest for power generated a sordid struggle within the armed institutions between the so-called moderates and the hardliners. One of the main institutional challenges faced by the military government during the entire period 1964–85 was to find and maintain some sort of balance between these two factions in order to ensure the regime's internal cohesion and particularly to protect the unity of the Brazilian armed forces.

The readiness of the military leaders to stage a military coup was nurtured by a sense of threat produced by the left-wing radicals' influence on President Goulart. Koonings also stresses the importance of the past in this respect, as this threat brought to mind to many military officers the role played by the communist military in the 1935 uprising and its harmful consequences for the military corporate integrity and unity. He also illustrates how a military regime which was initially thought to be a short-lived interim solution until a democratic restoration, evolved into a long-term authoritarian political project. This was mainly the result of a marked shift in the balance of power between moderates and hardliners within the army, symbolized by the figures of Castelo Branco and Emílio Médici, respectively. From 1969 onwards, the consolidation within the government of the hardliners' faction was reflected in the growing influence of the intelligence and counter-insurgency services and in targeting the crushing of communist subversion as a top state priority. They used the 'logic of war' to legitimize repression against their political enemies (leftist political parties, union leaders, intellectuals and so on) and the abuse of human and civil rights. However, in the early 1970s the regime had to face a serious problem of institutional legitimacy, forcing the military to initiate some sort of political opening. This facilitated the comeback of the moderates' faction represented by Generals Geisel and Figueiredo but the strong counterbalance still exerted by the hardliners determined the gradual and slow pace that characterized the Brazilian democratic transition.

In Chapter 9, Francisco Rojas explores the very complex nature of civil–military relations in Chile during the democratic transition and the first two democratic governments led by the Concertación coalition in the period 1990–2000. Previous to the 1973 military coup, civil–military relations in Chile were characterized by what has been called 'formal constitutionalism', representing the existence of a factual subordination of the armed forces to the civil authorities, but without an effective commitment by the armed institutions to the democratic system. Instead of adopting and absorbing the democratic values and norms ruling civil society, the Chilean armed forces opted to isolate themselves from the rest of society. Following the coup, civil–military relations were profoundly damaged due to the extreme repressive nature of the new regime and the gross violation of human rights by the Pinochet regime. However, civil society itself became extremely divided between those sectors which almost unrestrictedly supported the coup and subsequent military government, on the one hand, and the rest of society who never accepted the military's self-conferred right to rule the country, on the other. After more than 17 years in power, the military regime dramatically changed the country's socioeconomic, political and even cultural landscape. In that period Chile's export-oriented economy experienced a powerful expansion while at the same time income inequalities reached extreme levels. The Concertación governments of Patricio Aylwin and Eduardo Frei attempted to democratize the institutional and legal structures left by the authoritarian regime but had only mixed results. Current civil–military relations in Chile remain under severe stress as the armed institutions strongly resist the Concertación governments' attempts to eliminate the remaining authoritarian enclaves in the legal and institutional system, and to discover the truth about the location of the remains of those who disappeared during the Pinochet years. Pinochet's arrest in London even further increased the tensions between the government and the military institutions as the army and right-wing sectors felt the government had not done enough to obtain the General's liberation. Following his return to Chile civil–military relations seem to have gradually improved.

In the final chapter, Paul Cammack assesses the future role of the armed forces in South America, analysing in retrospect the main factors that made possible the political intervention of the military in most South American countries in the 1960s and 1970s, and the structural changes which have occurred in South American societies ever since. Cammack criticizes O'Donnell's BA thesis as in his opinion it overemphasizes the role of the crisis of import-substituting industrialization in the establishment of military governments in the 1960–70 period. Instead, Cammack regards the breakdown of (semi-) democratic governments in those years to be rather the result of a general crisis of bourgeois hegemony in the region. In addition, international factors such as the cold war and the Cuban revolution also stimulated many South American armies to embrace doctrines of national security and encouraged the idea of staging coups in order to prevent the spread of communism in the continent. Since the late 1980s the situation has dramatically changed as a result of the neo-liberal system of global governance.

Today in Latin America, the neo-liberal project has been accompanied by a renewed commitment of the national elites to democratic politics. The current Latin American market economies would not know how to deal with a possible military intervention as it could easily provoke market instability, flight of capital and eventually a severe recession. In this manner, in the current neo-liberal era it is not in the interests of either national or international capital to provoke a breakdown of democratic rule in South American countries. Moreover, as the case of Fujimori in Peru has clearly shown, serious political and economic crisis does not necessarily have to lead to military coups: governments can also decide to severely reduce the democratic content of civilian regimes, from which new forms of 'low-intensity democracies' can emerge.

The contributions to this book clearly show the important role played by the armies in the shaping of South American nations and in their further political evolution since Independence up to the present. Most of the time, civil–military relations have been characterized by a lack of mutual understanding and the existence of deep mistrust. While military leaders have traditionally questioned the ability of civilian politicians to run affairs of state, the political class has often looked at the army as representing a constant danger for civilian governments because of its ability to stage a military coup. Civilian control and supremacy over the armed forces is an aspiration that has rarely been achieved in this region. This has been certainly related to the fact that in the last decades no general societal consensus has existed about the need to have and to maintain democratic political systems. Most military coups has taken place in deeply divided societies in which a part of the population actively or tacitly supported the active involvement of the army in the political process to find an extra-institutional 'exit' to the crisis.

During the last two decades, however, South American political culture seems to have gradually changed by increasingly accepting the idea that the search for solutions for the social, economic and political problems affecting their nations has to be confined within the boundaries of democratic rule. The recent authoritarian experience had strongly discredited the military option, as most of the military regimes did not manage to offer a firm solution for the countries' social and economic problems. In addition, the severe violation of human rights in countries like Argentina, Chile and Uruguay created deep wounds and traumatized vast sectors of the population making clear once and for all how high the price would be if social conflicts were to lead to another military intervention.

The recent past continues to determine the nature of current civil–military relations, as the victims of the former authoritarian regimes continue to demand justice from the democratic governments implying the judgement of all those military men involved in the 'dirty wars' of the 1970s. Regardless of the solution to this question, it seems that a quite long period of time will have to pass before the South American nations will be able to find a stable and sustainable pattern of civil–military relations which satisfies the demands of this new century.

2
Foreign Influences on the South American Military: Professionalization and Politicization

Frederick M. Nunn

Introduction

As we look back over the past hundred years of Latin American history it is easy to see the significance of professionalization of the armed forces in the context of military–civilian relations.[1] Early in this century a professional ethos had developed within some of the region's armies to the point where this, as much as events in the civilian sector, would propel professional officers into governmental and, sometimes, formal political roles. Latin America's idiosyncratic military–civilian heritage notwithstanding, this was not unique to the region. The French and German armies, models for South American military professionalization, were themselves never fully insulated from the effects of government and politics, never fully free from politically ambitious or professionally protective military leaders. Their institutional influence on armies of the ABC countries (Argentina, Chile and Uruguay) and their political behavior can still be readily discerned, as this essay seeks to confirm.

Central American and Caribbean armed forces organized by US advisers began to participate actively in civilian affairs at about the same time as Europeanized South Americans, that is in the decade following the First World War. But the latter would evolve professionally more than their circum-Caribbean counterparts between early-century experiences in military professionalism engendered by Prussianization and Francophilia, and the experiences in institutional *golpes de estado* and manifestations of professional militarism

13

that mark off the 1964–89 quarter century. This is especially true in Argentina, Brazil, Chile and Peru, that is to say in the Southern Cone (in its broad definition).

If we are to understand the internal political roles assumed by army officers of the ABC countries in this century, due attention to institutional history must be paid in full, for much of what has transpired in recent decades has deep roots in the past. In the past ('pasts' may be more appropriate, given the disparity of historical evolution within Latin America), armies always played some political or governmental role. A quick survey of the nineteenth-century historical experience makes this clear. But it was not until the military became a profession – with the army being the principal force – that this role became more than armed might applied for personal or partisan reasons.

This is to say that professionalization of the military in Latin America would result in 'militarization of the profession' from the late nineteenth century forwards, to different degrees according to locale. We still have as much to learn about these different degrees and locales as we do about the similarities in Latin American military–civilian relations – nationally, regionally and thematically. The more we learn about these differences and similarities, the more we will know about the relationship of foreign influences on internal roles played by the professional armed forces. The more we understand the historical qualities of European-style professionalism in South America, the more we will understand the qualitative distinctions in political behavior of Latin American armies and their uniformed allies.

Military professionalism and professional militarism

About thirty-five years ago this writer began, in a modest way, to study the military's participation in politics and government. As fate would have it, it fell to him to write a doctoral thesis on civil–military relations in Chile between the Civil War of 1891 and the Popular Front electoral victory of 1938. This was a thesis about relations between a professionalized army (and a navy, of course) and one of South America's most 'democratic' (and fractious) civilian-dominated political systems (Nunn, 1963). When the then director of Chile's Biblioteca Nacional, a historian by profession, heard the explanation of the thesis topic, methodology and so on, he replied that access to the library was of course granted, but that the research would result in little of scholarly substance. There was no 'military problem' in Chile, no significant example of a military internal role playing since independence, and not much substance to a cause and effect relationship between professionalization and political action.

Greater attention to the recent past might have stood that Chilean in good stead, for barely a decade later, deep into the cold war, the Chilean armed forces would overthrow both their country's government and its 'democratic' and fractious political system. Not only did military leaders destroy a political system, they proceeded to enforce the creation of a new one over the next sixteen and a half years, all the while continuing to flaunt their European-style 'roots'.

Only Brazil, among Latin American countries, has had a longer sustained experience with professional militarism. Only Peru has had a more militarized regime (one steeped in French colonial military theory, let it be said). Only Argentina has experienced a more violent protracted military–civilian confrontation.

Elsewhere this writer has analysed the phenomena of European-style military professionalism and professional militarism that mark some countries off from others in Latin America and beyond, so a few words of explanation beg expression here.[2] Military professionalism is a state, a condition based on education and expertise, autonomous institutional governance, a sense of career, and an explicit statist mission. Professional militarism is the willingness and propensity to provide solutions to a country's problems – economic, political, social – based on a military ethos. This ethos, sometimes called a mentality or spirit, is a result of professionalism in conflict with civilian sociocultural tendencies that are probably most discernible in the political sphere of the most developed countries of the region: the countries of the Southern Cone.

Without professionalism there can certainly be militaristic thinking and behavior, but not true professional militarism. The difference between militaristic thinking and behavior (*latent* professional militarism) and provision of solutions by force (*manifest* professional militarism) is determined heavily by relationships, both short- and long-term, between armies and the societies and polities of which they are a part, as well as by perceptions on the part of the military that national culture, values and ideals are under attack both from within and without (see Nunn, 1992: 11–75).

All armies have internal roles or missions that involve them in civilian sociocultural change – or confront them with the lack of it. These roles or missions may be minimal; they may be limited to narrowly defined 'civic action', 'nation-building', or the like. In Latin America such roles were called, more often than not in the early years of this century, the 'civilizing mission' *misión or missão civilizadora*. Minimally or not, all Latin American armies have laid claim to a social role, a *rol social*. Whether clearly articulated or not, social roles have encouraged army officers to pay attention to domestic affairs in order that national defense, more recently 'national security', be assured. There can be no separation of defense and security from internal roles or missions of Latin American armies or constabularies, at least not from the beginnings of professionalism onwards. Nor can these two elements be separated from foreign influences.

Back before the First World War, before the rise of the United States as the hemispheric and not just a Caribbean power, if Latin Americans wanted to reform, modernize or professionalize an army they looked either to the victor or the vanquished of the Franco-Prussian War. Chileans in the 1880s, and in the next decade the Argentines, contracted with German officers to teach, administer, organize, train and write up codes; to organize war games, tours abroad and exchanges; to create Southern Cone versions of Europe's military titan.[3] In the 1890s, Peru contracted with French officers, a number of whom had served in North Africa, to reform the army along French Republican lines.[4] There were German training officers in Bolivia, and a French-style Escuela Politécnica in Guatemala. By the time the European model armies went to war against each other in 1914, Prussianized Chileans were training Ecuadorans, Colombians and Salvadorans (see Nunn, 1970a; 1983). Soon after the Great War, French officers would begin a stint of nearly twenty years of military missionary work in Brazil,[5] and other French officers were contracted by Paraguay and Uruguay. A few Germans served privately (sometimes with the benefit of Danzig passports) again in Bolivia and elsewhere (see Nunn, 1983: 136–47, 212–13).[6] A few Chileans continued to serve in northern South America and in Central America. Just before and then again after the First World War, US military personnel began to organize constabularies in the Caribbean and Isthmian countries for the explicit purpose of maintaining internal order.[7]

By the time war broke out again in 1939 there were two distinct spheres of exogenous professional military influence in the region. Most of South America retained a continental European military heritage reminiscent of nineteenth- and early twentieth-century France and Germany. And most of the circum-Caribbean was under the organizational influence of the United States, thus having little traditional sense of professional separateness from the rest of society. This was of little positive value to either military or civilian sectors in countries like Cuba, Haiti, Nicaragua and the Dominican Republic. There, separateness of *uniformados* represented little more than a continuation of *fuero militar*-like immunities, little sense of role or mission, social or civilizing, beyond that expressed cursorily in writing or orally on formal occasions by praetorian lackeys of uniformed presidents or their civilian allies. Foreign influences are not all the same.

By this time, too, Europeanized South American armies had expressed their professionalism in a variety of ways. Their internal orientation was plainly the result of their professionalism in conflict with civilian political practices and socioeconomic realities, not simply the result of their assignment to keep the populace in its place and protecting vested interests as in the circum-Caribbean. On occasion, South Americans performed police-like functions; Caribbeans and Central Americans regularly did so. Over time it would become necessary for South Americans to assume a more prominent internal profile, but not until such time had passed to make that profile inextricable from professionalism. This has been of debatable value to Argentines, Brazilians, Chileans and Peruvians. There, separateness was the result of an elaborate combination of professional commitments to make a difference, not to perpetuate families or clans in power.

From the onset of professionalization in South America, national defense carried with it an internal imperative. Lessons of war learned by Europeans in the nineteenth century were transmitted to South Americans who were already familiar with war and, believing it might break out again, wanted to be prepared. Southern South America was the scene of three major nineteenth-century wars involving seven of the subcontinent's ten countries. Twice Bolivia and Peru allied to fight Chile (1836–39, 1879–84); and Argentina, Brazil and Uruguay allied to fight Paraguay (1865–70). Boundary disputes left over from the colonial centuries, power rivalries and geopolitics all played a role in these conflicts, and in the aftermath of each victors and losers realized that not all disputes and rivalries had been settled or dissipated. International cooperation was sporadic and limited, and South America was a lot like Europe in this sense.

South American defense policies can be pretty well-discerned by the causes and results of each war, especially those of the second half of the past century in which sizeable portions of territory changed hands. Bolivia, Paraguay and Peru all suffered significant dismemberment at the hands of Argentina, Brazil and Chile respectively. Of the victors only Argentina and Chile, and of the losers only Peru, had the resources to embark on the road to military professionalization before the century's end. In each case the South American recipient of military missionaries knew full well that if a conflict arose, a competent, well-trained and indoctrinated fighting force would be needed. No longer could bonuses, bounties or promises of freedom convince peasants, workers, Indians or slaves to take part in national defense. By the 1890s, moreover, a few South Americans had obviously read *A Nation in Arms*.

The army and the nation

A little over twenty years ago the writer was taking tea in the study of a well-known and widely published retired Argentine general. The conversation turned to Argentine military literature and the recurrence in it of themes present in Colmar Freiherr von der Goltz's *Das Volk in Waffen* (1st edn 1883). The general rose from the tea table, went to the bookshelves and found a copy of *La nación en armas*, thumbed through it and said 'we all read this as cadets or young officers. It's like the Scriptures.'

Goltz's late nineteenth-century treatise stressed relations between the people and their army, making it clear that national security could only be ensured if the populace were able to serve the interests of the state when needed. An entire nation in arms might be needed in future conflicts, and some kind of permanent force should stand ever ready. Based on lessons learned about mobilization, mechanization and obligatory service during the Franco-Prussian War, Goltz's little book became standard fare in early twentieth-century South America. It helped perpetuate a continental orientation to the external imperative, and legitimized professional military concern for internal conditions.

For how could South Americans have 'good armies' unless they had 'good countries?' A good army meant literate lower classes (whence most conscripts, after all); obligatory military service (in order that *the nation* participate as an organic whole); up-to-date military education, advanced training, foreign experience, materials, transportation and communications infrastructures; and pay and benefits appropriate to the profession of arms. A good country meant a political system committed to defense of the fatherland, an economy capable of supporting ever-increasing demands for new equipment, a culture that held in high esteem the army as the 'purest image of the state'.[8]

Years before the First World War, then, army officers in Argentina and Chile recognized that there was a serious gap between their aspirations and the capability and willingness of civilians to provide for them in a manner to which they wanted to become accustomed. They were reminded of this only too dramatically whenever they were called out to quell strikes and demonstrations by workers in Buenos Aires or miners up in the Atacama nitrate fields in northern Chile. Early in this century they began to ask themselves just what and who were to blame for the miserable conditions in which the majority of civilians lived? Such civilians made poor soldiers. And many civilians whose cultural level and health did make them suitable for military service never wore the uniform, for obligatory service schemes in place since the turn of the century were full of loopholes. Money, connections, educational deferrals, substitution rules – all made it possible to escape being an integral part of *the nation in arms*. What officers took so seriously, it seemed, civilians did not.

Nowhere was this more obvious than in Peru, where French missions toiled off and on between the 1890s and 1939, with time out for the First World War. The French who came to Peru brought with them a commitment to the social role of the officer and the civilizing mission of the army. They had all doubtless read two of the most influential pieces of French military literature ever published: 'Du rôle social de l'officier' and 'Du rôle colonial de l'armée' by Hubert Lyautey, 'the monarchist who created an empire for the Republic'.[9] Lyautey and Goltz form the most historically significant intellectual influence on the internal orientation of Southern Cone officers corps. Lyautey's essays, especially the first mentioned, have been cited, alluded to and plagiarized in Portuguese and Spanish more than any other sources in Latin American military literature. Goltz's book remains on professional reading lists, as this writer has confirmed on numerous occasions since that pleasant tea-time in Buenos Aires.

French officers, especially if they had served in Africa or Indo-China, believed that officers had an obligation to civilize their charges, to educate them, to be their moral and cultural mentors – to be a part of France's grand *mission civilizatrice*. But in Peru their charges were not Frenchmen or assimilated locals, they were illiterate peasants and *indígenas*, who often did not even speak the official language of their own *nación en armas*. The French and their Peruvian disciples knew from the outset that they were up against formidable odds. Not Bolivia or Ecuador, much less Chile, but topography, race, climate, culture, demography and language were the enemies they faced in their daily labors. To make an army they had to make a country.

Now, the same enemies existed to a degree in each of the ABC countries. Central America and the Caribbean were not all that different, nor was Mexico, although *La Revolución* would affect her army in a unique way. Indeed, second-generation Prussianization activities in Colombia, Ecuador and El Salvador led officers of those countries to many of the conclusions reached by their Chilean mentors. Historically speaking, Latin American armies have sometimes found themselves to be armies of occupation in their own countries early in this century.

The traditional, external role of South American armies soon became inseparable from their internal role of civilizing, educating, uplifting and *modernizing*. Wherever European-inspired professionalism took root, even if solely within the officer corps and for the army's own purposes, it did so always with internal ramifications. This was also the case in Europe, of course, but there domestic enemies were slightly less formidable than in South America because political systems were entrenched more firmly (although this might be debated for both France and Germany after 1930). Civilian primacy was a tradition in itself in Europe, but its credibility was diminished early on in South America owing to officer corps thought and self-perception. Brazil's 1889–1930 republicanism, Chile's 1891–1925 parliamentary system, Argentine radicalism of the 1916–30 years, and Peruvian political bankruptcy between 1919 and 1930 would lead military professionals to equate a country's shortcomings with democracy when mass participation became more significant through populist-reform, socialist and communist movements.[10]

By 1930, at which time Brazilians had been fully weaned from the short-lived, pre-First World War influence of young *germanófilos*, military leaders from the Southern Cone already had a taste of nation-building. Their internal roles had expanded in proportion to both the decrease in level of war threat and the increase of political activity by the populace. This was timely, for it was during the long South American peace, from the end of the War of the Pacific in 1884 to 1932, when Bolivia and Paraguay finally put their German and French lessons to the test in the War of the Gran Chaco (1932–35), that armies participated intensely in a variety of internal roles ranging from strike-breaking, riot dispersal, controlling political protests, frontier and hinterland colonization, road building and over-throwing governments. In these years, no South American country could boast a national police organization capable of controlling large-scale, politically driven civil disturbances. Chile's vaunted *Cuerpo de Carabineros*, an Italianate creation of the 1927–31 admin-istration of General Carlos Ibáñez del Campo, was the closest thing to a professional armed institution devoted solely to an internal mis-sion (see Nunn, 1970b: 149). Brazil's *Forças Públicas* served the same purposes on the state level there. Thus it was that from the outset, professionalized officer corps in South America would play impor-tant internal roles in countries with grave economic and social problems, under intense political disruption. Although armies were not specifically assigned police functions, civil disorder – and this could mean a number of things – could bring them to action against *internal enemies*.

It is not too strenuous a march from the protests and riots, and the internal disorder of a political nature of the pre-Second World War years to armed confrontations with ideologically-inspired inter-nal enemies later in this century. Just as Marxism–Leninism did not miraculously, as it were, spring to Latin American life in Cuba in 1959, the professional military's internal activities are not simply the results of post-Second World War causes. The cold war and the Cuban revolution did not cause the military–civilian crises of the ABC countries in the second half of this century. Poverty, misery, illiteracy and backwardness were eliminated neither by democratic experiences nor by military professionalization schemes begun nearly a century ago, and professional armies in South America have amassed nearly a century of accumulated, assigned or self-assigned role experience in internal affairs. Their own linkage of national defense to internal order and progress, as well as the willingness of political figures to manipulate 'the nation's finest' would have made this so, even if Marxism–Leninism had never been considered a menace. Such a sweeping conclusion, however tentative, needs some qualification.

In search of foreign models

Nearly three-quarters of a century ago, when the French mission arrived in Rio de Janeiro, the most widely read military journal of the time, *A Deféësa Nacional* (April 1919: 225–8) editorialized: 'A Missão Militar Estrangeira: Bemvinda Seja'. Despite their pre-First World War *germanofilismo*, based essentially on rivalry with the French-trained São Paulo *Força Pública*, Brazilian army officers, especially the younger ones, were enthusiastic about the French victors coming to Brazil. That editorial in the influential journal founded by *germanófilos* was the first piece of literature on Brazilian military evolution ever analysed by this writer. It remains a pivotal essay in the literature of the Brazilian army. The defeated army of 1871 (which for that reason had appealed to Peru's own losers of the 1880s) was now attractive in victory to the sole remaining South American great power lacking a European tie. Brazilian adaptability to a French model helped prolong in South America the intangibles attendant to a European continental military heritage. The Chaco War would do the same. So would Argentine and Chilean *Prussophilia*, even in the face of increased diplomatic and economic influence from North America. Peruvians clung to their French traditions too. So change began change and reinforced tradition simultaneously. European-style professionalism benefited from each change.

If the last two assertions have substance, they lead to questions about what constitutes change and what influences might arrest the effects of time's passage *vis-à-vis* foreign influences on an army's internal role. The fact that both praetorians and professionals have played these roles must not lead us to see them doing so for the same reasons. It is as hard to make conclusions on the topic 'military–civilian relations in Latin America' as it is to provide a comprehensive historical definition of the entire region. By associating certain trends in the civilian sector with others in the military, however, we gain insight into just what internal roles mean to professionals and citizens over the course of our own century. In doing this we may more readily discern long-term effects of a variety of foreign influences.

Social and cultural change in countries where direct European military influence was of relatively long duration, or was maintained following the departure of the French and Germans, made armies adapt, if grudgingly, to changing times. Prolongation of social dichotomies more representative of the early part of the century meant that constabularies and armies of the circum-Caribbean countries, however, did not have to begin even thinking about adapting to changing times until later than their South American confreres. From the external side it was never the intention of the USA to create the kind of armies in the circum-Caribbean area that Europeans had once envisioned for their own disciples' countries. Moreover, the European presence had been sought; the North American accepted. In South America it was accepted after 1945 with resignation, if not with outright occasional grumbling.

Economic development in the ABC countries was unmatched by that of the circum-Caribbean; the New World Mediterranean remained – to mix geopolitical metaphors – a Balkanized region.[11] Diversification, economic nationalism, the rise of organized labor, systemic political complexities, media sophistication and the like associated with changing times in South America were unmatched up north, with the exception of Revolutionary Mexico's leap forward. The Central American common market experiment came nowhere close to equalling the economic expansion and diversification enjoyed by most South American countries, either independently or, as today, in concert. Expansion of the middle sectors contributed proportionately to more political instability in South America than it did in the north. So did expansion of electorates. An essentially pre-First World War society maintained itself in most of the circum-Caribbean until after the Second World War, by which time the differences between European-oriented South Americans and US influenced Caribbeans and Central Americans were easily discernible.

Although strides toward professionalism were made in the north, then, fiscal resources, US influence and different paces of social, economic, political and cultural development precluded the attainment of levels of professional development so historically characteristic of southern South America. Challenges to the military's adaptive capabilities were not strong enough to produce an elaborate military lore like that which prevails to this day in the Southern Cone.[12] Superficially, roles both internal and external are defined comparably, but the fact remains that in and around the New World Mediterranean, military organizations with some exceptions continued to play roles similar to those played prior to the Second World War.

National defense in the north does not retain the continental flavor that prevails in the ABC countries. Problems peculiar to Costa Rica, Guatemala, El Salvador, Honduras, Nicaragua and Panama, and Haiti and the Dominican Republic, make defense forces more far internally than externally-oriented. The same must be said or at least contemplated for Cuba, despite the African adventures of the 1970s and 1980s. An examination of recent professional military literature shows that civic action programs and maintenance of order (civilizing mission and social role in modern guise) are assigned and accepted functions in the circum-Caribbean, all right, but in practice professional militarism at a Southern Cone level is impossible, for domestic conditions and foreign influence are simply not comparable. Despite the fact that all Latin American armies have the same roles in theory, historical and contemporary influences preclude their practice within the North American sphere of influence. Internal roles, however they may be defined, are still played according to a mix of domestic conditions, foreign influences and professional thought and self-perception. This last factor is the essential institutional and historical ingredient, and in the ABC countries and Peru, thought and self-perception of the officer corps are still more comparable to French and German than to North American models.

Internal roles

One day, just a few weeks after his discussion of Goltz with the Argentine general, this writer was reading away an afternoon at the

Centro de Estudios Histórico-Militares in Lima. At the same table a social science colleague from England was likewise poring over issues of the *Revista Militar del Perú*. Over the course of frequent conversations the writer and his colleague had been comparing impressions and notes, for, it seems, they were seeking answers to the same question: whence the intellectual origins of the Peruvian *golpe de estado* of 1968?

On this afternoon the colleague declared that he had found a document containing the answer. It was, he said, an article published in 1952 appropriately entitled 'La función social del ejército'. Upon examining his find and discussing with him its ramifications, the writer summoned a beadle and asked him to bring out the 1933 issue of the journal in which this revelation appeared. A few minutes later it became clear that the 1952 essay was a reprint of a pre-Second World War piece derivative of Lyautey's assignment of a social role to officers and a colonial role to armies.[13] The 1968 military movement's roots went deeper than the cold war or the founding of the Centro de Altos Estudios Militares.

An archival epiphany like this one argues the case for old ways dying hard. It also illustrates the potential significance of European-style professional thought and self-perception in both theoretical and practical internal role fulfillment. Domestic conditions urging the playing of an internal role by armies exist throughout Latin America. Professional responses to these conditions are essentially alike in theory, but in practice they differ, and there is no evidence of anything closely resembling Peruvian professional militarism, latent in 1933 and manifest thirty years later, emanating from within the US sphere of influence. Supporting a civilian dynasty, showcase civic action, fighting a civil war, counter-insurgency and seizure of power at almost predictable intervals just do not equal attempts to create regimes designed to administer an entire country based on a military ethos derived from European sources. Maintenance of an existing order just does not equal the imposition of a new order; police functions do not adumbrate creation of a police state. Constabularies and civil guards cannot be possessed of deeply rooted institutional traditions like those that enable military professionals to become professional militarists. Foreign influences are not all the same.

Both the cold war – in many respects an era whose significance in Latin America may still be misunderstood – and the US military presence – the impact of which has certainly been exaggerated – reinforced internal role assignments dating from early in this century. In the ABC countries and Peru these were patterned after those associated with, but rarely played by, European armies.

US military influence by no means initiated South American interest in internal roles, except perhaps in Colombia and Venezuela. Internal roles played most often in Argentina, Brazil, Chile and Peru have been based on commitments to the civilizing mission and the social role. Often resentful of police inability to maintain order, however, Europeanized South American armies would ultimately blame civilians for nearly all their countries' shortcomings. Fearful of professionalized police as potential competitors for scarce resources and the allure of power, armies did not overwhelmingly support modernization of police forces. In South America, clearly, an army's internal role could easily become one that overlapped and duplicated police functions in exceptional circumstances. Ideologically charged exceptional circumstances characterize the second half of this century.

The post-1945 era added little of substance to extant role definitions in the circum-Caribbean area. Denied a balance of European and US influences, defense forces there had less heritage to fall back on when called out by civilian politicians and presidents in uniform to protect a *status quo* partially of their own making. This is in direct contrast to the situation in South America where, by the 1960s, officers took action to alter the *status quo*, or at least to rearrange it. There simply is no case of an armed institution in the circum-Caribbean area contemplating anything like what the Argentines, Brazilians, Chileans or Peruvians attempted between 1964 and 1990.

Professional literature corroborates this assertion. The net effect of cold war inter-hemispheric ideological conflict was, in the final analysis, both simplification of internal roles in much of the circum-Caribbean, and complication of them in South America. Exceptions to this conclusion can be made for Paraguay, whose military–civilian relations resemble Nicaragua's and the Dominican Republic more than those of neighboring states. Mexico is an exception to most conclusions reached herein as well, and Bolivia constitutes a lapsed case of European-influenced professionalization owing to domestic upheaval and abject underdevelopment.

So far we have utilized geographical and historical breakdowns to examine the origins and nature of foreign influences on armies from South America and the circum-Caribbean. Another two perspectives have been alluded to and require some treatment before proceeding to speculation on the present and foreseeable future ramifications of foreign influence. These are those of countries that have been through either a protracted revolutionary or praetorian experience.

Praetorianism

About a quarter-century ago the writer had an opportunity to present a paper on military intervention in Latin American politics to a professional meeting.[14] In the concluding remarks he stated that if the military could do what it had done (six months earlier) in Chile, the military could conceivably do the same anywhere in the region. In the question-and-answer session immediately following scholarly commentary, a scholar in the audience asked if the writer had intended to include Mexico in his sweeping conclusion. When the latter replied in the affirmative the panel chair (a Mexicanist) gave him an incredulous stare: '*en México jamás!*' was the unspoken message. All exceptions excepted, Mexico has become in the early 1990s more and more like other Latin American countries than at any time since 1910. Before then, Mexico's was a praetorian-style army of occupation akin to others of the circum-Caribbean. What distinguishes Mexico for so long in this century is *La Revolución*, a unique, protracted, trans-generational, ethos-building experience that followed the writing and promulgation of the Constitution of 1917. In this sense, Mexico, her military–civilian relations and the internal orientation of her army have had more in common historically with post-1952 Bolivia, post-1959 Cuba, and Nicaragua between 1979 and 1989 than they have had with South America or the rest of the circum-Caribbean. But in another sense it is rejection of a nearby (and willing) foreign influence that characterizes the development of the Mexican military profession. Foreign influences are not all the same.

In Somozan Nicaragua (1937–79), Stroesssnerian Paraguay (1954–89), Trujillan Dominican Republic (1930–61), and Duvallierian Haiti (1957–86), family dynasties, clans and cliques controlled national guards and armies, making a mockery of professionalism. All but one of these examples fell well within the US orbit; Paraguay's unique history places it both within and outside the European sphere of influence. Venezuela under Juan Vicente Gómez (1908–35), then Marcos Pérez Jiménez (1948–58), and Panama under Omar Torrijos (1968–78) might be considered as much marginal members of this, the praetorian category, as are Ecuador, Colombia, Bolivia and Uruguay of the Europeanized South American group, and as El Salvador, Guatemala and Honduras are of the US-influenced circum-Caribbean group. Thus, in addition to historical and geographical qualifications of professionalism, we need to consider praetorian and revolutionary control of armed forces, as well as a number of exceptions, when we go about examining foreign influences on internal role definition and fulfillment: no mean feat this for a region as complex as Latin America.

In the Southern Cone, we know, European-style professionalization helped create an institutional identity, a separateness based on education, mission and attainment of higher rank through merit. The truly professionalized officer corps has a solid theory base with which to consider itself both *apart from* and *a part of* the society it serves. Praetorian systems and revolutionary regimes envelop the military, but the latter make the military part of an ideological revolutionary process, wherein professional education and orientation are built around defense of the revolution as synonymous with defense of the fatherland. Historical, political and economic reasons make this imperative, for revolutions are menaced both from within and without. Forces of reaction and anti-revolutionary foreign influences are everywhere. Cubans might have fought in Africa, but they also defend their fatherland against internal dissidents, exiles and 'Yankee imperialists'. Nicaraguans had to struggle between 1979 and 1989 against *Contras*. Bolivian *uniformados* were ultimately absorbed by the home-grown 1952 revolution through rebuilding of the army, then came to be significant interpreters of that revolution from the mid-1960s forwards.

Regardless of future events there can be no full turning back of the clock on significant revolutionary achievements like agrarian reform, economic nationalism (in varying degrees and depending on place) and social reform. The collapse of Marxist–Leninist schemes in Europe may or may not presage the future dismantling of Cuba's economic structure. The failure of statist socioeconomic schemes in South America by no means foreshadows imminent pri-vatization of the Bolivian tin mining industry, not yet anyway. Electoral ouster of the Sandinistas in 1989 does not mean that all they fought for will wither away.

The reconstruction of the Mexican army (accomplished with min-imal US input) that accompanied the institutionalization of *La Revolución*, resulted in effective linkage of the army to Mexico's great movement (see Lieuwen, 1968; 1984). The army's internal roles were defined first and foremost by its existence as a revolutionary force, part of the 'revolutionary family' within the official party. Whatever its professional level may be, deep into this century the Mexican army has remained incapable of offering Mexicans any alternative preferable to revolutionary politics and government. The image of the army is still based heavily on its revolutionary ties and its civic action capabilities, not on any foreign professional or ideological influence. Codified internal roles – ample in emergencies – have not encouraged army leaders to assert themselves against the wishes of the regime. To do so would still be counter-revolutionary and, despite all Mexico's current problems, still against the popular con-sensus (see Nunn, 1992; Camp, 1992). Revolutionary Mexico's prox-imity to the United States (a nineteenth-century foe, after all) has not resulted in the creation of a defense establishment designed to counter aggression from without, unless forces located near Guatemala are taken into serious account. Revolutionary successes in socioeconomic affairs have precluded any successful insurgency movement, and Marxism–Leninism has never proved a viable alter-native to the home-grown revolution. Thus, the internal imperative is still a strictly limited one in Mexico. That this can change goes without saying for, as asserted above, Mexico is more like the rest of Latin America than it has been at any time since 1910.

Neither Cuba nor Nicaragua have enjoyed revolutionary Mexico's privileged position within the orbit of US influence. A principal rea-son for this is that they did not achieve revolutionary status until the cold war was well under way, when the specter of Marxism–Leninism loomed large in the Isthmus and the Caribbean. Defense of their revolutions in the critical pre-institutional stages, therefore, meant confrontation with a world power, not a war-weary, isolation-ist, hemispheric ambivalent one as in Mexico's case. Their armies' internal roles have been more limited by foreign revolutionary myths and ideology than was the case in Mexico. To have opposed the Castros or Ortegas would have been suicidal as well as counter-revolutionary. Thus, internal roles in Cuba and Nicaragua, and in Bolivia and Mexico, have been shaped by both imported and domestic dogma in ways distinct from the ABC countries and Peru.

Clearly praetorianism has not been limited to the circum-Caribbean. Is it possible for personalism to obtain well within the European sphere where decades of professionalism should ostensibly preclude it? The cases of Argentina's Juan Perón (1946–55), and Peru's Juan Velasco Alvarado (1968–75) come to mind. So does that of Chile's Augusto Pinochet Ugarte. A length of tenure exceeded only by the likes of Juan Vicente Gómez, Rafael Trujillo, Anastasio Somoza and Alfredo Stroessner made it impossible for the Chilean army to avoid taking on a tinge of personalism. The officer corps of the 1990s is a creation of the Pinochet years. Its schooling, mindset, lore and role definition is a result of the national catharsis of 1973 and measures taken to secure and defend the fatherland against any and all internal enemies. Width and depth of participation in internal affairs gave Chileans a taste of professional militarism that will last for a generation at least.

Foreign influences dating from the days of the later Kaisers had an impact on the Chilean army of the cold war – and later. Many *uniformados* see this legacy as a result of forceful leadership *á la* Francisco Franco or Charles de Gaulle as much as stemming from professional tradition and expertise (see Nunn, 1992; Arriagada, 1988; Correa and Subercaseaux, 1989).

Some resent the lack of appreciation shown by civilians, especially erstwhile political allies, for the army's efforts at infrastructural and technological modernization of a country that sorely needed it. For these reasons and others, something of a cult surrounded Pinochet into his last months as commander-in-chief, and particularly following his arrest in London in October 1998. This gave a new dimension to military *caudillismo* and indicates that it may not be a thing of the past. Recent events in Argentina, Peru and Venezuela indicate that *caudillismo* may endure in new forms in countries where (re)democratization is occurring. If this is so, internal roles for the experience of professional armies may not be out of the question. If they are not out of the question, foreign influences of a historical nature will merit continued scrutiny.

The post-cold war period

¿Y el mañana?. The future is a risky thing to be predicting right now. The end of the cold war and experiments in (re)democratization occurred so closely to the *quincentenario* that some observers have leaped to the conclusion that democracy is (yet again) the wave of a new paradigm. Events in Europe show the dangers of such a leap. In the Balkans, the Baltics, the Caucasian republics and in Russia itself, armies are asserting themselves as guarantors of order. Ethnic and religious differences, muted during the existence of the USSR and Yugoslavia – and the Austro-Hungarian and Russian Empires before – or held in check in the pre-Second World War Middle East, now threaten to tear apart fledgling democracies across Eurasia and continue to plague authoritarian states everywhere. Democracy in its current guise is by no means inevitable anywhere.[15] All of this indicates that armies in these parts of the world, whether or not they are prepared to do so, will play internal roles in important ways. This may include police functions. Where there exists a strong sense of profession, militarism and *caudillismo* cannot be perfunctorily ruled out.

It does not appear that either democracy or civilian control of the armed forces faces too bright a future in Africa and Asia. This means that internal roles will probably not diminish there. The tortuous road from military to civilian rule travelled by Africans during the 1990s serves as but one example of African politics and government continuing much as they have since independence: as an adjunct of military–civilian relations, not vice versa. The same might be said for Turkey, Pakistan and other countries of the Islamic world.

In the immediate post-Gulf War years the US armed forces, hitherto bastions of proper military–civilian relations, were also beset with controversy. The design and execution of new external roles were controversial enough, and suggestions that an internal, developmental role was appropriate were taken more seriously than at any time since 1941. Embroilment of the armed forces in controversies surrounding women in combat and homosexuals in uniform (much less combat) brought the army closer to domestic sociocultural and political issues than the Vietnam War ever did. The Tailhook scandal did the same for the navy. Similar controversies have plagued the air force and the marines during this decade. A new president in 1993 involved himself in growing military–civilian controversies both because of his Anti-Vietnam War stand as a young man and his support for the rights and obligations of homosexuals in uniform. These issues – unheard of in Latin America – exposed the US armed forces to focused observation and criticism – and gamered some civilian support. They led some South Americans to see the United States as an undependable ally, and led some US personnel to opine on military–civilian relations in ways that resembled the treatment of controversial issues in Latin American military journals.

For example, in the November 1992 issue of the *Marine Corps Gazette* there appeared a brief essay, 'Tailhook: The Larger Issue' (Lind, 1992: 38). Therein the author likened the reaction to this documented episode of sexual harassment at a US navy function in the summer of 1992 to a subversive warfare assault by feminists on the armed forces. 'The battlefield', the author claimed, was 'culture, and the strategic battlefield is between traditional, Western Judeo-Christian culture on the one hand and an ideology that seeks the destruction of that culture on the other. Feminism is an element in the coalition, and the feminists see the military as a bastion of traditional Western culture', he observed. Such opinions strongly resemble those of military writers from the Southern Cone who look nostalgically on the European-influenced professional past as their *bella época*. Foreign influences may flow in more than one direction, may they not?

Military internal role-playing does not always have to flow from a putsch. If, however, an army is pulled into controversies of a socio-cultural and political nature, it is extremely difficult to maintain relations among officers and soldiers, politicians and civilians in an ideal status quo of mutual trust. Most parts of the world are now entering a new era of military–civilian relations. Latin America is no exception; nor is the USA, for that matter. This does not signal the demise of the military as a political interest group; nor does it diminish the significance of historical or contemporary foreign influences as variables in the assessment of political behavior. These remarks apply to the ABC countries and Peru as much as they do elsewhere.

With the cold war over and Southern Cone experiments in professional militarism exposed as frustrated attempts to impose military values and ideals on resistant and resilient civilian populations, two features make the present and near future distinct from the past. For the first time in a half century Latin American transitions to civilian, popularly conceived government are taking place in an ideologically neutral ambience. Army officers educated to fear and loathe Marxism by any name, can no longer cite the 'Red Menace' as justification for their actions. Nor can they justify their actions by claiming that they alone have the expertise to solve the *grandes problemas nacionales*. The failures of the 1964–89 quarter-century testify to this in Argentina, Brazil and Peru: war, shattered economies, internal dissent. Attempts by Argentine and Venezuelan *coroneles* to oust civilian leaders and the calculated stances of Guatemalan and Peruvian *uniformados* in recent crises showed that, for the time being, civilian support for renewed military involvement in government is not strong across the region. This does not mean that it remains so permanently.

It may come to pass that civilian institutions prove incapable of coping with Latin America's various dilemmas. The fact that many of these dilemmas are not at all unique to the region causes an element of surprise. The world may not be, strictly speaking, smaller, but economic, environmental and social problems are probably more comparable continent-to-continent than they ever were before. If civilians do falter in (re)democratizing Latin America and improving the human condition there, what can happen? Which foreign influences will be brought to bear, and which will be rejected by military leaders then?

Built into Latin American constitutional systems and national budgets – and that are significant to the restoration of civilian government and politics – are professional military role potentials even more elaborate than in the past.[16] Internal disorder by whatever name remains under the ultimate jurisdiction of the armed forces. This is the case in the Southern Cone, where Argentines, Brazilians, Chileans and Peruvians – the Europeanized archetypes – monitor what goes on in the civilian sphere.

Loathe to involve themselves too deeply in attempts to thwart the Shining Path guerrilla movement, Peruvian officers understood President Alberto Fujimori's 'de-(re)democratization' of civilian politics and government early in this decade. They have never had much faith in either – nor are they all that enchanted with him. They take much credit, rightly or wrongly, for the crushing of the

Shining Path and for the 1997 resolution of the *Tupac Amaru* Japanese Embassy hostage incident. Down the coast a national security council still has wide powers over Chilean political activity, and a blue ribbon committee of army officers still renders advice to their commander-in-chief on all manner of national and international affairs. The army shows a good deal of interest in the presidential succession of 2000. Across the Andes, chastened by their underwhelming performance in the Falklands War and their flagrant abuses of human rights between 1976 and 1982, Argentine military leaders are temporarily quiescent. Little wonder that some of those who used to be called 'young officers', colonels like Aldo Rico and Mohamed Alí Seineldín, showed impatience with their superiors and lashed out, *cuartelazo*-style, against both the military and civilian leadership that was guiding the armed forces towards an international peacekeeping role, away from an internal, political one. And to the north in Brazil, the army still has a lot at stake in the meanderings of civilian government and politics through scandal after scandal. *Interiorização*, once one of the army's dreams, has become enmeshed in an ecological and environmental disaster of world proportions. Brazil's frontiers still need defending; not against Bolivians, Paraguayans or Venezuelans but, say some, against foeign non-governmental organizations and entrepreneurs, both national and international, and their Brazilian allies.

In short, despite the manifest failures of professional militarism, armies in Latin America have come out of the 1964–89 epoch in a potentially stronger position than they enjoyed in the early stages of the cold war. The techniques available to military leaders who deem it necessary to provide solutions to national problems may not (in the meantime) include the *golpe de estado*, although this does not mean they do not have means to do so. Means lead to ends, as tactical measures lead to strategic goals. Latin America from the Rio Bravo to Cape Horn is no longer a cold war battlefield. The United States is an ambivalent hemispheric giant.[17] European models of all types contend anew with North American ones, and electronic media all but eradicate the regions relative solitude. The quincentennial has passed; a new century looms (see Nunn, 1992: 239–61). Beyond those mentioned, are there other conceivable foreign influences on armies of the Southern Cone, especially with regard to their internal roles?

Final remarks

Early in this decade, for three years running, the writer asked a number of high-ranking Chilean officers, 'Who is the enemy now that Marxism–Leninism no longer poses a threat to your fatherland?' Back in 1991, the answers had been cautious. Communism might still resurge...but in the quincentennial year and again in 1993, with the Soviet empire in a state of collapse and Boris Yeltsin struggling to hold on (a lot like early nineteenth-century Spanish American nation-founders had done), the answers tumbled out. The enemies of the fatherland were readily ticked off by officer after officer, not always in the same order. Pornography, drugs, homosexuality, premarital sex, abortion, feminism (not women's rights) importation of alien culture via electronic media, consumerism and materialism, destruction of family values, and 'internationalism'. The undermining of national values by forces from both outside and inside the country constitutes an identifiable menace to public and national security, to the existence of the fatherland. These 'enemies' are not unique to Chile.[18] The presence of these influences encourages an internal role as elaborate as any contemplated at the dawn of the age of military professionalism late in the last century or during the heyday of professional militarism 100 years later just as it is folly to discount foreign influences on armies of the ABC countries in the pre-Second World War decades, it would be unwise to do so now, basing one's hopes for the future unperceived US influence in South America. The Chilean case being as extreme as it may be, the potential for foreign influences on professional armies and their internal roles has not faded away in the Southern Cone. Subversion does go on, disorder accompanies democracy, freedom begets licentiousness, say more than a few officers. Foreign influences on military professionalism and professional militarism are by no means a thing of the past.

Notes

1. Recent research for this essay took place in the following locations: Biblioteca del Círculo Militar, Buenos Aires; Biblioteca do Clube Militar, Rio de Janeiro; Biblioteca Central del Ejército and Biblioteca de la Academia Nacional de Estudios Políticos y Estratégicos, Santiago; and Biblioteca del Centro de Estudios Histórico-Militares del Perú, Lima.

Earlier research is noted in cited sources. Thanks go to directors and staff members for their interest and assistance, with special thanks to Ms Mary Krug, *sine qua non*, Office of International Affairs, Portland State for her extraordinary efforts in the processing of several versions of this essay.

2. Much of this essay is drawn from themes and discussed in Nunn (1983, 1992, 1995).

3. See Nunn (1983: 100–12, 122–31) for a discussion of pre-First World War German military missions in the Southern Cone. See also Nunn (1970a: 300–22) for a detailed case study of the initial impact of European military thought on a Latin American army.

4. See Nunn (1983: 112–22) for information on pre-First World War French influence in Peru. See also Nunn (1979: 391–417) for information on the perduration of French influence.

5. See Nunn (1983: 131–6). See also Nunn (1972) for a similar treatment of Peru in n. 3, supra.

6. A brief synthesis of early twentieth-century European military influence in South America is Nunn (1975).

7. First systematically discussed at length in Lieuwen (1961).

8. This term is used to describe the *eischswehr* by General Hans von Seeckt in his *Gedanken eines Soldaten* (Berlin, 1929).

9. Louis Hubert Gonzalve Lyautey, 'Du rôle social de l'officier', *Revue des Deux Mondes* (15 March 1891): 443–59; and 'Du rôle colonial de l'armée', *Same* (1 January 1900): 308–29. The first essay was published anonymously and resulted in Lyautey's posting to Indo-China.

10. See Nunn (1983: 249–86; 1992: 151–77, 205–37) and Loveman and Davies, Jr (1997) for wide coverage of Central and South American military–civilian relations in the twentieth century.

11. The terms 'American Mediterranean' and 'New World Mediterranean' have been applied to the Caribbean in Domínguez (1993).

12. Military lore is described and analysed at length in Nunn (1979).

13. Lieutenant Colonel Manuel Morla Concha, 'Función social del ejército peruano en la organización de la nacionalidad', *Revista Militar del Perú* (October 1933): 843–72; 'La función social del ejército' (April 1952): vii–xxv.

14. Presented at the annual meeting of the Rocky Mountain Council for Latin American Studies, Texas Tech University, Lubbock, Texas, March 1974, and later published as Nunn (1975).

15. For comments on military–civilian roles of the future, see Nunn (1995).

16. Loveman (1993) makes a solid case for the nineteenth-century origins of the professional military's constitutionally mandated internal role assignments. He has done the same in a forthcoming volume dealing with the twentieth century. An excellent country case study on transition from military rule is Stepan (1989). See also Stepan (1988).

17. What follows is but a sampling of implicit and explicit questioning by South Americans of the US' hegemonic position *vis-à-vis* hemispheric

defense and security priorities in the wake of the cold war: Major (r) Sergio Toyos, 'Fuerzas armadas y guardias nacionales', *Revista Militar* (Argentina) (April–June 1995): 57–8; General Ricardo Etchevary Boneo, 'El Tercer Mundo dentro del pensamiento estratégico de los EE.UU', *Revista Militar* (January–June 1996): 46–52; Colonel (r) Roberto Miscow Filho, 'A Funçao e O Papel das Forças Armadas', *A Defésa Nacional* (Brazil) (July–September 1993): 89–95; Colonel Valmir Fonseca Azevedo Pereira, 'O Relacionamento Militar Brasil x Estados Unidos', *Revista do Exército Brasileiro* (4th trimester 1996): 11–16; Lieutenant Colonel Cristián Le Dantec G., 'El NAFTA, los tratados de libre comercio y su posible repercusión en la defensa nacional', *Política y Estrategia* (Chile) (May–August 1995): 33–5; Colonel Juan R. Galecio Araya, 'La situación mundial actual: Algunas reflexiones', *Memorial del Ejército de Chile* (2nd quarter 1996): 187–205; Lieutenant Colonel Otto Guibovich Arteaga, 'La doctrina militar propia: Necesidad o imperativo', *Revista del Ejército del Perú* (7 June 1995): 42–7; and 'Chavín de Huántar', *Actualidad Militar* (Peru) (May–June 1997): 8–9; a paean to the 22 April operation that freed hostages of the Tupac Amaru Revolutionary Movement held in the Embassy of Japan without either 'advice or assistance from any foreign power with experience ...'.

18. For examples of consistency in argument see the following Argentine, Brazilian and Peruvian sources from the 1980s and 1990s: Colaboración Curso Básico de Comando 1980, 'El euro-comunismo', *Revista de la Escuela Superior de Guerra* (Argentina) (January–February 1981): 15–42; General Ramón G. Díaz Bessone, 'Guerra revolucionaria en la Argentina, 1959–1978', *Revista Militar* (January–June 1988): 7–20; General (r) Héctor Rodríguez Espada, 'Las fuerzas armadas y la subversión terrorista', *Revista Militar* (October–December 1995): 45–9; Colonel Nelson Abreu do O' de Ah-neida, 'Forças Armadas: Apenas Segurança Externa?', *A Defésa Nacional* (March–April 1989): 23–34; Lieutenant Colonel Osmar José de Barros Ribeiro, 'O Tráfico de Drogas no Mundo e no Brasil', *A Defésa Nacional* (October–December 1995): 51–64; Dr Jesús Lazo Acosta, 'Análisis sicosocial del terrorismo', *Revista Militar del Perú* (September–December 1985): 3–15; and Lieutenant Colonel Roberto Vizcardo Benavides, 'Ejército del Perú: Seguridad, paz y desarrollo', *Revista del Ejército del Perú* (30 November 1995): 5–8. For Chilean sources see Nunn (1995).

3
War, Society and the State in South America, 1800–70

Hans Vogel

Introduction

There is a close, triangular relationship between the State, Society and War. Thucydides and Livy have already made observations to that effect, and they have been followed by many others such as Machiavelli, Montecuccoli and Hans Delbrück (Pieri, 1963). After a period when military history – even if related to state and society – was shunned by the historical profession for being old-fashioned and traditional, today one notes a kind of comeback of the subject.[1] So far, attention from this point of view has been mainly given to the history of Europe and North America. The military history of Latin America is still largely the domain of retired army colonels, uniform freaks and old-fashioned battle-historians.

The military history of Latin America ought to be rewritten, if not to be written, period. This vast field has hitherto hardly been worked. The situation is, however, not a desperate one. Much useful material is to be found in the sheer limitless numbers of biographies of nineteenth-century figures. Nor is there a shortage of traditional institutional studies, dealing mainly with the military in times of peace.[2] Most work by non-Latin Americans falls into this category, as it tends to deal exclusively with the army as an institution in peacetime.[3] If there are any studies of the military at war, these tend to be 'general staff' histories, military history written from the top looking down, with lots of details about the functioning of the command structure, but little eye for the experiences of the man in the field (see for example Best, 1960; Lecuna, 1960). But as John Keegan has shrewdly pointed out, the military historian ought to look at the way the army performs the tasks for which it is intended, that is fighting, and holding up under duress. This can be done most fruitfully by looking at the way the individual soldier behaves on and about the battlefield (see Keegan, 1976; Holmes, 1986). Besides the social and psychological approach to military history as advocated by Keegan and Holmes, there is a parallel approach analysing the relations between war and society, or armed forces and society, pioneered by George Clark, Piero Pieri and André Corvisier in the 1950s. Along these lines, the Chilean historian Alvaro Jara has published a classic work on the theme of colonial society and war: *Guerra y sociedad en Chile: La transformación de la Guerra de Arauco y la esclavitud de los indios* (Santiago, 1971). Despite there being an earlier French version, this book is still largely unknown outside the rather limited field of specialists.

At the same time that the army and society approach was initiated in Europe, US historians and political scientists such as John J. Johnson and Samuel Huntington began to look at the relationship between army and politics. Departing from this research angle, the eighteenth-century military reforms in the framework of the 'Bourbon Reforms' have been a favorite topic with a number of North American scholars belonging to the 'McAlister school': Lyle McAlister, Allan Kuethe, Leon Campbell and Gary Miller.

Few scholars working on Latin American military history have asked, let alone tried to answer, some of the key questions to be asked by modern military history: how was discipline maintained, what was morale like, and how was it affected by the particular experiences of the different units? What about leadership, was it effective or inept and inefficient? What about the medical perspective, and what about the natural circumstances, such as terrain and climate? What about food, fatigue, equipment and weapons? Such details have decisive influence on the performance of the individual soldier and his unit.

'State' and 'society' in the early nineteenth century

As far as Latin American history is concerned, the subjects State and Society are far more familiar and better understood than War. The state, to begin with, is generally understood to have been weak or even absent, prior to the advent of modern tools of state control, such as the railway, the telegraph and the breechloading repeating rifle with smokeless ammunition. The integration of Latin America into the world economy brought about phenomenal economic growth, making some countries relatively rich. By the early 1900s, for instance, Argentina alone accounted for more than half of the continent's combined foreign trade. Together with Chile, Uruguay and Southern Brazil (inclusive of São Paulo), this region – which we might call the Southern Cone or, neglecting Uruguay, the ABC countries – had become what it still is today: the economic power-house of Latin America. The contrast with the situation in the first half of the nineteenth century could hardly be starker.

Although in name these countries were sovereign states with a substantial national territory, in reality the authority of what could hardly be called the 'central government' did not extend far beyond the capital. Chile occupied merely the Central Valley and some out-lying regions, such as Concepción; Argentina was a congeries of 14 quite autonomous provinces, with only Buenos Aires remotely able to participate in a process of modernization, whereas the authority of the Emperor of Brazil did not reach far beyond the city limits of Rio de Janeiro. Uruguay was little more than a port with some sur-rounding countryside. To refer to these political configurations as states may be correct in an abstract sense, and for want of a better term, but neither their authority nor the number of their civil ser-vants could stand comparison with contemporary states in other parts of the Atlantic world.

The dismantling of the colonial state – which was a state by any standard – had led in many places to a total or partial breakdown of public order and civilized life. One of the first victims of the revolu-tions for Independence was the humble task of day-to-day paper work. As clerks could not be paid their salaries, or were chased out of the country by hardship or for being of suspect loyalty to the new order, bureaucracy evidently suffered. Needless to say, the reverse was true in Brazil where the arrival of the Royal family, the Royal government and its staff in 1807 contributed to a strengthening of the state.

Perhaps it would be better not to speak of 'the' state, but instead to use the plural 'states', since it could be argued that every auto-nomous Argentine province and each Brazilian province constituted a separate state. Though at first glance less obvious than in Argentina, provincial autonomy in Brazil was far-reaching, with some prerogatives, such as having an independent armed force, only abolished in the 1930s. It might be worthwhile to compare Brazil and Argentina with medieval France, where the authority of a central state (Île de France) was in theory recognized by the other regions of the realm. In practice, however, the central government could exert little if any authority outside the area under its immediate control.

What may be said of the state also holds true for society. It might be more useful to think of Brazil, Argentina and Chile as groupings of different societies, rather than as single, unified ones. The terms 'national identity', nationality and nationalism can hardly be applied to Argentina or Brazil as a whole. The case of Chile is doubtful. At any rate, not even in Chile was there a true nationwide public opinion, which seems one of the main conditions for the existence of national identity. Public opinion existed in the national capitals and in a few major ports and inland towns, but detailed historical knowledge of its extent and functioning is lacking. The extent to which there was a network connecting the various local elites is likewise still largely unknown. For all practical purposes, therefore, it is at best doubtful if one may use the term 'society' to denote the whole of a population living within the borders of the newly independent countries (Deutsch, 1966). In many cases it was the vestiges of the Spanish colonial state and society somehow holding the various countries together. The longevity of such mechanisms ought not to be underestimated, as they continued to be in operation throughout the nineteenth century. Foremost among these mechanisms is the rule of Spanish law. As of today, knowledge of this subject – the survival of colonial legal practice and its position within a Latin American 'moral economy' – is practically non-existent.

Such was the background of the long series of civil and international wars in the Southern Cone in the nineteenth century, beginning with the British invasions of Buenos Aires and Montevideo in 1806, and ending with the Paraguayan War of 1864–70. It may be argued that the War of the Pacific (1879–83) and the Aparicio Saravia rebellion of 1903 in Uruguay deserve to be included and discussed as well. However, these conflicts took place in the midst of an otherwise tranquil period, and as economic developments had already drastically changed many regions in the Southern Cone. At best, the latter conflicts are to be regarded as distant echoes of a process that had begun a century earlier, and that had largely run its course before the 1880s.

War and the shaping of the nation

Organized collective violence was an essential feature of life in Argentina, Brazil and Chile for the better part of the nineteenth century. Chile, a relatively compact and small society, was used to a special kind of organized violence over a much longer period than either Argentina or Brazil. Ever since the Araucanian Indians had pushed back the Spaniards north across the Bío-Bío River in 1598, Chile had been a militarized society. Nowhere else in the Spanish Empire was there such a constant and real threat of falling victim to a fierce indigenous warrior nation, and nowhere else was military alertness and preparedness such a central feature of life as in Chile. Chilean and foreign historians have tended to consider this circumstance as the major factor in shaping Chile as a nation, and perhaps it can be argued that Chile is the only true nation-state in Spanish America, possibly alongside Mexico.

The colonial roots of nineteenth-century collective violence may also be detected in Southern Brazil and in Argentina. The southern part of Brazil was the area where the bandeirantes operated since the seventeenth century, pushing back frontiers and blazing trails for further colonization. Argentina was plagued for a long time by incursions by hostile indigenous communities who disrupted trade and communications between the coastal settlements and those in the interior, such as Córdoba, Tucumán and Salta. Border conflicts between the Spanish and the Portuguese, resulting in major military operations in 1750 and 1775, are further proof that the River Plate was far from peaceful even in the second half of the eighteenth century when the economy prospered.

The Independence Wars in the River Plate came close on the heels of a border war involving the biggest single troop transport (some 10 000 men) ever to have been undertaken by the Spaniards prior to the reinforcement under Pablo Morillo sent to Venezuela in 1816. The British invasions of 1806 and 1807 carried on the tradition of major military encounters in the Southern Cone even before the

Independence Wars had begun. However, the British invasions brought about a massive mobilization of the civilian population (though within the spirit of the Bourbon military reforms), especially in Buenos Aires. Thousands of local inhabitants spontaneously took up arms and donned uniforms, confronting the invaders in rapidly raised units organized along ethnic and regional lines. These militia units formed the backbone of the revolutionary army that was created in the wake of the proclamation of an autonomous government at Buenos Aires in 1810 (see Halperín Donghi, 1968).

The new *juntas* taking power in Spain's American kingdoms were the answer by American creoles and those sympathizing with them to the crisis that affected the Spanish Empire as a whole. This crisis was not a mere political one, but it was felt in every facet of Spanish civilization. New forms of political organization had to be found to replace the old absolutist system. The obvious and immediate answer – a product of the Enlightenment as much as the Absolutist system it was seeking to replace – was Liberalism. However, it took some generations and a lot of violence to have it adopted as the guiding principle for the organization of state and society. The opposing forces were diverse and, above all, formidable (see Annino, 1995).

The Independence Wars, immediately following the installation of autonomous regimes in the Spanish American capitals, were essentially civil wars. They also had an international dimension in that they were at the same time wars of decolonization, but their main distinguishing feature was their internecine character, pitting the members of a single society against each other. In order to understand the way these wars were fought, it is as helpful to be aware of the issues as it is to take a closer look at the armed forces of the first half of the nineteenth century and the late eighteenth century.

Southern Cone armies: the colonial heritage

To begin with, the traditional standing army in the Southern Cone was made up of relatively small units stationed in a number of towns. This so-called *ejército de dotación* had units in three Chilean cities (Valparaíso, Santiago and Valdivia), on Chiloé Island and along the frontier, mostly concentrated in the town of Concepción. In the Platine region, small units were to be found at Buenos Aires, Montevideo and along four frontiers: the Luján frontier, the Chaco, the Banda Oriental, and in Corrientes. From the 1760s, reinforcements were also despatched to Buenos Aires, totalling more than 4000 soldiers. The Bourbon Reforms created an additional military force, the militias, in order to be better able to resist possible attacks from overseas. Thus, in the River Plate and Chile, some 55 new units were formed between 1760 and 1810. Brazil could hardly muster military force superior to those of its Spanish neighbors, even after the arrival of the Court from Lisbon in 1807.

Obviously, the colonial troops, both peninsulars and creoles, were organized according to prevailing Spanish and Portuguese military doctrine and tradition. It is hardly surprising that both armies were strongly influenced by the leading military powers of the day in the second half of the eighteenth century: Prussia and France. In Spain, French influence was probably prevalent since the Bourbon dynasty had begun drastic reforms, with the French example foremost in their minds. In 1768, King Charles III decreed a new set of military laws and regulations, the so-called *Ordenanzas de Carlos III*, that were to have a decisive influence on all armies of the newly independent Spanish American republics. For instance, the Ordenanzas remained in force in Argentina until 1888, and even afterwards continued to form the backbone and the essence of the new regulations. As a matter of fact, together with Chile, Argentina is considered to be among the countries where Spanish military influence has been strongest (Gárate Córdoba, 1986: 128).

American troops were trained according to the same principles and standards as those of Spain. Most attention was given to the drilling of infantry soldiers, especially those destined for service in *Line Regiments*. In accordance with prevailing battlefield practice in Europe, the main task of troops of the line was to exert supreme self-control. They were expected to hold their terrain and to advance when possible. Firing was supposed to be done in a very controlled way, with the troops arranged in three rows behind each other, the first row kneeling and the other two standing. The first row was to fire a volley first, then the second and finally the third. While one row fired, the other two could clean and reload their rifles, the maximum rapidity of fire being about two to three shots a minute. When subjected to artillery fire, line regiments were expected to stand still and not to dive for cover and run away. Regiments quietly standing as they were being massacred by ricocheting and caramboling round shot had a demoralizing effect on the enemy. However, only the best regiments in the most renowned armies were capable of such battlefield conduct. Constant drilling enabled line regiments to perform delicate manoeuvres, transforming from a marching column into a line and back, on both flat and undulating terrain. It is not surprising that it was extremely costly to train and maintain effective line regiments, and it took at least four years of intensive drilling and training to form a good soldier of the line. Although economic and tactical reasons moved states to field other kinds of troops, operating in a more unorthodox and flexible way between the lines and in broken terrain, the so-called *cazadores* (from *Jäger*, or *chasseurs*, also called *tirailleurs*) line regiments continued to form the backbone of armies until the middle of the nineteenth century. Even so, actual fighting did not proceed in textbook fashion, and warfare was not nearly as orderly as accounts and engravings would have us believe.

Warfare in the Southern Cone was hardly ever carried out by the rules of military theorists. Most engagements involved more horse than foot soldiers. Battles involving linear tactics were few and far between; some battles in Upper Peru and north-western Argentina, and the Battle at Caseros in 1852, constituting the clearest examples; although it has to be stressed that even in that battle, horses were involved in staggering numbers. Urquiza's allied forces had over 50 000 horses and more than half (17 000) of his troops (28 000) were mounted. Part of the explanation can be found in the poor quality of troops recruited in the area. Most foot soldiers were cityfolk, and for that simple reason less resistant to fatigue and hardship than rural people. Montecuccoli, for instance, always emphasized that country boys were far superior as soldiers to men recruited among urban populations.[4] Moreover, during and after the Wars of Independence, governments seldom had the time or the funds, often not even the instructors and experts, to build up an army of the line.

From a technical point of view, there was no discontinuity between the American colonial armies and the armed forces of the independent countries. Around 1810, Southern Cone armies still used the standard Spanish army flintlock musket, firing a round lead ball weighing some 25 grams (a caliber of about 18 mm). Such weapons were accurate up to a range of 100 meters. As for mounted troops, in addition to a carbine and a sabre they carried a three-meter long lance, which in fact was the most effective weapon for horsemen, making full use of the animal's momentum. Artillery units used bronze cannon of various calibers, firing round shot weighing 3, 6, 9 and 12 pounds. It should be borne in mind that major breakthroughs in armament technology did not take place for about a hundred years, from 1750 to 1850. The middle of the nineteenth century saw the introduction of the breechloading rifle firing prefabricated aerodynamically shaped bullets from brass shells. In fact, there was not a great difference in equipment between the Spanish American fighting men of the first half of the nineteenth century and the soldiers of Frederick the Great of Prussia.

Material conditions of warfare

If armaments and equipment in America were hardly different from those found in Europe, there was a world of difference regarding the other material conditions of warfare. In the first place, the road infrastructure in America was totally incomparable to the situation obtaining in Europe. Roads were often non-existent, and if there were roads they did not cover great distances, making most troop movements at best cumbersome; it was practically impossible to move large numbers of soldiers. Since logistics – the provisioning of troops – was correspondingly difficult, it is only too obvious that warfare could only take place under quite restraining conditions. Given the complicated logistical situation it is not surprising that a network of magazines such as sustained warfare even in the most densely populated areas of Europe could not be set up in the Americas. Thus, in contrast with Europe, where campaigns often took place in the richest and most densely populated regions (such as Belgium and Northern France, Germany, the Po Valley), there was hardly a place where war found a natural environment. The only place springing to mind is probably the Rio de la Plata. There, conditions were ideal for operations involving great numbers of horses, where fodder was abundant on the endless grassy plains.

Again, in contrast to Europe, there were hardly any good and reliable maps available for Spanish and Portuguese America. With France and Austria leading the way in the 1760s, the major European powers had initiated massive cartographical programs mapping the entire national territory, producing, as in the case of

France, a set of superbly detailed maps on a scale of 1:85 000. Such maps were an essential tool for warfare as they enabled commanders to make full use of the terrain, to select the best place for a battle and to direct and coordinate intricate troop movements. The newly created general and divisional staffs, moreover, could produce detailed maps on demand, using triangulation and observation. Even if artillery officers had received thorough training in such skills, also in Spanish America, they were seldom able to put their knowledge to as good a use as their European counterparts, for the simple reason that campaigning in America was often rapid and did not permit armies to stay in any one place for any length of time. Consequently, engagements mostly had a more improvised nature in the Americas than in Europe.

From the point of view of health, it was also advisable not to stay in any one place too long, thus putting an extra premium on a war of movement. For instance, in north-western Argentina, especially in the scant oases of this arid region, malaria was endemic, threatening the health of soldiers as they passed through and decimating their numbers if they stayed too long. As late as the 1880s, a French naval medical officer stationed in the Rio de la Plata noted how military camps set up near estancias could be suddenly affected by outbreaks of typhoid fever, causing many deaths and driving men to suicide (Devoti, 1885). During the Paraguayan War, the contending armies were visited by cholera, yellow fever, malaria and smallpox, in addition to the usual flagellations of syphilis, asthma and tetanus. It goes without saying that scant regard for hygiene in the semi-permanent abodes associated with many military campaigns created a hospitable environment for fleas, lice and rats, the most unwelcome of guests for any household, and the carriers of deadly diseases.

Since distances in the Southern Cone were great, and displacements cumbersome, troops that could move swiftly, strike rapidly and disappear as quickly were extremely useful and valuable. In other words, by nature, cavalry was the Queen of the Battlefield, unlike in Europe where it was rather the infantry. It is especially in the 'pure' civil war phase of fighting in the Southern Cone, that is, after the Independence Wars, that cavalry fully took this position.

American armies, though dressed and equipped in the same manner as their European counterparts, were radically different. In many respects their social makeup, their recruitment and their values were a throwback to long-forgotten periods in European history. In the first place, armies were relatively small. It was quite expensive to maintain a substantial armed force, and most American governments of the early Independence years were faced with serious financial problems. Most national armies did not exceed a few thousand men. Brazil, which had the biggest army in the 1820s, halved it in 1831 from 30 000 to some 14 000, and even then most soldiers were assigned to garrison duties and could not be assembled into a field army. As during the Wars of Independence, effective field armies seldom exceeded the 10 000 mark.

Officers and rank and file

In knowledge, customs and tradition, neither officers nor the rank and file differed a great deal from their counterparts in the late colonial armies. In general, Spanish American and Brazilian commanders, whatever their formal training or bookish knowledge and inclinations, were as good as anyone when it came to practical knowledge. The nature of war in the Southern Cone demanded high adaptability (as all wars tend to do) and flexibility. If anything, traditional military wisdom as could be found in European manuals had to be abandoned. Such conditions helped to nurture a kind of military officer unknown in Europe itself, but rather to be encountered on its colonial fringes. It may not be far-fetched to compare Southern Cone military commanders of the first half of the nineteenth century with the officers of the French Foreign Legion on duty in Northern Africa, the so-called 'Africains', who had risen through the ranks on their own merit and valor and on whom Emperor Napoleon III relied so strongly. Other comparisons spring to mind as well, such as the officers of the British army in India, the Russians fighting in Central Asia and the Caucasian foothills, and even Helmuth von Moltke since his service on the Ottoman Kurdish frontier in the 1830s.

As for the rank and file, their recruitment was never easy, nor was army life. Armies everywhere were rather grim organizations, where harsh corporal punishment was the order of the day. This was true especially of armies operating far from their natural home base, such as the frontier armies of European powers and the armies of the Southern Cone governments in the first half of the nineteenth century.

Small wonder that a career as an army soldier held few attractions, save perhaps for the social flotsam and jetsam. The few who signed up out of their own free will, and the many who were forced to do service through *enganche* or as a *destinado* (arrested under the various vagrancy laws), were not ideal soldiers. They were rather the dregs of society, quite unlike the ideal of the citizen soldier as advocated by Jourdan in France in 1798 and practised in the post-Jena Prussian army. Nor were they the kind of hardened but well-paid, proud professionals that made up the Austrian army stationed in Italy until 1859.

Early nineteenth-century Southern Cone soldiers were subjected to the only language it was felt they could understand: violence. Hence the corporal punishments, ranging from whipping and beating to branding and worse. Small wonder that many tried to run away at the first opportunity. There are few figures on desertions but, even so, the term was frequently defined and interpreted differently. In the end, all we have are some rough indications and estimates. During General Manuel Belgrano's campaign in Upper Peru and north-western Argentina in 1812 and 1813, for instance, desertion rates reached up to 40 per cent in selected companies (total annual desertions expressed as a percentage of average strength). It seems, however, that most deserters eventually reported back for duty and were pardoned. When General José Rondeau, nicknamed '*mamita*', led his army to the north-west of Argentina in 1815, almost half the men had vanished into thin air before the destination was reached. Desertion was also quite high in the Brazilian army fighting Buenos Aires in the Banda Oriental in 1827, and in the Argentine forces fighting in Paraguay in the late 1860s. Of course, desertion is a perennial companion of armies, not a phenomenon to be found only in the rickety armies of the early nineteenth-century Southern Cone governments. Desertion, for instance, was notoriously high in the French army of the 1730s, and in Frederick the Great's army of the Seven Years' War. On the other hand, desertion in the French revolutionary armies of the 1790s was about 2 per cent.

In all likelihood, desertion declined in the *caudillo* armies of the 1820s, 1830s, 1840s and 1850s. Warfare between the *caudillos*, for all that is known about it from the writings of men like General José María Paz and General Tomás de Iriarte, did not resemble the still rather organized fighting of earlier years. Local commanders would call up their men (now usually numbering hundreds rather than thousands), assemble them for a lightning raid into neighboring territory, and then return laden with loot and booty. After carving the booty up among the raiding party, the soldiers (all horsemen and all preferably armed with lances and sabres) would return to their homes and cabins. This kind of warfare recalls early medieval or even Germanic practice, when every free man had to answer a call to arms, fight a brief campaign, and could then return home. Long campaigns were impossible under this system. Of course, Domingo Faustino Sarmiento had already noticed the medieval character of civil war in the Rio de la Plata, but he merely interpreted it as proof of his country's backwardness.

If historical data tend to be unreliable, those on the casualties of war are even more so, while historical data on nineteenth-century Latin America have to be used with the utmost caution. It is, therefore, no easy task to provide accurate estimates of war casualties for nineteenth-century warfare in the ABC countries; there is an endless series of major and minor battles and insignificant 'combates' to be analysed. Still, such data would be quite helpful in understanding the significance of armed conflict in the Southern Cone. Needless to say, in order to better understand the complex relationship between war, society and the state in the ABC countries in particular and in Latin America in general, military history is the field to turn to.

Notes

1. There is a marked increase in the number of monographs dealing with war in general, such as Keegan (1993) and Cardini (1995), as well as new encyclopedias, such as Cowley and Parker (1996).
2. Access to this body of literature is provided by such useful tools as Etchepareborda (1984).
3. For example, Campbell (1978). A good example of a recent Latin American work is Suárez (1984). See also Marchena Fernández (1983).
4. Raymond de Montecuccoli, the savoy general in Austrian service, hero of the wars against the Ottoman Turks in the seventeenth century and a classic authority on the art of war, insisted on the need for high quality men: '... on ne doit pas enrôler des hommes de la lie du peuple, ni au hazard: mais il faut les choisir entre les meilleurs; sains, hardis, robustes, à la fleur de leur age, endurcis aux travaux de la campagne, ou à des arts pénibles; qu'ils ne soient ni faineans, ni effeminez, ni débauchez ...' (1712: 19).

4
The Army as a Modernizing Actor in Brazil, 1870–1930

Celso Castro

Introduction

During the period between the end of the Empire and the First Brazilian Republic – that is, in the six decades from the end of the Paraguayan War in 1870, going through the military coup of 1889 until the 1930 Revolution – the army was the most active social agent in the modernization of the country.[1] Before examining this affirmation, it is necessary to clarify two points. Firstly, by 'modernizing' I understand the affirmation of values and an implementation of practices linked to individualism, discipline, rationality, bureaucratic organization and merit in a society, like the Brazilian one of that period, marked by a strong colonial heritage, slavery-oriented and patriarchal, where aristocratic values and personal relations predominated. Secondly, it would be a mistake to treat the army as a whole, without acknowledging the minor group that, in fact, best fulfilled this role: the young officers with higher education in the Military Academy.

The affirmation of individual merit as a value can only be correctly understood in a wider context of historical and cultural processes leading to the progress of *individualism* in modern western societies. These values held the center of the political arena after the French Revolution: the affirmation of value attributed to the singularity of an individual, who considers himself independently from the groups that he belongs to. Instead of passively suffering from the influence of this process, the military institution has been, in reality, one of its most active agents.

The officer corps which graduated from the new military academies created at the end of the Napoleonic Wars differed in many
aspects from their own societies, assembling 'isles of modernity' in
the middle of an ocean of traditional values. In the non-European
societies, the action of the young officers educated in military academies as modernizing vanguards was very important, especially
when they took political power. In these countries, the superior military academies have always been one of the first and more important institutions to disseminate 'modern' practices and values,
opening, in this way, new channels of social mobility to individuals
not belonging to the traditional elite. The conflicts resulting from
this factor have often led to dramatic effects (cf. Ralston, 1990).

In the process of professionalizing modern armies, the existence
of military academies with egalitarian access – more specifically,
without demanding an aristocratic background from their students –
accomplishes an absolutely central role. Consequently, the *spirit* of
the officer corps – their social identity – was less frequently referred
to as an aristocratic spirit of class and, instead, focused more on its
own institution. The hierarchy of the military institution tended to
be disassociated from social hierarchy. If in premodern armies the
body of officers was 'anchored' in society because of its aristocratic
origin, with growing professionalization, a specific *ethos* was developed. In this way they became a professional group with relative
autonomy in relation to the rest of society. Aristocracy through
birth was progressively substituted by an aristocracy through merit,
conferred through education. Around 1870, this process was reason-
ably consolidated in the majority of western armies.[2]

The Military Academy

Although it had been created in 1810, the Military Academy in
Brazil only became a prerequisite for entering the officer corps and
for building a career as of 1850. In 1889, the professionalization of
the officer corps had advanced considerably, with the growing adoption of bureaucratic criteria for promotion and for the merit system.
This resulted in an opening of a military career to people who did
not belong to the elite; to anyone who wished to have an official
position, this was a career open to talent. The same modernization,
in fact, did not occur in the rest of the army corps; it would take

some decades to change the profile of the rank and file through the introduction of universal conscription. Besides this, a series of reform measures and the modernization of the Army – like the creation of a General Staff, the adoption of new instruction doctrines, the construction or recovery of old installations and the purchase of efficient armaments – would only be implemented with the advent of the Republic.

In the period from 1874 to 1904 the Military Academy functioned at Praia Vermelha, in Rio de Janeiro. It was here that the formation of the *mocidade militar* ('military youngsters', to use the language of that period) took place and played an active role in the Republican conspiracy that led to the 1889 coup, ending the last monarchy of South America. The social profile of this group deserves close attention. A typical member of the 'military youngsters' came from the north, the least developed region of the country, and was less than 30 years old at the time of becoming involved in the conspiracy that led to the Republic. Many were still students; the rest were still in the early stages of their careers. Many students came from modest homes and took up a military career from necessity rather than actual vocation. Because it was gratuitous (in reality, the students even received a small salary), the Military Academy was practically the only route in the Empire for people of non-aristocratic birth to achieve higher education. The ethnography of life in the Military Academy, is therefore, absolutely essential to an examination of the professional socialization and the cultural universe of the 'military youngsters'. Below, I will attempt to clarify how a young man, when entering the Military Academy in the final years of the Empire, became a follower of visions that were considered modern.

Tabernacle of Science

Documents found in personal archives give us a very good understanding of this process. One can refer, for example, to the case of José Beviláqua. He was a 16-year-old, who arrived for the first time in the city of Rio de Janeiro (then the court and capital of the Empire) to study in the Military Academy. He was born in a small town in the province of Ceará, in the north, and his parents were of humble origin. Through letters written to his parents, we learn of his first impressions regarding the Court. Upon first visiting the

Military Academy, he found everything 'very beautiful and amazing', the food was very good, and he was impressed with a painting depicting the Paraguayan War – the painting was bigger than the living room of his house. The city dazzled him even more. He wrote about the first time he rode in a street-car, went to the theater and of a 'marvelous invention' he saw when going out for a walk in Ouvidor Street (the most fashionable street and heart of the city): a gramophone, a 'machine that talks'. He synthesizes this new world he discovered: 'Rio de Janeiro is Brazil and Ouvidor Street is Rio de Janeiro. Everything here is very beautiful.'

For the great majority of military students coming from the provinces, especially from the north, arriving at the Court for the first time implicated not just a spatial, but a *cultural* displacement. Among other things, it meant experiencing a different social pace from that of the province: more 'modern', 'advanced' and 'fast', contrasting with a slower and backward quasi-colonial pace. The preference is clear: for José Beviláqua, Rio de Janeiro becomes Brazil's reflection, getting closer to Europe than to the *sertões* (hinterland).

Another great change occurred upon entering the Military Academy. Away from the family and from his homeland, the basic referential group of the new student was composed of his colleagues. It was through intense daily interaction with his peers at the Academy that he became part of the 'military youngsters'. It is quite obvious that there is no such thing as a perfectly harmonious and uniform collective body, but the *esprit de corps* among the students of the Military Academy seems to have been quite strong. The dull image they kept of professors and commandants contrasts vividly with their remembrance of the interactions between colleagues during the hazy period, leisure time, in lodgings and associations; and all this contributed significantly to the formation of the social identity of the 'scientific' youngsters of Praia Vermelha as a specific group.

These elements were not the only ones. As previously mentioned, during the Empire the Military Academy was the main institution to develop modern characteristics at the heart of a predominantly traditional society – rural, patriarchal and hierarchical – remaining so well-beyond the institution of the Republic. Among those characteristics, there are two which must be emphasized: the predominance among students of a 'scientificist' mentality and the supervalorization of the merit principle. Those two elements constituted a basis for social identity among the young educated officers.

I will attempt to give an idea of how these cultural elements informed the political action that led to the end of the monarchy and to the installation of a republican regime in Brazil, in 1889. One may begin by referring to 'scientificism', presently understood, in the sense of the supervalorization of science: 'Not that scientifisists value science for science, – what they acknowledge is the innocuousness of any "non-scientific" solution to human problems' (Barros, 1959: 323). The very expression used informally by students in naming the Academy as the 'Tabernacle of Science', reveals the high regard for the study of the sciences.

The Brazilian Military Academy, was for a long time the only engineering school in the Empire. There was a clear superiority in the curriculum of the so-called scientific branches (artillery and engineering) on the study of infantry and cavalry. The course was known for its complexity, especially in relation to mathematics. Theoretic studies received better attention than practical ones, which seem to have been in reality, consistently deficient. It is enough to say that those students who graduated received the title of 'Bachelor, in mathematics and physical sciences'.

In this way, there was an enormous gap between the Military Academy graduated officers and the rest (the majority) of the army officers who had no higher education and held a fundamentally *troupier* profile. With the lack of what was considered attractive perspectives for professional promotion within the army, the young 'scientifics' became less interested in the military profession (their lack of vocation was frequently declared) and more interested in belonging to the Brazilian intellectual elite. It was with members of that elite that they disputed socially and symbolically, space and power.

During most of the Empire in Brazil, the hegemony of the Bachelors of Law within the Brazilian elite was clearly evident. While the social status of military personnel was low, the young Bachelors of Law had easy access to public charges and functions in all political and administrative posts of the country. So the young 'scientifics' of the army fought for a better position inside a social field dominated by Bachelors of Law. Not only was the Praia Vermelha Academy a military academy, it was also a rival to civilian academies.

Opposition between young 'scientific' military personnel and Law Bachelors, frequently appears in the writing of students of that period. They always mentioned 'scientific' elements as being the ones deficient in Bachelors of Law. It is important to notice that the *form* assumed by the kind of discourse and characteristic thought of the military youngsters was very close to the model so much criticized in the law majors, whom they would have liked to differ from. In the Military Academy, for example, there was no sort of practical study or any significant scientific experimentation; the same conventional 'bachelorism' so much criticized in the law courses predominated. The title of 'Bachelor in mathematics and physical sciences' conceived in the Military Academy, even though it emphasized the importance of the study in mathematics and science, also placed its title in the academic fields of 'Bachelors'. The military bachelors disputed social prestige within the civilian Bachelors, using different arms but subject to the same rules. The similarities in thought and discourse, however, must not obscure important differences in discourse and contents – in the curriculum of the Military Academy and in the form of language used by the student, 'scientific' elements still predominate – and also of professional and scholar *socialization*. In addition, and in contrast to the practices existing in the law schools, the Military Academy was well-known for its sternness and seriousness in the evaluation of individuals.

Euclides da Cunha – future author of *Os Sertões* (one of the most important books in Brazil), then a 20-year-old student – wrote an article criticizing the 'sad state of our law academies, where society is studied without notions of the most simple natural laws' (Cunha, 1984: 54). The study of sciences, especially mathematics was therefore a powerful symbolic element of differentiation for the military students of that time, a constitutive element of their social identity. It is solely for this reason that, as we have seen, students called their school at Praia Vermelha a Tabernacle of Science.

The study of mathematics and sciences was attributed a greater importance than we can conceive nowadays. It was seen as an essential value in the forming of mental states and for psychological predispositions, as fundamental to the formation of the mental structure of the young military men. Mathematics and the study of sciences seem to parody an image from Durkheim: the 'skeleton' of the spirit of the military youth who dwelled upon the Tabernacle of Science. The young military graduates from the Military Academy at the end of the Empire shared the same cultural background of metaphors, examples, images and exemplary narratives taken in

great part from mathematics and the sciences and applied to particular situations.

According to the scientificist mentality, the world of values would
be reducible to the plane of physical and natural phenomena, which
it would only differ from because of its being more complex, and
not because of being of a different nature. Philosophy, politics
and moral values should also become 'scientific'. This project had
already been present during the European Enlightenment. The novelty of the nineteenth century was the incorporation of history to
nature, mainly through the notion of *evolution* and the idea that the
same determinism present in the natural world would be the same
that conducts the development of humanity. In this way, moral,
political and philosophical values had come to be seen as manifestations of the place where humanity was at that point. This nourished
a feeling of intellectual superiority among the scientificists, who
naturally considered themselves products of the most 'advanced'
place in humanity.

The intellectual style characteristic of scientificism was a strong
force during the second half of the nineteenth century, materializ-
ing in diverse *isms*: materialism, positivism, Darwinism, evolutionism, monism. They were all looking for a *law* that could determine
progress and evolution. With Comte, for example, the law of three
stages would take form; with Darwin and Haeckel, the fight for survival of the fittest; with Spencer, evolution from the homogeneous
to the heterogeneous, of differentiation. Applied to Brazilian reality,
these different scientificistic interpretations pointed in one direction: national history was thought of as being part of the universal
movement, and not a distinct entity. Concerning the identity
between the national and international, Brazil's specific situation
came to be seen as one stage in the course which the so-called more
developed societies had already gone through. For the scientificist,
the objective was to quicken the pace of the country's progress, so
that it would start to actively take part in universal history.[3]

The writings of students from the Military Academy, as already
mentioned, reveal a diverse intellectual environment. Even though
there were some orthodox positivists, they never formed a significant
group among the students. The predominant scientificism was the
eclectic mixture of diverse doctrines: positivism, evolutionism, monism, and so on. Of most importance to the young scientifics was the

general spirit of these doctrines and not the doctrinary intricacies. The difference between authors was minimized in relation to what they had in common: the faith in progress and the emphasis given to science. They were all in accord regarding this point of view.

Meritocratic vision

We will now deal briefly with the supervalorization of the merit principle, the second element that, in my opinion, was a base of social identity among the young educated officers, and that together with scientificism informed their political action.

As mentioned before, the development of meritocratic values inside modern professional armies and, more specifically, in military academies was a well-diffused historical phenomenon. Ideally, power based on relations or wealth was no longer as important as individual merit, reaffirmed primarily by intellectual aptitudes through the school system. With the new emerging social elite, social positions would no longer be attributed to those enjoying the privilege of birth, but would be acquired only due to individual capacity. The meritocratic society would be one where this principle would predominate.[4]

The introduction, in Brazil from 1850, of bureaucratic mechanisms based on merit for advancement in a career, may be considered a fundamental mark in the differentiation process of the 'scientific' official corps in the army in relation to the civilian elite. Within the army, the majority of officers without higher schooling and of a *troupier* profile, mostly belonged to the infantry and cavalry. In spite of this, officers of the 'scientific arms' did not become professionally privileged. In fact, the reverse is true; the valorization of academic performance did not result, for example, in a significant increase of units and vacancies in positions of command. Consequently, many of the 'scientific' officers had to remain in bureaucratic positions for long periods, or to dedicate themselves to the role of instructor. There was, however, an enormous distance between this affirmation in the Military Academy course about the superiority of merit and scientific studies, and its true effectiveness in the reality of a predominantly *troupier* army that was slow in modernizing.

The memoirs and records of ex-students of the Military Academy enables us to see the exceptional value attributed to the merit principle. Not that this principle functioned as a whole in the Academy, nor that opposite values to the meritocratic were not engaged at certain times. The image that students, professors and other military persons normally had of the Academy was that of a kingdom where individual merit was the sovereign, a good academic performance being enough for career advancement. The mother of José Beviláqua, the freshman student referred to earlier, once recommended her son to a general. He answered that 'the student should be reminded to study with value and courage and, in that way, he alone would already be recommended'.

The merit principle was not merely an ideal; the title of 'alferes-aluno' (ensign-student), exclusive to students of the Military Academy, emphasized that they should be outstanding in the initial years of the course.[5] Another letter from José Beviláqua (from 1884), now in the middle of the course, proudly informs his parents of his success in his studies, communicating that, consequently, he would soon be eligible for the title of 'alferes-aluno': 'This post ... is a *prize* given to students who are *absolutely* approved during the first two years; ... it is a highly regarded promotion in the Army, because it is given by law and studies, independently of the minister, who in other cases promotes his protégés' (emphasis in the original). The ascent by merit represented, in this way, a fundamental symbolic good for the construction of the social identity of these young military men.

Therefore, the 'military youngsters' with higher education suffered double marginalization: as part of the army inside a monarchic order dominated by law bachelors, and as a group of officers with higher education, inside an army that would not modernize. The resulting isolation and resentment facilitated the development of distinct ideological characteristics that contrasted greatly with those of the civilian elite.

The channelling of these cultural elements in collective projects of action followed a specific path. In the Military Academy, informal socialization outside classrooms was organized by the students themselves, and was far more important to the formation of the characteristic mentality of the military youngsters than that learned from the teachers. At least, there are two indicators which point to that. Firstly, the much smaller number of references, in the memoirs of ex-students, about teachers and formal schooling than that of informal socialization – ragging, associations, intra-students relations and so forth. Secondly, the fact that much of what was intensely discussed in magazines and in student reunions was not part of the school syllabus nor taught by professors. For example, when discussing more modern scientificist theories, like those of Spencer and Haeckel, the students' writings show us a more heterogeneous and diverse intellectual environment than that of their masters. The horizontal strings of comradeship and loyalty also materialized in scientific, literary and philosophical societies formed by students at the Military Academy. And even if the directorate permitted these, they were not dependent on them and neither did they originate from them.

More advanced students, though also young, played an active role in the socialization and intellectual formation of younger students. These, coming mainly from the small provinces, often experienced a real intellectual shock when arriving at the 'Tabernacle of Science' – this denomination, we recall, was given to the Academy by students, signifying an informal school rather than a formal one. The intensity and speed of this process gave these young men the sensation that their youth would be compensated for by great experience acquired through the individual effort to advance in both learning and in professional life, from the new and intense sociability developed in school and, mainly, through the contact of 'scientific' and 'modern' doctrines. The 23-year-old student, Lauro Sodré, for example, in some articles from 1881 arguing with the clergy, provides another example of how contact with scientific doctrines gave the young men a feeling of intellectual superiority, in spite of their youth:

> a short but well driven observation has more value, than long years of disoriented experiences. Therefore, it is not surprising that this obscure youngster, author of these lines, knows the positive philosophy that is unknown to priests of the catholic religion. (Sodré, 1896: 149)

Republican ethos

The republicanism of the 'military youngsters' was, in my opinion, born from the symbolic valorization of individual merit plus a hegemonic scientificist culture among the young scientific officers. The last decades of the nineteenth century saw the growing approximation between the 'cult of science' and republicanism. Since France was then the cultural center of the 'civilized world', the emerging Third Republic elevated the cult of science, reason, evolution and progress to an official ideological condition. 'Science' became a common word in the Republican manifestos, parallel to the popularity of evolutionist biology, and served as an ideological weapon against Monarchists and Conservatives (Clark, 1984; Paul, 1985).

In Brazil, the narrow link between republicanism and science was also frequently affirmed. In 1885, the now lieutenant Lauro Sodré, who criticized the priests, wrote a 'Letter to the Emperor', through a provincial newspaper, where he stated, based on natural science methods, the inevitability of progress, 'the indefectible march forward of civilization'. Quoting Spencer, monarchy is 'a mental inferiority certification and lowness of character' (Sodré, 1896: 145–54). Lauro Sodré was also editor of a Republican manifesto in 1886, where he affirmed that his purpose was 'to eliminate royalty, because that represented the cause of our backwardness' (1939: 29–35). The certainty that the Republic would be implanted was justified in scientificist terms:

> because the virtue of evolution, this eternal law conducting all natural phenomenon, from the microcosms to the macrocosms, from the differential atom to the great whole named universe, the light of civilization may come through antrums of despotism and sweep from the earth's surface the shadow of autocrats. (p. 30)

A change of regime, nevertheless, would not occur 'without a commotion and disturbance': 'Those are natural factors of social order, those violent shocks called revolutions.'

Some articles written by Euclides da Cunha in 1888–89 provide great examples of how the scientifistic culture of the 'military youngsters' was projected in their vision of politics. Firstly, the absolute certainty of Republican democratic ideas being scientific must be highlighted – a formula admirably outlined in the affirmation: 'a democrat is made of the same material as a geometrician.'

> As is known, XIX century politics is called democracy; for a long time the collaboration of all sciences and natural tendencies of

our temperament, stripped it of the fragile character of party opinion, to redress it in an unbreakable logical fortress of scientific deduction. In sociology, I believe that ... you arrive at it as naturally as Lagrange did to the general formula of dynamics. It is not a form of government that is adopted, but the philosophical result that one must adopt; a democrat is made a geometrician, by observation and study; and, in this strenuous fighting between political parties, in the end the Republicans will not win – they will convince; and, when finally dominating his enemies, won't send them to be guillotined, but will send them to school. (Cunha, 1966, I: 545–6)

My aim is to show – through a brief ethnography of the Military Academy in the final years of the Empire – an indication of the links and coherence between cultural elements and the political action developed by the 'military youngsters': merit versus privileges, science and progress versus metaphysics and backwardness, the future versus the past.

Another letter of the student José Beviláqua written in early 1886 – about three years before the Republican coup – is even more elucidating in this respect. He aims to reassure his practicing catholic mother after the shock she got upon receiving news that her son, now 'alferes-aluno', would soon leave his lodgings at the Military Academy to live with some colleagues in a 'Republic' (this word, in Brazil, designates still today, community lodgings kept by students outside the University). The way in which this 'scientific' youngster of 23 years solved this misunderstanding is quite remarkable:

There is no reason for you to be fearful when hearing the word Republic; firstly because it symbolizes the form of government where rights of citizens are better defined, therefore not admitting any privileges from family or from class, the law makes every citizen equal and the only distinction is that which is born out of merit and individual virtues ... besides, a Republic is only a student home, where it is customary to designate it by that name.

The 'military youngsters' were frankly Republican. Since 1878, students from the Military Academy had created secret Republican clubs and, on diverse occasions, sang or tried to sing the revolutionary French *Marseillaise*. The radicalism of their actions was noticeable and the fact that, in the writings and memoirs of the young scientific men, there is a lack of references to professors and politicians converting them to republicanism. References to this subject always lead to books and, mainly, to other 'scientific' youngsters grouped in associations and clubs from students of the Military Academy.

There was no understanding among the military youngsters of how the coming Republic would be organized. It seems to have been enough to know that it was a scientific method of government, where merit would reign as regulator of all social life. The lack of definition in regard to the Republic made it easier, in one way, for unity in thought and action of the military youngsters before the 1889 coup; and, yet, it helped quicken the pace of its fragmentation as soon as the Republic was established.

It was with the scientific and republican spirit previously described that the military youngsters actively participated in the Republican conspiracy that led to the end of the monarchy in Brazil. In this process it attracted some non-politicized officers – like the Military Academy professor Benjamin Constant – and others of a more *troupier* profile, like Marshal Deodoro da Fonseca, who would become the first president of the new Republic.[6] Despite their small numbers, these officers were important for conveying to the nation and army the idea that they represented the 'military class'. In reality, they represented a small part of the army, but were successful in linking the movement to a *resentment* within the military towards civilians in general, particularly politicians, and when monopolizing extremely important symbolic elements of the military *ethos*, like the idea of 'honor'.

In the first five years of the Republic, the 'scientific' youngsters not only progressed rapidly in their careers, but also began to occupy some positions generally reserved, in the Empire, for Bachelors of Law: in Congress, in state governments, in ministries. According to Joaquim Nabuco (cf. Freyre, 1959, I: 51) what could be called a 'neocracy' was created in Brazil. This meteoric social ascension took place in the midst of chaos. Even though it might seem exaggerated, this is the most appropriate term to designate the first decade of the Republic. They were years characterized by conflicts in all areas. The fragile unity of the military class forged just before the coup among the military youngsters led by Benjamin Constant and a small group of *troupier* officers, close to Deodoro, disintegrated rather quickly.

The anarchy of the initial years of the Republic led to the emergence, within the civilian elite, of a consensus: it was necessary to distance the military from politics and regain control of the political system. The state oligarchies, led by the *paulista* oligarchy, began to regain control of the situation with the election of Prudente de Morais who succeeded the second military president, Floriano Peixoto, in 1894. Some time later, with the second civilian president, Campos Sales, who took power in 1898, the phenomenon that came to be known as 'governors' politics' began, which would characterize the First Republic in Brazil and would last until the 1930 Revolution.

The majority of the young Republican military officers of 1889 were soon removed from the positions they had acquired right after the coup. They were still politically active, although decreasing in strength until the end of 1904, with the failure of the Vaccine Revolt led by old 'scientific' officers who preached the return to an ideal Republic dreamed about by the 1889 conspirators. With the defeat of the Vaccine Revolt, the Military Academy of Praia Vermelha was finally closed.[7] Thus, the history of the 'Tabernacle of Science' was over.

Military and politics in the 1920s

During the first decade of the twentieth century, the still politically active 'scientifics' were defeated twice: both in the political arena and within the army. There were two historical landmarks: at the end of 1904 what remained of the old political radicalism from the end of the Empire was defeated together with the Vaccine Revolt; and at the beginning of 1905, Marshall Hermes da Fonseca, Minister of War, organized the first military manoeuvres of the Brazilian Army and initiated a series of measures aiming to modernize the institution. Despite the remarkable similarities in relation to the intellectual and social professional formation of generations from the end of the Empire and from the first decades of the twentieth century – such as the valorization of sciences, of merit and from the symbolic opposition to the elite of law bachelors – some significant differences came into place. The main one was a more *professional* institutional orientation and the introduction of European military doctrines that slowly began to create a more career-oriented body of officers than the 'scientifics' of the end of the Empire. Furthermore, if the initiative of modernizing the political action was mainly in the hands of the Military Academy students and young officers, at the beginning of the twentieth century these initiatives would also be encouraged by some generals. In this way, the army – or rather, groups inside the army – maintained a strong performance as a modernizing element, but in a different sense.

The military European scenery was, at that time, dominated by the notion of 'Nation in Arms', by which the Armed Forces, besides being responsible for defense, should also be a sort of 'school of Nationality'. Ideally, they would recruit elements from all sectors of the population, from all social origins, giving them a feeling of national unity. With this, the Army looked upon itself as directly linked ideologically to the *Nation*, an entity which was not merely its guardian but also its creator. Despite this vision, the official corps continued to be, quoting a sentence from Nunn, 'too clearly part of, yet apart from, the society surrounding them. Education and career experience counted more *vis-à-vis* their thought and self-perception than did social backgrounds ...' (1983: 289).

The army reform movement initiated in 1905 developed in the following years by sending some dozens of Brazilian officers for internships in the Prussian Army. From 1913, many of these officers began to voice their ideas through the magazine *A Defesa Nacional*, beginning a long argument for the introduction of universal conscription together with the modernization of the army and nation. For this reason, they were nicknamed 'the young Turks'. Some of them, or some officers who formed this group, joined as instructors in military schools at the end of 1918, through competitive examinations which were then still a novelty. This group was known as the *Missão Indígena* ('Native Mission'). Various officers who had great influence in the political history of contemporary Brazil left school in 1919, and were already influenced by this new background: Luís Carlos Prestes, Eduardo Gomes, Cordeiro de Farias, Juarez Távora e Siqueira Campos. According to a testimony of one of them,

The officers who graduated in 1919 would go to the troops, masters of what they had to do. It was a heavy shock, because we would arrive at the units with a technical formation that made us

stand out from other officers ... Everything began to change. A
new renovating influence irradiated from the inferior squadrons
to the top, creating a more military and technical mentality. In
this sense, the lieutenants of 1919 emerged as an elite inside the
Army. (Farias, 1981: 66)

The reform process of the army culminated in the contracting of a
military French Mission, arriving in Brazil in 1920. The Brazilian
Army followed, though somewhat later, the example of various
other South-American countries (Nunn, 1983).

In the three first decades of the twentieth century, the institutional profile of the army altered significantly as a result of these
measures in relation to its modernization and professionalization.
The selection and training of officers went through a phase where
professional aspects predominated; universal military conscription
was finally initiated in 1916, and in the decades that followed slowly
led to the modification of the troops' profile. The introduction of
systematic and obligatory physical education in Brazil was also the
work of the military, who saw it as closely linked to *national defense.*

During the 1920s, the official corps still being professionally
incipient within the Brazilian Army once again faced the world of
politics, through diverse *tenentes* (lieutenants) revolts. This was a
considerably different Brazil from that of the end of the Empire,
with significant economic changes and urbanization, the first problems arising due to the uncontrolled growth of cities. With the
ascension of many 'lieutenants' to power in the 1930 Revolution,
the modernizing role of Brazil's military assumed different forms.
The institution itself suffered profound transformations, which
resulted in the consolidation of hierarchy and discipline practices
and principles, to the framing, and finally to the domestication of
structural radicalism of the young officers educated at the Military
Academy. At the end of the 1930s, the army became more active as a
unifying actor. In the formula of General Góis Monteiro, who, with
the installation of the *Estado Novo* dictatorship of 1937 obtained the
consolidation of a hegemonic project for the institution around the
idea of avoiding politics *in* the army, however making the politics *of*
the army.

The political radicalism of the 1889 'scientific' youth and of the
1920s 'lieutenants' had therefore inscribed permanently on Brazil's

political history the vision that an enlightened military group was able to save the Nation, in its name.

Notes

1. This chapter outlines arguments developed mostly in Castro (1995) and later publications.
2. There is a vast body of literature on the professionalization of Western armies. See, for instance, the classical contributions of Huntington (1957) and Janowitz (1960).
3. For a more comprehensive analysis of these ideas, see Barros (1959).
4. Besides the faith in progress and in the cult of science, another common point to all scientificist doctrines, as perceived by the 'military youngsters', was an opposition to metaphysics and to the Catholic religion. Living in a country where Catholicism was the official religion, the absolute majority of the young 'scientific' military men were agnostic or atheist.
5. This title, created in 1840, establishes the focus of 'scientific' studies in the Military Academy. Received by the wholly approved students at the end of the initial years of the course (therefore, infantrymen and cavalry-men, could not be *alferes-alunos*), it was a representation of a substantial growth of remuneration besides being a prize for school performance.
6. This interpretation differs from that of traditional historiography, that presents Deodoro and Benjamin Constant as the ones who converted and attracted the young officers to the republican cause, and not the contrary. My perspective is focused not on the leaders, but in their supposed followers as the most dynamic element of the conspiracy.
7. Two years later it was re-opened in another location.

5
Military Governments: Continuity and Change in Twentieth-Century South America

George Philip

Introduction

This discussion puts forward the argument that there existed a distinctive type of political system in South America from around 1925 until 1982, a system which no longer exists. The system in question can be characterized as civil–military and distinguished from the genuine democracies which have come into existence in most South American countries during the 1980s and which operate today. This civil–military system must be understood primarily through the way in which political power was organized rather than via a study of legitimation. The system operated only partly through formal rules entrenched in clearly-defined value systems, and for this reason the legitimation of power during this period was patchy and imperfect. By the same token, the nature of social power only partly explains the workings of the political system. The stress placed here on specifically military factors is not by any means intended to suggest that societal power was irrelevant to politics. However, societal factors did tend to operate at a distance from the immediate exercise of power, which they influenced and constrained but did not directly determine.

Key elements in understanding the civil–military system of South American politics include the type of military rule under which power was – for much of the time – exercised, and the type of military organization which developed over the period. We consider these in turn before going on to consider the civilian aspect of the civil–military system. The final part of the chapter considers some of the contrasts between the civil–military system of the past and the more authentic democracy of today.

Some characteristics of military rule 1925–82

South American military rule, during a historical period spanning around six decades from the 1920s to the 1980s, has had several distinctive characteristics. One of these is that the military organization continued to exist largely independently of whoever occupied the presidential palace. At the same time, the military organization remained the ultimate arbiter of state power. In other words there was always a potential military veto on any government, whether military or civilian, but the military itself was subject to little or no accountability from civilians. For this reason, military government never evolved into a different form of rule. On those occasions when it looked like doing so, the military elite intervened and blocked any such change. This meant that fascism, for example, never developed in South America. Some military officers were certainly influenced by fascism, but the military in South America did not (for long) tolerate autonomous coercive organizations run by civilians – such as played a key role in European fascist movements. A further consequence of military autonomy was that the military hierarchy successfully maintained control over its own organization. No NCO movement succeeded in South America, and even the 'junior officers' who were so important in Chile and Brazil in the 1920s were in fact mostly captains and majors. Attempts by civilians to encourage junior officers to turn against their military seniors never succeeded and were often heavily punished. In contrast, generals whose coup attempts failed were likely to suffer nothing more than forced early retirement from the military.

During the 1930s, it is true, some alternatives to military authoritarianism and elected government did reach the political agenda. Some officers were influenced by communism (notably Marmaduke Grove in Chile), others by fascism (Uriburu in Argentina), and others again by separatism (notably in São Paulo in 1932). There were also NCO revolts in Chile and Brazil. However, none of these prevailed, and after 1945 no such options were seriously on the political agenda. The 1963 sergeants' revolt in Brazil, which was believed by some academic observers to be a major threat to military hierarchy in that country (Stepan, 1971), turned out in the end to have been orchestrated by Brazilian military intelligence.

Continuing with the organizational theme, military rule in South America has never, with the exception of Bolivia in 1952, led to the fusion of military, party and state such as happened in Mexico and some parts of the Middle East. Nor, again with the exception of Bolivia, has military rule ended either in civil war or the overthrow of military government by force. Even when under the most extreme pressure, as with the Argentinean military after defeat in the South Atlantic in 1982 and the Chilean military in 1932, retreating military governments have generally been able to organize elections and hand over power to a civilian in at least a semi-orderly way. Military factions have at times squared up to each other and exchanged some gunfire, but (with the already-noted Bolivian exception) this never led to a situation where armed civilians could influence the outcome of conflict. Nor have the outcomes of intra-military disputes been in doubt for long. In short, the military institution in South America during this period clearly meets the Weberian criteria of 'organized force' securely in control of a territorial unit. This criterion was not threatened by the fact of military government itself.

As a result of the strength of the military high command, only two alternative forms of rule were possible. One was military and the other was a very cautious form of elected (if not always very democratic) government. Military governments always came to an end with the handing over of power, either voluntarily or under some degree of duress, to civilian government. In return for its willingness to return to barracks when times became difficult, the military retained much of its organizational autonomy and protection against serious accountability for its previous behavior in power. Where civilian governments, even popularly elected ones, did not sufficiently respect the independence of the military organization they could be overthrown – as happened to Perón in 1955. For this reason, there were no human rights trials of military officers by civilians during 1925–82. When some such trials did take place, in Argentina after 1982, this change was important evidence that the old civil–military system was no more.

South America is unusual but not wholly exceptional in having had a bureaucratically autonomous and politically interventionist military. Similar patterns have existed in such countries as Turkey and Pakistan. However, South America does indeed seem to be exceptional in the extent to which military officers in some countries came to be considered an ordinary part of the power elite. This was more true of Brazil and Argentina than of Chile and Peru (at any rate prior to 1970). In the former cases the military took an active part in policy-making under civilian as well as military governments. They were also active in running important economic fiefdoms of their own. By the 1970s a large part of the (extensive) state-owned enterprise sector in both countries was directly run by military officers. Moreover the senior military academies – notably the Escola Superior de Guerra (ESG) in Brazil – played a major part in the socialization of military and political elites (Stepan, 1971).

If one were to seek out explanatory factors for the operation of this kind of system, it would be necessary to look at the earlier historical evolution of the South American military (Nunn, 1997). An explanatory factor of a different kind would be the relative absence of war in South America during this period; the military enjoyed considerable prestige without the inconvenience of being called upon to fight. The one case of large-scale warfare was in the Chaco (1932–35), and the different political trajectory of Bolivia thereafter had much to do with the consequences of military defeat. Much the same could be said about Argentina after 1982; the South Atlantic conflict was one of the key factors behind the replacement of civil–military rule by genuine democracy. The military bureaucracies which developed during the twentieth century in South America were organized for politics, not war. By the same token, this military bureaucracy could not easily emerge in the previous century because the South American state did not invariably monopolize force. *Caudillo* revolts could and did overthrow governments, setting at nought formal ranks and hierarchies.

The bureaucratic and political organization of the military

Then, finally, there is the organization of the military itself. The key point to make in this context is that political actors other than the military had to operate in an environment in which it was clear that the military was both technically capable of imposing dictatorship and possibly willing to do so. While giving due weight to the importance of social (and on occasion international) factors, it nevertheless seems appropriate to discuss the outcome of this situation in a narrower framework, focusing on issues of force, physical control of a territorial unit, bureaucratic organization and the quest for legitimacy.

Some of the best work on the military has started by putting organizational analysis at its center. The point is not to try to answer historical questions by purely deductive means, but rather to find an appropriate starting point for further research. Any minimally-sophisticated organization of force involves some bureaucracy, but the military bureaucracies of South America have become highly sophisticated – a requirement which seems to have been driven more by their political role than any purely military objective. The increasing sophistication of the military bureaucracy explains much about the changing character of military government between the 1930s and 1960s (and later). This theme has been explored fairly thoroughly in earlier works focusing on the so-called 'new professionalism' of the 1960s (Stepan, 1971).

More recently, Remmer (1991), Arceneaux (1997) and others have explored the relationship between the institutional characteristics of military rule and the nature of military government. Probably the most important contribution here is to highlight, yet again, Chilean exceptionalism. In other countries (Argentina, Peru and Brazil) military factions competed for power intensely, and politics within the military was an important factor in explaining government decisions. However, Pinochet never had to worry excessively about military factions, at any rate after the early years, any more than Franco did. 'Sultanistic' military rule is more effective in policy terms but less in the interest of senior military officers than the more collective form of military government seen in Argentina under Videla, Brazil under Costa e Silva and Medici, and Peru under Velasco Alvarado. Ultimately, though, collective forms of military leadership tended to lead either to disastrous policy-making (as with the South Atlantic adventure), or to a backlash from disciplinarian military officers dismayed at the barbarous and corrupt behavior of the worst of their colleagues. When General Geisel in Brazil began the process of 'decompression' which led to an eventual return to barracks, he did not do so because of any belief in democracy but out of intense dislike of the way in which particular military commanders (particularly the military command in São Paulo) were operating.

Institutional determinism, like other forms of deductive reasoning, is an inherently limited approach to human affairs. One way of making it more satisfying is to explore the consciousness of military officers themselves, and to try to understand the relationship between organizational questions and the political outlook of particular individuals. The third Potash volume on Argentina (Potash, 1996) provides evidence of how this interaction worked in respect of one important case. One important conclusion to emerge was the observation that military officers are fallible humans (more than averagely fallible, perhaps, at least in respect of their political judgement) who made a significant number of mistakes and misperceptions. However, it is also clear that at decisive political junctures the weight of senior military opinion was against seeking to maintain military dictatorship *tout court*, and in favor of seeking some institutional bridges between the military and civil society. This preference, in the end, allowed the return to power of Perón in 1973.

Across the region as a whole, the 1930–82 period did see significant political change within the overall context of a civil–military system. One theme is the continuing increase in the bureaucratization of the military. Alongside other factors, this facilitated increased military intervention in politics after the mid-1920s, at first in alliance with civilians and then increasingly autonomously. As time went on, the 'civilian' element in civil–military coalitions become more and more subordinate without ever disappearing entirely. It seems unlikely that fresh research will significantly alter the finding of increasing professionalism and reducing civilian influence over military government. Another key finding is that most officers proved to be more committed to the military institution itself than to political movements of any kind. This doubtless explains why the inherent tendency towards the factionalism of the military when in power has been kept in some kind of check, or why steps to limit the impact of factionalism generally occurred when this was perceived as having gone too far. The same notion of organizational

autonomy in the face of stresses introduced by active military participation in politics also helps explain the eventual decision by
the military to return to barracks after a period of government – particularly after the incumbent military government was discredited
by policy failure, evident unpopularity or changing international
circumstances.

Another general theme, which links institutional scholarship with
broader themes, is that of legitimacy. Military rulers never worked
out a completely satisfactory form either of organizing themselves
in power or of satisfying themselves about their right to rule. The
notion of legitimation offers a key perspective on the impermanence of military rule, although it is important not to confuse
attempts at state legitimation with the kind of democratic legitimacy that we accept today, at least in the First World. Nevertheless,
while democratic values were never universally accepted in South
America, they were never completely forgotten either. For this reason, it is a constant theme in the politics of military rule that generals in power needed to find some sort of democratic *imprimatur*.
General Franco advised Argentina's Onganía to put aside schemes
for social reorganization and concentrate on running a tight ship.
This may have been good advice, but it is not what most senior
Argentine military officers wanted to hear. They wanted to be popular as well as powerful, and therein lay the seeds of a disorganized
retreat from power during 1970–73: therein, a decade later, lay the
seeds of the disastrous (for them) South Atlantic adventure of 1982.

In Uruguay, similarly, Bordaberry called for the permanent institutionalization of a form of authoritarian corporatism in 1977 – and
was promptly removed from office. When the Uruguayan generals
lost their 1981 plebiscite, they slowly prepared to leave power.
General Pinochet, too, remained in power as long as he could win
plebiscites, as in 1978 and 1980, and left power when he lost the
vote in 1988. In Brazil the generals kept local and Congressional
elections going during most of the post-1964 period, and left power
once it became clear (at the beginning of the 1980s) that their popular support was collapsing. Where generals did not want to risk an
open political contest, they still sometimes sought popular approval.
The Velasco government's experience with the National System for
Support of Social Mobilization (SINAMOS) – which in the end
proved a major embarrassment to the regime – is a case in point. In

the 1930s, it is true, it was for a time easier for authoritarians in power to talk of 'New States' and to appear to discount democracy for good, but even then the demand for elections continued to be heard. In the 1930s military governments returned power to civilians in Chile, Peru and Uruguay. Overall, it may be said that military encounters with popularity, populism or elections were most instrumental than anything else in bringing periods of military government to an end.

The military and economic performance

The picture of South American politics just drawn does help explain the relatively poor policy performance of authoritarian government in South America. The experience of Pinochet, Franco and (until the last few months) the Asian Tigers does seem to suggest an affinity between at least one type of authoritarian politics and rapid economic growth. O'Donnell, famously, identified the 1970s governments of South America as 'bureaucratic authoritarian' and developmentalist (O'Donnell, 1973). But, Pinochet apart (and Pinochet was more 'sultan' than bureaucrat), South America's bureaucratic authoritarians did not deliver. Argentina's military rulers were seriously destructive of the country's previous prosperity; Velasco left behind a litany of problems in Peru; while the military rulers of Brazil did not really succeed in turning in a better economic performance than the majority of civilian rulers who had preceded them – though their record in government was the least bad of the three.

Where military rule failed in performance terms, the main reasons seem to have been similar in all cases (Chile apart). They included extensive government spending on developmentally useless projects which were satisfactory to the military, popularity-boosting measures financed by fiscal deficits, and over-sensitivity to the potential opposition of veto groups when considering reforms. Obviously individual stories are different in each case, but the tendency of military governments to build up debt during the 1970s was a common factor. There was also a general reluctance on the part of even autonomous-seeming authoritarian regimes (Pinochet accepted) to avoid the kinds of institutional reform which might have helped a developmentalist project. To take one example among many, much of the state bureaucracy in South America under military rule remained clientelist and politicized even though the military itself was run along the principles of a professional bureaucracy. The overall picture is one of a pattern of policy-making focused excessively on the short term as a result of weaknesses in legitimate authority. These weaknesses both stemmed from, and reinforced, an essentially factional approach to policy irrespective of who occupied the presidential palace.

This diagnosis would fit in well with the argument made by some recent scholarly commentaries on the Asian economies (Amsden, 1989; Wade, 1990; Evans, 1995) which place a great deal of emphasis on the role of the state. There is, after all, no known antidote to serious state failure. Research into the Asian experience stresses the importance to development of Weberian bureaucracy, and positive state–private sector interaction. However 'Weberian' bureaucracies need to be soundly based in civil society, and the manifest political problems associated with both military and civilian rule tended to prevent their emergence in South America.

Democratic breakdown and military rule

Scholars who have written about military rule in South America have mostly asked 'why not democracy?' There have been many studies of democratic breakdown, and where the literature has discussed the question 'was authoritarianism only to be expected?', the formulated answers have varied. Huntington (1968) famously posed his answer in terms of the impact of social mobilization upon weak institutions. Other writers have phased the answer primarily in economic terms – most notably O'Donnell (1973) in the early 1970s. However, in my view the question has been formulated most fruitfully by Rueschemeyer *et al.* (1992), building on (but also partly rejecting) the earlier work of Barrington Moore (1967). Rueschemeyer's work is largely 'structural' (in the sense that it gives significant weight to societal forces) but allows cultural factors to define the nature of class politics and is less determinist than Moore (and indeed O'Donnell). South America has until recently had many social and institutional conditions likely to lead to the emergence of authoritarian government. These include a powerful class of large landowners, a concentrated pattern of income distribution, ethnic divisions (more pronounced in some countries than others), a Catholic Church which was no friend to democracy until the late 1970s, and successive governments in Washington about which much the same could be said. (It is worth noting, incidentally, that British governments were no more interested in helping democratic forces in the Southern Cone in the years when London had real influence than was Washington either then or later.)

Military rule for the most part served elite interests though it did not invariably do so. Civilian elites had no brief for democracy *per se*. They were sometimes willing to tolerate elections, but where the lower classes were seen to provide any kind of political threat then the dominant classes were quite willing to call in the military. Where military governments clashed seriously with elite interests, then this was generally an important factor behind military decisions to return to barracks (Frieden, 1991). Drastic elite disaffection with a previous military government, when this occurred, also reduced the likelihood of an early military return to power. Chilean elites were strongly opposed to the ten-day 'Socialist Republic' briefly imposed in 1932 by some radical military officers; the military left power later in that year and did not return until 1973. Similarly, elite rejection of the military regimes of General Velasco Alvarado in Peru and Pérez Jiménez in Venezuela helps explain why the return to barracks in Peru (in 1980) and Venezuela (in 1958) have so far proved definitive. An open letter by the powerful Mesquita family in 1973, ironically congratulating Brazil's military government for reducing Brazil to the status of a banana republic, was followed soon afterwards by a significant easing up of the Brazilian dictatorship.

Stepan (1988) is right to caution against a purely class-based interpretation of military rule. This is so for two reasons. One is that the military during 1925–82 progressively acquired organizational interests of its own which made the institution more impervious to civilian pressures. The other is that non-elite interests also at times flirted with military intervention. The phrase 'knocking on the doors of the barracks' eventually described behavior indulged in, at various times, across the entire political spectrum (Imaz, 1964). The fit between dominant class interests and military rule is neither definitionally unambiguous nor empirically convincing, but it would be naive to discount the relationship completely. The thesis that best fits the facts is that dominant class interests could not control military-political behavior in every detail, but that they were an important long-term influence on the formation and breakup of military governments.

What may appear surprising about the civil–military alternation in power is not so much the weakness of democracy (for which there are persuasive structuralist explanations), but the repeated failures of dictatorship. With the signal exception of Chile under Pinochet, the region's alternative to democracy has been surprisingly tentative. While twentieth-century South America has not seen the institutional continuities experienced by some of today's First World democracies (France, Britain, the United States, Canada, Australia), neither has it seen the determined efforts to institutionalize non-democracy which has characterized many others – such as Germany, Italy, Spain, Japan and the former Warsaw Pact countries. The key point is that South America's civil–military system was shaped by weaknesses in the legitimacy of *both* democracy *and* authoritarian government. The result, much of the time, was unstable politics and mediocre policy-making. Let us then provisionally conceptualize the 1925–82 period in South America as being characterized by a conflict between dominant social and institutional forces on the one hand (favoring authoritarianism), and dominant political ideas on the other hand (favoring democracy except perhaps for a few years in the 1930s). To make this idea more satisfying we need to look at the weaknesses of democratic rule over this period in order to compare these to the weaknesses shown by military government.

Elected government in South America during 1925–82 had its own characteristics, one of which was impermanence. Civilian rule was frequently punctured by military coups, or coup attempts, in Brazil, Argentina and Peru, whilst continuous civilian rule was more evident in Chile, Uruguay and post-1958 Venezuela. However, if one regards democracy as genuinely secure when the overwhelming majority of the population is fully committed to democratic principles, then it is difficult for us to reach this conclusion even in respect of Chile because of restrictions on suffrage during the 1940s and 1950s and also the banning of the Communist Party during

1947–57. It is quite obvious that these principles were not fully accepted anywhere else in the region. Finally, such elected governments as did exist found themselves subject to an 'anticipated reactions' effect. If they made enemies, the enemies would turn to the military and the military might intervene. This provided an all-too-successful constraint on the freedom of various elected governments.

There were, as already noted, structural factors militating against successful democratization. The cold war did not help either. However, the suggestion here is that democracy did not really have enough chance to prove itself; the possibility of military intervention short-circuited the problem-solving facilities of the region's democratic systems. Whenever there was a problem, opposition politicians tended to call for the military, and when this happened, they generally came. Civilian as well as military perspectives therefore seem to confirm the appropriateness of this attempt to categorize political system in South America during 1930–85 as 'civil military'. Just as military rulers could not rely wholly upon authoritarian principles, civilian politicians tended not to rely purely on democratic ones. An authoritarian was often a democrat who had been defeated at the polls. Individuals such as Brazil's Lacerda in 1964, Peru's Belaúnde in 1962 and Chile's Eduardo Frei in 1973 come to mind. In contrast, a democrat was often an authoritarian who had fallen out with his military colleagues – figures such as Perón, Vargas and Ibáñez serve as examples.

South American democracy since the mid-1980s

The most important reconceptualization of South American history during the past decade has not been so much the product of academic research as of actual politics. Despite various problems, the new democracies in South America have on the whole worked well. At any rate they have neither been replaced by military rulers nor have they performed less successfully at economic management than their military predecessors. Although there are still some problems with rights issues and judicial systems, the democratization which has taken place during the past decade is much more complete than in previous historical periods. A decade or more of uninterrupted civilian rule has also permitted a learning process to occur which has enormously increased the sophistication of policy responses to a range of issues as diverse as corruption, inflation and political decentralization.

All of this rather casts into relief the pattern of politics which existed in the region prior to the recent democratization. The contrast is even more telling when one notes that several South American republics had functioning electoral systems before 1930 and might have been expected to undergo a relatively smooth transition to fully democratic politics thereafter (Rueschemeyer *et al.*, 1992; Mouzelis, 1986). While there were undoubtedly policy failures under elected governments at various times between 1930–82, these would not have triggered military intervention had the impetus to intervene not already existed. After all, in the whole of twentieth-century South America there were no inflations worse than those of Peru in 1990 or Argentina in 1989. Nor were there many worse constitutional crises than those which hit Venezuela in 1992–93, Brazil in 1992 or Ecuador in 1997. Factors which would once have predictably brought the military into government no longer do so, which surely constitutes evidence that the nature of politics in the region has changed fundamentally. Also important, as already noted to some extent, is the considerable reduction in military non-accountability. While military officers who may have been responsible for criminal acts when in power have been dealt with more gently in South America than they were in Greece after 1974 or Germany after 1945, there is no longer such an aura of untouchability either locally or nationally. General Pinochet discovered this to his cost in London in October 1998.

The questions of why the civil–military system came into existence in South America at the end of the 1920s, and why it came to an end in the 1980s, would need to be discussed at more length than is allowed here. This discussion concludes with a brief treatment of the issue and a note on civil–military relations under post-1980s democratic government.

The breakdown of elective systems during 1925–33 probably needs to be explained in international terms. There were significant differences in the internal political and social systems of the various South American republics at this time and also in their levels of economic development. The gap between Argentina and Uruguay on the one hand, and Brazil on the other, was much wider in 1930 than it is today, yet the triumph of authoritarianism was a feature of the entire region. The Great Depression cannot be blamed entirely, since the overthrow of the civilian government of Chile preceded the Great Crash, and the Argentinean and Brazilian coups of 1930 both took place before the worst effects of the world economic downturn could be felt. It is likely that more emphasis should be given to the intellectual prestige of the Mediterranean authoritarians (Mussolini and Primo de Rivera in particular) and to the indifference of both Britain and the United States as to the most appropriate form of government in the region. There was no suggestion at all that the authoritarian rulers of South America in the 1930s risked turning their countries into international pariah states – which was a very real consideration for Pinochet's Chile after 1973. The 'New Deal' administration of F.D. Roosevelt coexisted quite happily with non-democracies across much of the region.

The general democratization of the 1980s may have more to do with domestic factors. The structural factors which made authoritarian government relatively likely in a rural region dominated by landlords clearly no longer apply to anything like the same extent. Moreover, the whole region was wealthier and more urbanized at the beginning of the 1980s than a generation earlier – whatever the differences between them in this regard. Vanhanen's index of power resources suggests that South America has simply modernized beyond the stage where democratic breakdown is likely (Vanhanen, 1997). This may be too sweeping, but the tendency towards social modernization cannot be ignored. Moreover, global factors seem to have been important as well. The ending of the cold war, for example, made it easier for the United States to distance itself from the 'if he is a son of a bitch, then let him be our son of a bitch' attitude which characterized its foreign policy for much of the postwar period. The most important factor, however, may be domestic and international at once. The cold war was significant for the region not merely via its impact on US policies, but also through its effect upon political legitimacy. A failure to agree on the respective merits of capitalism and communism was surely a key component on a failure to agree on a set of democratic 'rules of the game'.

Taken together, these factors would seem to have contributed to a decisive shift in political consciousness which was catalysed by the defeat of the Argentine military in the South Atlantic. Suddenly, military rule came to be seen as part of the region's problems rather than part of the solution, and border disputes have come to be seen as dangerous anachronisms. While the South Atlantic dispute has not been settled, nobody seriously believes that there will be a return to hostilities. Other territorial disputes in the region – Chile vs Argentina, Peru vs Ecuador, Peru vs Bolivia – have indeed been settled. Domestically, moreover, the patriarchal principles which underlie military government hold ever-reducing appeal to civil society; the greatly enhanced political role of women is both symptom and cause of the change. Finally globalization has enormously undermined the emotional significance of 'national sovereignty' kinds of political argument which served to legitimize the internal role of the military. While much of what the military in power actually did relate to social control and internal policing, the rhetoric and imagery of military rule tended to be based far more on conceptions of nationalism in which Latin Americans today seriously believe. There is today a psychology as well as an economics of globalism.

If it is true that South America's long legitimacy crisis is over, then we may need to be less surprised by the ability of different democratic governments to carry out reforms at least as effectively as authoritarian rulers ever did. Critics of democratic rule were wrong to see civilian governments as necessarily softer and less focused on economic essentials than their military counterparts. What matters to economic policy is the existence or otherwise of a consensus upon which any society can build. The chief significance of military rule after 1930 was that it impeded the development of such a consensus by allowing the emergence of expedient-based rule which may have seemed clever at the time but which eventually proved progressively more damaging.

Nevertheless it would be wrong to end this discussion on a note of unconfined optimism. It is surely right to see democracy as inherently superior to military rule; however, the military was – in the days when it exerted political power – one of the very few undoubtedly bureaucratic and professional aspects of the South American state. The removal from the scene of the military has not led to its replacement by a professional civilian state, and the lack of such a state can be a serious problem.

The kinds of problem to which the application of military force was in the past seen as a solution have not automatically vanished with the onset of democratization. The development of a large-scale narcotics trade is a good example of a problem which has not been resolved. In Colombia, for example, the Weberian definition of a modern state does not hold; the state cannot plausibly claim a monopoly of force within its boundaries. Since Colombia has been governed by civilians since 1957, a legacy of authoritarianism cannot be blamed for the problem. Rather, the Colombian example does seem to show that democracies cannot just forget about the need for an effective security apparatus. The problems which other South American militaries were called upon to resolve in the past may have been to a large degree imaginary, exaggerated, or the product of previous authoritarian misgovernment. However, it would be dangerous if an over-reaction to previous military excesses were to handicap efforts by existing democracies to defend themselves when they are facing genuine threats and pressures.

6
Forging Military–Technocratic Alliances: The Ibáñez and Pinochet Regimes in Chile

Patricio Silva

Introduction

Despite the many differences existing between the several military governments the ABC countries have experienced during the present century, the ample presence of civilian technocrats in top decision-making positions seems to represent a common feature among these regimes. Since the late 1920s, the emergence of military governments in these countries was accompanied by the increasing colonization of the public administration by engineers, financial experts and, later, by professional economists.

The existence of a kind of 'elected affinity' between military men and civilian technocrats has often been suggested, though generally in implicit terms. It is assumed both groups share quite similar world visions as well as coinciding societal goals. This should constitute one of the main factors explaining the emerging coalition between the men in uniform and civilian technocrats in many South American military regimes. Although the existence of shared values and objectives could certainly have facilitated the collaboration between both sectors, I do not believe this to be the main explanation for the phenomenon. I think much more attention has to be given to the very specific political and economic circumstances under which this distinct rapprochement between military men and civilian technocrats usually takes place. In addition, the degree of 'affinity' existing between military men and civilian technocrats requires a critical reappraisal as their mutual relationship has not been spared continuous tensions and disputes.

This chapter has three main purposes. Firstly, to explore the alleged 'elected affinity', existing between military men and civilian technocrats. For this purpose I shall analyse the elements which both have in common as well as the factors which tend to keep them separated. Secondly, I describe the specific politico-economic circumstances in which the 'marriage' between the army and civilian technocrats has been sealed, and the consequences this has for the type of relation between both groups. And, finally, I want to examine the elements of continuity and change one can observe in the military–technocrats relationship in both old and new military regimes.

I shall deal with these issues by focusing on the Chilean case. For this purpose, I will illustrate several aspects of the relation between the military men and civilian technocrats by referring to the military governments of Colonel Carlos Ibáñez del Campo (1927–31) and of General Augusto Pinochet Ugarte (1973–90).

Encounters and clashes between warriors and technicians

When we briefly look back at Latin American history we find that the presence of technocrats in governmental circles is a relatively old phenomenon. In addition, we find that authoritarian regimes in particular have shown a marked inclination to rely on the support of technocrats in the running of state affairs. For instance, as early as the 1890s, Mexican dictator Porfírio Díaz incorporated in his government a group of intellectuals and professional men, known as the *Científicos*, who aspired to introduce a 'scientific' state administration (cf. Jorrín and Martz, 1970: 132–8; Zea, 1976: 399–406). In the final event, the Mexican Revolution brought little change in this situation as it resulted in the generation of new undemocratic political structures and facilitated the formation of a huge techno-structure which, even today, continues to exert firm control over the country's political system (cf. Smith, 1979; Camp, 1985; Centeno, 1994). In the 1920s and 1930s Latin America experienced the emergence of several authoritarian regimes which were also characterized by an alliance between military men and civil technocrats. This was the case during the first government of Colonel Carlos Ibáñez del Campo (1927–31) in Chile, in which a group of

young technocratic-minded *ingenieros* was appointed to top positions within state institutions in order to implement profound economic and administrative reforms (cf. Ibáñez Santa María, 1983;
Silva, 1994). The existing 'elective affinity' between technocracy and
authoritarian regimes became even more apparent during the 1960s
and 1970s as a series of 'bureaucratic-authoritarian' regimes were
established in the Southern Cone countries. In his seminal work on
this new type of political regime, O'Donnell (1973) identified the
civilian technocracy as one of the military's principal allies in the
'pro-coup' coalition, and as key figures in the execution of the military regime's economic policies. Under the military regimes of
Argentina, Chile and Uruguay, a select group of economists and
financial experts acquired unprecedented discretional powers in the
formulation and implementation of radical financial and economic
reforms (cf. Vergara, 1985; Valdés, 1995). In the case of Chile, a
group of young technocrats, the so-called *Chicago boys*, emerged as
the main designers and executors of the neo-liberal economic policies applied by the government of General Pinochet. In addition,
they eventually evolved as key ideologues of the regime as they
attempted to provide an ideological answer for the coexistence of
economic liberalism and political authoritarianism (Silva, 1991).

But what is the main common ground between the military men
and the civilian technocrats? In the Chilean case, the modernization
of the army initiated in the late nineteenth century under the supervision of Prussian officers led to the adoption of modern forms of
organization and warfare. This produced confidence among younger
officers; a growing confidence in their own professional abilities and
awareness of their own role in Chilean society as a whole. As a result
of the increasing professionalization of the army, officers with technical expertise increased both in numbers and importance. At the
beginning of this century the goals of modernity and technical and
social progress had increasingly begun to become assimilated among
the corps of officers (cf. Nunn, 1970).

Apart from the military itself, the civil engineers were undoubtedly the technically most sophisticated professional group which
also possessed the most clear sense of mission to achieve modernization of the country (Ouweneel, 1995–96). For decades, they had primarily worked in the northern mining activities, which were mainly
under control of foreign-owned companies. At the beginning of the

century, Chilean *ingenieros* already constituted a well-entrenched pressure group which defended the idea of economic independence and state protectionism and demanded the development of large-scale programs of public works (Crowther, 1973).

Together with their common sense of mission, both actors also shared an almost innate rejection of party politics and the belief in technical and apolitical solutions for the country's problems. While the military detested the alleged lack of patriotism shown by most politicians, civil engineers rejected political leaders because of their lack of responsibility and the immense ignorance displayed in the decision-making process. They had personally witnessed the structural inability of the late aristocratic political system to solve the national problems and to prepare the country for the new challenges of the twentieth century.

Young military officers and civil engineers, who largely came from middle-class backgrounds, rejected the weak, slow and inefficient oligarchic structures. In addition, both actors shared a clear meritocratic vision on personal efforts and rewards and hence repudiated the very restrictive nature of Chile's political class, which was still dominated by a traditional Basque-Castilian aristocracy in the 1910s. Against the dominating principles of social ancestry and wealth, they defended the principles of personal capacity, effort and merit. In this manner, their meritocratic *weltanschauung* was only reinforced by the social barriers built up by the ruling oligarchy.

But, over the years both groups have demonstrated that they have a structural reticence towards democracy and mass participation in the national political process. The military has seen democracy as an auspicious arena for corruption, demagogy, anarchy, and eventually communism.[1] On their part, engineers and, later, professional economists, have often questioned the ability of democracy to impose and to maintain the application of rational developmental policies despite their potentially high electoral costs.[2]

Nevertheless, the differences existing between the military men and civilian technocrats have not been insignificant. To begin with, the very nature of a military hierarchy and its ruling principle of following orders from superiors without question has constantly clashed with the technocrats' postulate to follow no other path than that of scientific knowledge. In the cases of Ibáñez and Pinochet, the military–technocratic coalition worked relatively well as both rulers provided unprecedented room for manoeuvre and relative autonomy to the technocrats in charge of economic policy and reform of the state. A kind of division of labor among the military and the civilian technocrats was established, in which the former provided order (repression), and the latter applied policies directed at rationalizing and modernizing the state apparatus and the country's economy. So by separating the strictly military spheres from the administrative and economic 'fronts' conferred to civilian technocrats, many potential conflicts were avoided. Communication between the army and the technocratic team took place at the highest level; so while Ibáñez communicated directly with his Minister of Finance, Pablo Ramírez, Pinochet primarily discussed matters related to the performance of the economic team with the Chicago boys' uncontested leader, the Minister of Finance Sergio de Castro.

Despite this workable solution for sharing power between the army and civilian technocrats, the classical deep division existing in Chile between the 'mundo militar' and 'mundo civil' impeded, at least from the point of view of the military officers, full acceptance of the presence of those 'clever civilian youngsters' in a government of the armed forces. However, the strong 'verticalidad del mando' and discipline existing in the Chilean army inhibited any possible open expression of the mixed feelings many military men had *vis-à-vis* the group of young engineers during the Ibáñez government, and the Chicago boys during the Pinochet regime. This military discipline also prevented a major clash between the army and civilian technocrats on a very sensitive question on which they had been defending opposing views: the control of Chile's natural resources. The Chilean army has consistently defended nationalist positions on this issue, by supporting state control of saltpeter production and later of many industries considered strategic for national security. Notwithstanding this position, when Ibáñez authorized Pablo Ramírez to pursue his attempts to establish a joint-venture between the Chilean state and American interests in the exploitation of saltpeter in the late 1920s, and when Pinochet openly supported the Chicago boys in the privatization of state-owned industries; the armed forces simply obeyed the decision of their superiors.[3]

However, as I will try to show in the following section, even more important for the constitution and maintenance of the military–technocratic alliance are the specific political and economic circumstances in which this had been sealed, and the particular state of mind existing among the population *vis-à-vis* politics, politicians and technocratic solutions.

The 'exceptionality' of military interventions

As a general rule, military interventions only occur under very exceptional circumstances. In the Chilean case, the establishment of the Ibáñez and the Pinochet regimes occurred amidst unprecedented political and economic crises. Additionally, in both cases the establishment of the military government marked the end of a long-standing type of political regime (oligarchic and democratic regimes, respectively), and the beginning of quite revolutionary changes in the Chilean state and society. Ibáñez put an end to the oligarchic order, consolidated the ascendancy of the urban middle classes, modernized the public administration, and took the first steps towards a process of state-led industrialization. Ironically, Pinochet put an end to the developmental path initiated by his 'camarada de armas' in the late 1920s, inaugurating a radical transformation of the Chilean economy and the bases of the country's political and ideological structures, what has been labelled the 'neo-liberal revolution'.

In my opinion, the existing general awareness about the 'exceptionality' of both periods, and the marked sense of mission shown by the armed forces on both occasions, produced a particular state of mind among the supporters of those regimes, and particularly among right-wing civilian technocrats, about the unique possibilities for change created by this political event. The idea of the moral renewal of the country and the creation of a 'Chile Nuevo' proclaimed by Ibáñez encouraged many engineers to collaborate with the modernization project of the military government. On the other hand, the fall of the Allende government was seen by many of its opponents as an act of national salvation carried out by the military leadership, and which required the unambiguous support of all 'free' Chileans.

Technocracy under Ibáñez

The rise of the public technocracy in Chile in the late 1920s took place under very specific historical and political circumstances which, in my opinion, proved decisive in facilitating its consolidation. The crisis and the final breakdown of the oligarchic state in the early 1920s had produced a deep feeling of discontent among Chileans with respect to the parliamentary system, politicians and the so-called 'aristocratic frond' (Edwards, 1952). The general dissatisfaction with the existing order was reflected in the publication of several critical essays denouncing the social, political and moral decline of the nation. A vivid expression of this particular state of mind is Francisco Encina's *Nuestra inferioridad económica*, published in 1911, in which he strongly criticizes the weak and inefficient parliamentary system, stressing the need to strengthen executive power and to modernize governmental institutions. Clearly, the prestige of parliamentary democracy in general, and the politicians in particular during those years, had completely evaporated. As Góngora concluded in his reflection about this particular period, 'parliamentarism was morally, intellectually, and politically, completely discredited, according to the most varied testimonies' (1988: 130).

Following the First World War, the crisis of the oligarchic order reached its final phase when the state's main financial basis abruptly disappeared as a result of the collapse of the saltpeter economy. This produced a severe economic crisis, which led to the dramatic reduction of incomes, and to an explosive exacerbation of the social and political tensions in the country. The overall dissatisfaction with politics and politicians, combined with an all-embracing appeal for the modernization of the state, created a very propitious climate for the adoption of so-called 'technical and apolitical' policies by the post-oligarchic governments. Indeed, the administrative reforms and the expansion of the state institutions initiated under the first government of Arturo Alessandri (1920–25) were mainly legitimated by arguments stressing the need to achieve efficiency and technical excellence in conducting state affairs.

Besides the general 'anti-politics mood' of the country, the official emphasis on technical expertise was also motivated by the government's objective of eliminating the traditional bureaucracy, which constituted an unwanted remnant of the old oligarchic order, from the state apparatus. The government initiatives in this direction led to a veritable *empleomanía*, as large contingents of new public employees from middle-class backgrounds invaded both the existing and the newly created state institutions (Urzúa and García, 1971: 44–52). Furthermore, the decision to integrate people with technical backgrounds into the state apparatus was to pursue a clear-cut political objective, as their professional competence and authority could function as a force for pacification in a polarized polity. The government hoped that the *técnicos* would be able 'to solve the fundamental problems affecting national stability and harmony through technical planning and the successful execution of their administrative tasks' (Ibáñez Santa María, 1984: 57). The search for 'technical mediation' also implied a call for technical advice from foreign experts. For instance, this was the case of the 'Kemmerer mission', led by Professor Edwin W. Kemmerer from Princeton University, who was asked by the Chilean government in 1925 to conduct a far-reaching reform of the country's monetary, banking and fiscal systems. As Drake points out, the Kemmerer mission received warm support from all political and social sectors 'because most Chileans saw these outsiders as more objective and skilled than nationals ... Kemmerer enjoyed a reputation as a scientific, dispassionate mediator between conflicting government and private economic interests' (1989: 91).

The valorization of technical expertise was to become even more explicit during the first government of Colonel Carlos Ibáñez del Campo (1927–31), who stressed the need to construct what he called a strong and efficient state. For this purpose, he attempted to completely isolate public administration from political involvement in order to avoid its subordination to parliamentary debates and party interests. As Loveman summarizes, 'Ibáñez rejected liberal democracy, detested radicalism, and blamed politics for Chile's decadence' (1979: 251). By banning 'politics' from the functioning of the state apparatus, Ibáñez gave the state activities a purely administrative character. The emphasis placed by the Ibáñez regime on administration was such, that Góngora could conclude categorically: 'from May 1927 until July 1931 Chile had to live without national politics; there was only administration' (1988: 170).

Ibáñez's project for the institutional modernization of the state obviously required the presence of a techno-administrative bureaucracy to take charge of and to give form to the plans for expanding the public sector. Ibáñez therefore invited a new generation of technicians and professionals, committed to the building of an efficient public administration, to conduct these reforms. As Pinto indicates, the Ibáñez administration gave central stage to a public technocracy which emerged from the highest strata of the middle classes. This occurred throughout the entire bureaucratic machine, leading to the improvement of both the technocrats' own socioeconomic status and to the strengthening of the state apparatus (Pinto, 1985: 13). As a result of this, an increasing number of state institutions were to gradually achieve a sort of relative autonomy by which managers, technicians and professionals in general acquired plenty of room to manoeuvre in formulating and applying developmental policies. In this way, the public technocracy began to exercise a decisive influence in the decision-making process in ministries, state enterprises and the public administration at large.

The key figure in the formation of the state technocracy was Pablo Ramírez, Ibáñez's Minister of Finance (see Silva, 1998). This young man, who was relatively unknown at the time of his appointment, became the main architect of the administrative reforms implemented by the Ibáñez government. While Ramírez was the key person in the formation of the state technocracy, the group chosen to take over the top positions was mainly recruited from a contingent of young *ingenieros*, all in their thirties, who became known at that time as 'the *cabros* [boys] of Pablo Ramírez' (Ibáñez Santa María, 1984: 9n).

Minister Ramírez repeatedly stressed the competent and outstanding technical performance of this group of *ingenieros* and his desire to expand the level of participation of technicians within the state machinery. In a letter of December 1927 to the president of the Instituto de Ingenieros de Chile, the professional association of university-trained engineers, Ramírez praises the 'efficient contribution' of the *ingenieros* to the administration of state agencies. After mentioning an impressive list of *ingenieros* who occupied key positions in state institutions, he implicitly stressed the meritocratic and apolitical nature of their recruitment when he added: 'they were called to command important positions, which in the past were occupied only according to the political pressure exercised by the different political parties' (Ibáñez Santa María, 1984: 9).

The fact that the rise of these *ingenieros* to top positions within the state institution was mainly determined by a series of political factors beyond their own control, does not mean, however, that they were a passive instrument in a larger political game. At the beginning of this century, Chilean *ingenieros* already constituted a well-entrenched pressure group who defended the idea of economic independence and state protectionism and demanded the development of large-scale programs of public works (Crowther, 1973). So what they did from 1920 onwards was simply to take advantage of a favorable political and institutional climate to expand their influence within the state apparatus in order to foster their professional interests and aspirations. Given sufficient time they would develop a self-assigned 'mission' to achieve the overall development of the country. The interesting point is that this 'mission' to accomplish modernity and progress was presented in a nationalistic guise, which perfectly matched the government's goal of fostering national industrial development by and for Chileans.

The efforts of Pablo Ramírez and his team of *ingenieros* were specially directed towards the creation of the basis for a broad program of a state-led industrialization throughout the country. In his economic program, announced in 1927, Ramírez mentioned the 'active protection of industry' by the state, and financial and tax reforms as the key elements of the new economic policy. In order to achieve this, he created the Department of Industry in 1927, assigning it the task of formulating a plan for industrial development. A year later the Ministerio de Fomento (Ministry of Development) which was the direct predecessor of the Corporación de Fomento de la Producción (Chilean Development Corporation, CORFO), was founded.

Technocracy under Pinochet

Civilian technocrats acquired key roles in the formulation and application of governmental policies. In clear contrast to the anti-technocratic political discourse of the Frei and the Allende governments, Pinochet presented the technocratization of decision-making as the only guarantee for setting up 'rational and coherent' policies. In stressing the need to 'technify' the entire society, the military government intended to convince the population of the uselessness of 'politics' (and, hence, of democracy) to solve the problems of the country.

Following the military coup, the first economic team appointed by General Pinochet was mainly constituted of uniformed men and civil technocrats associated with the National Party and the

Christian Democrats. The Chicago boys were initially given only secondary positions as advisers in several ministries and state agencies, but after a period of time they were able to master the direction of the State Planning Agency, ODEPLAN, which became their operational base within the government. ODEPLAN was later used as a springboard for obtaining control of the rest of the state apparatus.

The relatively moderate economic policies adopted after the coup did not yield the expected results, while the international crisis (producing a strong increase in oil prices and a dramatic fall in the Chilean export revenues) made the situation even worse. In this critical scenario, the hard recipes proposed by the Chicago boys began to gain a broader audience and support among the military leaders. By the end of 1974, the Chicago boys controlled most of the strategic centers of economic planning, and finally, in April 1975, their leader, Sergio de Castro was appointed Minister of Economic Affairs. Immediately afterwards he announced the introduction of the neo-liberal recipes, marking the initiation of what later became known as the neo-liberal revolution.

The Chicago boys presented themselves as the bearers of an absolute knowledge of modern economic science, thereby dismissing the existence of economic alternatives. All possible criticism of their economic model was rejected by portraying it as the product of ignorance or an underhanded defence of particular interests. The increasing degree of influence of the Chicago boys within the government and among rightist political organizations and entrepreneurial circles was directly related to their ability to manage the crisis and to produce economic growth. The supporters of the military government also realized that the neo-liberals could count on the support of the international financial system (cf. Silva, 1991).

The strongest supporter of the neo-liberal plans inside the military junta was general Pinochet himself. He was well aware of the fact that for the definitive consolidation of his personal rule he needed a continuous string of successes on the 'economic front'. A landmark in the attempt of the military–technocratic alliance to institutionalize the new order was the adoption of a new constitution in September 1980, which was officially named the 'Constitution of Liberty' in a clear act of acknowledgment of Von Hayek's philosophical thought.

It is important to stress here that the maintenance of the 'affinity' between military men and civilian technocrats depended mainly on the ability of the latter to provide the results expected by the former. This became clear after the economic crisis of 1981. The collapse of a leading financial group in March 1981 resulted in a speculative wave which provoked, in its turn, general panic within entrepreneurial circles. Many financial institutions (*financieras*) and companies became bankrupt, global production declined dramatically and underemployment jumped to critical levels. At the end of that year the Global National Product decreased by 14 per cent.

Despite the intensity of the crisis, the Chicago boys continued to argue with dogmatic confidence that economic difficulties were only temporary, and that 'market mechanisms' would produce automatic adjustment to restore economic equilibrium. However, the economic situation became even worse as a result of the international banks' decision to cut down the stream of loans to Chile. The confidence of the population in the government and its economic policies rapidly began to dissolve and in April 1982 Pinochet was forced to reshuffle his cabinet. Sergio de Castro lost his post as Minister of Finance and his position as leader of the economic team, and the Ministry of Economic Affairs was placed under the command of an army general. This shows that the 'marriage' between the Pinochet government and the Chicago boys was based on pragmatic considerations on the part of the military, and the previous affinity between soldiers and civilian technocrats could rapidly change into discrepancy when the country's economic performance was at stake.

The government's marriage with the civilian technocrats was also the product of necessity. The military coup implied the abrupt displacement of the entire political class and the political parties from the public administration, and this created huge problems with respect to the managing of the state institutions and the formulation of a new national project. Like Ibáñez in the late 1920s, Pinochet came to power without a clearly defined program. The Chilean armed forces had scarcely participated in the political arena before, and therefore they lacked the experience required for ruling a country. So how and with whom could the armed forces govern Chile? The alleged 'apoliticism' of the technocrats was undoubtedly an important factor in their favor when being chosen by the military as their main associates in this political adventure.

The final choice of Chicago boys did not have much to do with the previously mentioned 'elected affinity' between the military and the civilian technocrats, but with Pinochet's personal efforts to consolidate his position within the military junta. Like his companions at arms, Pinochet possessed a deeply-rooted aversion towards politicians whom he called in denigrating tones the 'señores políticos'. According to him, the *políticos* were the main people responsible for the collapse of the former democracy. In fact the armed forces never felt comfortable with the presence of (right-wing) politicians in their government, as was the case during the very first period of the Pinochet government. Pinochet was particularly afraid that the contact between generals and politicians could lead to the politicization of the armed forces and hence to the fragmentation of its institutional unity. By replacing these political figures by civilian technocrats, Pinochet not only eliminated that threat but he also isolated possible power contenders within the armed forces from the support of Christian Democrats, the National Party and extreme right-wing groups.

The Chicago boys offered Pinochet a 'technical, scientific, and above all a non-political' approach which guaranteed the non-politicization (in terms of party politics) of the main policy issues. So the fact that the Chicago boys were relatively inexperienced and did not possess strong ties to political parties and leaders became, under these specific political circumstances, one of their major assets.[4] Moreover, the Chicago boys possessed a 'universalistic discourse' in which '*all* Chileans' and not certain political or social segments of society would become the main beneficiaries of their policies. Not a 'political struggle', but what the assumed impartial laws of the market would procure for the adequate socioeconomic development of the country.

In this way, the neo-liberal discourse of the Chicago boys was clearly functional for Pinochet's purposes, namely to guarantee a large degree of relative autonomy for his government *vis-à-vis* organized pressure groups. This would allow him to play the role of a 'supra-party' over the different interest groups in society.

Continuity and change in military–technocratic relations

When we try to assess the continuities and changes that existed in the relationship between the military and civilian technocrats during the Ibáñez and the Pinochet governments, one has to take into consideration a series of historical, structural and conjunctural factors which distinguish both military regimes.

Obviously, the degree of institutional development of the Chilean armed forces during both governments was not at all similar. In contrast to the late 1920s, the Chilean military institutions in the early 1970s possessed a very complex structure, having also a much higher level of professionalization. In addition, and despite the fact that the 'socialist threat' had also been an important concern during the Ibáñez regime, the Chilean armed forces adopted during the cold war, and particularly following the Cuban revolution, a much clearer and doctrinaire anti-communist position (mainly organized around the so-called Doctrine of National Security).

Simultaneously, while the left-wing political parties and the organized labor movement constituted a threat in the late 1920s, in the early 1970s they had already achieved power with the Unidad Popular government. So in contrast to the situation faced by the military in the late 1920s in which they confronted disorder in general terms, in the early 1970s their enemy was definitely communism. Moreover, Ibáñez had to fight against both the left-wing forces and the traditional oligarchy, while Pinochet came into power in an extremely polarized country with almost unconditional support by all the social and political forces which had fought the Allende government.

But despite these and other differences existing between both regimes, they curiously shared a similar ruling style which could be called 'low-intensity populism'.[5] They both talked in a very direct and unsophisticated manner, without trying to show a higher level of culture than they had. What has not been stressed until now is the fact that both Ibáñez and Pinochet, in contrast with most of the twentieth-century presidents (including Allende), spoke the language of the common people. This is certainly due to their lower-middle-class and provincial backgrounds, as well as their particular military way of talking (men of few words). Nevertheless, and despite their power, neither Ibáñez nor Pinochet allowed the establishment of political cults around their own persons, as Mussolini, Hitler or, much closer, Somoza, Perón and Stroessner did. Nor did they permit the constitution of parties or 'movements' (like the Francoist Falanje) to organize and mobilize the people.

Finally, these military leaders rarely addressed a large gathering and they did not really appreciate the concentration of large masses expressing their support of the military governments. I think this was clearly connected with the way they understood the role of military men in positions of power: to show the people their concern for their problems, but to maintain distance from the crowd and the civilian political organizations. At the same time, the idea of the 'impersonalidad del poder' built up by Portales in the 1830s and cultivated by most Chilean presidents ever since, certainly also constituted a source of inspiration for these military leaders.

In the case of Pinochet, the way he ruled the country strongly contrasted with the leaders of other military governments in neighboring countries during the 1970s such as Argentina, Uruguay and Brazil who ruled for a preestablished period of time and did not achieve such a central role as Pinochet did in Chile (cf. Remmer, 1991). Like Ibáñez in the late 1920s, Pinochet managed to become the uncontested single leader of the military government. As some authors have suggested (for example Arriagada, 1988), Chile's 'need' to have a single individual source of highest authority is related to both Chilean political culture and the specific characteristics of the country's armed forces. It can safely be stated that Chileans are accustomed to obeying the authority of the President of the Republic. Both Ibáñez and Pinochet were very aware of this and officially took possession of the designation of president of the country in order to obtain the required legitimation of their rule *vis-à-vis* the Chilean population. Besides, the strong tradition of 'verticalidad del mando' within the Chilean armed forces only admitted a pyramidal power structure with the figure of the Commander-in-Chief of the Army at the top. In this manner, the lack (and dislike) of structures of collegiate decision-making, which have been characteristic in other armies in the region, led to the almost natural ascendency of the person of the Commander-in-Chief of the Army (Pinochet) to a position of single ruler.

As has already been pointed out, Ibáñez's and Pinochet's decision to surround themselves with an army of young civilian technocrats could not have been contested by the army of any other institution due to this pyramidal power structure. Moreover, their strong aversion for both politicians and political parties only facilitated their relationship with the civilian technocrats.

The fact that civilian technocrats placed different emphasis on their tasks within the two governments (the Ibáñez's *ingenieros* in the modernization of the public administration and Pinochet's *Chicago boys* on the radical transformation of the economic order) was due to the different nature of the economic situation both military leaders had to confront, and the professional expertise and interests of both groups of technocrats.

While Pinochet had to face one of the most profound economic crises the country had experienced for many decades, the largest part of Ibáñez's short government enjoyed a situation of a relative economic bonanza, which was eventually and abruptly concluded in 1931 by the dramatic effects of the Great Depression. Although Ibáñez took firm steps towards the expansion of the role of the state in the industrialization and overall development of the Chilean economy and introduced a series of economic and financial reforms, this did not constitute his main passion and concern. As a man of his time, he firmly believed in the expansion and improvement of Chile's infrastructure (constructions of harbors, railways, bridges, roads, and so on) and the deep restructuring and modernization of the public administration, as the way to achieve progress and prosperity in the country and to put an end to political corruption. In contrast, Pinochet's main concern was to disarticulate the left-wing forces which had supported the Unidad Popular government and, particularly, to face the deep economic crisis affecting the country. So the centrality of the Chicago boys and their emphasis on economic reform and the activation of the economy arose from the specific situation confronted by the Pinochet government. Moreover, the neo-liberal formula promoted by the Chicago boys obtained the generalized support of the international financial community as neo-liberalism had begun to become hegemonic in mainstream economics by the end of the 1970s. As Stallings points out

> ... technocrats who had long argued for more open economies and a bigger role for the private sectors suddenly found increased backing from the outside. They could count on political support from the United States and other advanced industrial countries, intellectual reinforcement from the IMF and World Bank, and

empirical evidence of successful performance from countries that had followed an open-economy model. (Stallings, 1992: 84)

These technocrats have played a strategic role in conducting negotiations with industrialized countries as a means of rescheduling existing debts and obtaining new credits and financial aid. As Kaufman indicates, these technocrats are

> more than simply the principal architects of economic policy: they [are] the intellectual brokers between their governments and international capital, and symbols of the government's determination to rationalize its rule primarily in terms of economic objectives...Cooperation with international business, a fuller integration into the world economy, and a strictly secular willingness to adopt the prevailing tenets of international economic orthodoxy, all [forms] a...set of intellectual parameters within which the technocrats could then 'pragmatically' pursue the requirements of stabilization and expansion. (Kaufman, 1979: 189, 190)

In this manner, local neo-liberal technocrats have become the national counterparts of foreign financial experts from lending institutions who assess the performance of the Latin American economies which are currently executing adjustment programs. As Centeno points out, the communication between foreign financial experts and local technocrats has been clearly facilitated by their common academic backgrounds. They

> not only share the same economic perspectives, but perhaps most importantly, speak the same language, both literally and metaphorically...The technocrats do not necessarily have to represent one ideological niche or the other, they simply share a familiarity with a certain language and rationale...The graduate degrees from U.S. universities...enable these persons to present arguments that their fellow alumni at the World Bank...understand and consider legitimate. (1993: 325, 326)

In the case of Ibáñez, technocrats, and particularly his Minister of Finance Pablo Ramírez, played the same function in conducting negotiations with the international business community (see Silva,

1998). Ramírez was very aware of the fact that the solution for the national economic problems should not be sought only through internal means. Chile also needed to adopt a more active attitude towards both financial partners and economic competitors. In mid-March 1929, for instance, Ramírez launched an extended mission to the United States and several European countries. In New York he met bankers and investors, while in Washington he had a meeting at the White House with President Herbert C. Hoover. He followed this stage of the trip by going to London, where he had talks with nitrite producers and bankers. Abroad, Ramírez explicitly stressed the technocratic nature of the Ibáñez's government, presenting it as one of its greatest assets. In London he stated:

> our government today is exclusively technical; the engineer, the banker, and the expert in economic affairs have replaced the professional politician. In this way, the government has been able to restore economic activity, to solve the saltpeter crisis, to initiate a huge plan of public works, to obtain an adequate return on tax revenues, to control the money resources, and to organize the credit system. (*La Nación*, 17 May 1929: 10)

In both cases, the dictators always maintained, for the sake of public opinion, a certain distance from the technocratic team. This allowed both Ibáñez and Pinochet to replace these people as circumstances demanded, protecting their own position in this way, as well as the honor of the armed forces.

Concluding remarks

Despite the many differences that existed between the military governments of Ibáñez and Pinochet, they show a striking resemblance with respect to their predilection to govern with the assistance of a team of civilian technocrats. Both the *cabros* of Pablo Ramírez and the *boys* of Sergio de Castro determined to an important extent many of the key decisions adopted by both Ibáñez and Pinochet in the fields of administrative reform and economic policy. The remarkable degree of power and influence obtained by both groups of civilian technocrats in these regimes was definitively made possible by the unusual level of permanent *personal* backing and support given to them by Ibáñez and Pinochet. For instance, and despite the mounting criticism against Ramírez and his policies of reducing public sector personnel, Ibáñez openly supported his Minister of Finance until the very end. Similarly, Pinochet dismissed the growing criticism from entrepreneurial circles (and in covered terms from the armed forces) against the consequences of the 'shock treatment' policies of the Chicago boys in the first years of their reform program. And despite the unsatisfactory results of the neo-liberal policies until the end of 1977, Pinochet decided to maintain the chosen neo-liberal path. I think that this show of steadfastness of both military leaders is intimately related to the way military leadership functions within the Chilean armed forces – the Commander-in-Chief of the Army is considered infallible, and hence his decisions are almost by definition correct. Erratic policies and constant shifting would have damaged their personal image *vis-à-vis* the armed institutions – their 'don de mando'.

On the other hand, Ibáñez and Pinochet were convinced that the only way to depoliticize the country in general and the public administration in particular was to get rid of the unasked cooperation of politicians and people with connections with political parties. The civilian technocrats supported a plan for profound economic and administrative reforms which went beyond and above the particular priorities posed by each political group. Ibáñez and Pinochet not only chose civilian technocrats, but particularly *young* civilian technocrats (*cabros*, *boys*) as they hoped their young age would prevent them from becoming a part of the corrupt machinery and vested interests. This also facilitated the relative insulation of these technocratic groups from the direct pressures coming from interests groups and political organizations.

From the point of view of the civilian technocrats, both military governments provided them a unique chance to put into practice their ideas about how to modernize the country and to improve their professional aspirations within the state apparatus. Both the *ingenieros* under Ibáñez and the Chicago boys under Pinochet sustained right-wing positions and the dictatorial nature of those regimes did not prevent them from collaborating with it. On the contrary, they visualized the dismantling of the democratic fabric as a great opportunity to implement rational and scientific-based policies without the interference of pressures from labor unions, entrepreneurial organizations, political parties and a supervising parliament.

In short, it can be stated that on several issues there was indeed an 'elected affinity' between the military and civilian technocrats which made possible the establishment of a working alliance between both actors. Nonetheless, the existing affinities were not sufficient in themselves to allow the emergence of a common technocratic project. The existence of both a strong sense of emergency and of genuine opportunities generated by the military intervention helped to diminish the traditional mutual prejudices existing between the military men and certain sectors of civil society, as those who supported the coups adopted an exceptional collaborative stance *vis-à-vis* the new military authorities. As the governments of Ibáñez and Pinochet have shown, however, the civilian technocrats' support for their military masters has been mainly conditioned by the ability of the latter to show they are firmly in control of the political process. When the crisis of 1931 and the defeat of the 1988 referendum made it clear that the days of both military governments were numbered, many civilian technocrats gradually began to abandon the sinking ship and to embrace the general popular call for the restoration of democracy.

Notes

1. This vision, of course, only became explicit following the 1973 military coup.
2. This was one of the conclusions the Chicago boys took from President Alessandri's failure (1958–64) to maintain his technocratic-oriented economic policy, as a result of labor protests and left-wing opposition in Parliament. In other words, a profound neo-liberal reform of the Chilean economy and society was simply not feasible under democratic rule.
3. One of the main exceptions in the privatization wave of state-owned industries was the *Gran Minería*. Despite the many Chicago boys' attempts to convince Pinochet and the military authorities of the advantages of its privatization, the civilian technocrats did finally accept the political inviability of their plans.
4. This seems to have been the same motivation which encouraged Ibáñez fifty years earlier to invite the *ingenieros* into his government. In the late 1950s, Ibáñez remembered his attempt in the late 1920s to renew the country's politico-administrative class in the following terms: 'I managed to bring young and independent men to the top positions of the public administration, most of them from middle-class backgrounds. It did not

matter that they were not well known in the political scene or in the Santiago social circles. One had to introduce new habits, something one cannot achieve with people compromised with the political environment' (quoted in Correa, 1962: 151).

5. Despite the fact the Ibáñez government constituted the only single experience in military rule Chile had known this century previous to 1973, Pinochet rarely made any reference to that military leader. However, there are many similarities between both (for example, collaboration with young technocrats, distance from elite and political parties, and their peculiar type of populism) which make me think Pinochet took personal lessons from Ibáñez's experience.

7
Mourning and Mistrust in Civil–Military Relations in Post-Dirty War Argentina

*Antonius C.G.M. Robben**

'Often, as I returned to my house late at night, I saw lights burning in your windows and I asked myself who was living there, how the decisions that we had taken that day affected you, to what extent I was fulfilling my obligation to watch over the destiny of my fellow countrymen, and I would have liked to enter each and every house and talk to you, listen to you, and ask you about your joys and disillusions.'

Admiral Emilio Massera, member of the three-man junta, on 17 September 1978

Introduction

This confession by admiral Massera betrays the extent to which the Argentine military dictatorship sought to control the lives of its citizens during the dirty war that raged from 1976 to 1983.[1] The violence unleashed in that tragic decade penetrated deep into the homes of the Argentine people, and disrupted the relations of protection, safety, trust and love that dwelled there. Nearly two-thirds of all disappeared were abducted from home.[2] The violation of the home by the military shattered the intimate ties of its inhabitants, and caused a profound mistrust of the state and its institutions among a great segment of Argentine society. Civil–military relations

* This research in Buenos Aires, Argentina, from April 1989 until August 1991 was made possible by grants from the National Science Foundation and the Harry Frank Guggenheim Foundation.

remained damaged for more than a decade after the turn to democracy in 1983, in part because of the psychological consequences of the terror inflicted on the victims of the dirty war.

Even though the Argentine military turned the words 'dirty war' and 'disappearance' into household names, Argentina was not the only country in Latin America that instilled its population with fear and resorted to a brutal repression of the political opposition. Other military regimes had already paved the way. The Brazilian military who ruled between 1964 to 1985 were responsible for around 125 disappearances (Arquidiocese de São Paulo, 1985: 261); more than 1000 people disappeared in Chile after the 1973 coup d'état; while Guatemala set a sorry record with an estimated 42 000 disappeared since the start of the ruthless counter-insurgency campaigns in 1966 (Green, 1995: 119).

State terrorism and systematic repression were characteristic of most military dictatorships in Latin America, and in particular of Argentina, Chile, Brazil and Uruguay. The military in these four countries perceived a common threat of communist infiltration after the 1959 Cuban revolution, and agreed that the democratic governments were not doing enough to protect the national sovereignty and the region's Christian cultural heritage. Once the military came to power, they tried to silence the political opposition at great human cost, and cooperated closely to persecute political dissidents throughout the Southern Cone. Uruguayan citizens were abducted in Argentina and imprisoned in their own country, Chilean refugees were tortured in Argentina, and Argentine exiles in Brazil were traced through the SNI, the country's all-powerful National Information Service (see CONADEP, 1986; Arquidiocese de São Paulo, 1985, 1986).

The repressive methods of these four military dictatorships were at first inspired by the French colonial wars against liberation movements in Indo-China and Algeria, and later by US counter-insurgency strategies. Latin American military officers were trained in the 1960s at the US Southern Command in Panama, and at Fort Bragg, North Carolina (Loveman and Davies, 1989). The armed forces in all four countries thus received the same training in repressive methods, but each country developed its own practice of breaking the political opposition and armed insurgency for reasons that are beyond the scope of this essay.

Disappearances occurred in Brazil and Uruguay on a relatively limited scale. Brazil tortured suspects, held them *incomunicado*, and used death squads to kill political opponents. Uruguay preferred imprisoning nearly 50 000 people in detention centers between 1972 and 1983. About 5000 persons were convicted, and subjected to traumatizing prison conditions. The Chilean military carried out tens of thousands of executions, but made people disappear in far lesser numbers. Argentina was responsible for the largest number of disappearances (Fagen, 1992; Stepan, 1988: 14–16).

Disappearance was thus the preferred tactic of the Argentine military to combat the guerrilla insurgency that had emerged in 1969. The most immediate military objective was to sow terror and confusion among the revolutionary forces, but repression soon spread to civil society as a whole. The disappearance of combatants debilitated the guerrilla organizations because of the fear that under torture they would betray their comrades in arms. The operational goal of the disappearances was closely tied to the express wish to annihilate the enemy by breaking its will to fight.[3] This objective turned into the obsession to annihilate opponents also physically; not only by killing them but by destroying their remains. The disappearance of these corpses was seen as a means of paralysing the opposition. The military believed that the anguished search of relatives and friends for the disappeared would rule out any desire for further political action.

Paradoxically, the attempt to silence the political opposition had a reverse effect. Human rights organizations arose which demanded information on the whereabouts of the disappeared, a group of mothers held weekly protests in front of the presidential palace at the Plaza de Mayo, and a clamor was raised abroad. Apparently, the military had underestimated the human need for mourning and the moral obligation to care for the dead. The powerful need of parents to bury their dead children became the driving force behind a political opposition movement that hastened the eventual downfall of the military regime.

I shall argue that the disappearances carried out in the intimacy of the home invaded the relation of parent and child, and provoked intense guilt feelings among the surviving parents about having failed to protect their adult and adolescent children in the hour of their greatest need. Most disappeared were killed shortly after their detention by the security forces, and their bodies interred in mass graves. Parents were deliberately left in the dark about the fate of their missing children, and were thus denied the right to properly bury them. It was at this intersection of the political and domestic domain that parental trust and protection became mobilized, and led mothers either on a search for the human remains or to a vindication of the revolutionary ideals held by many of the disappeared before their abduction. I shall conclude that the dirty war tactics of disappearances politicized the human need of parents to bury their children, and deeply affected civil–military relations in the decades after the dictatorship by a continued refusal of the armed forces to hand over their former enemy dead.

Basic trust and mistrust

Erik Erikson (1951) considered the constitution of basic trust as essential to the healthy social and psychological development of a child. Basic trust is shaped during the earliest stage of childhood when the baby learns to rely on its main caretakers. Although basic trust is believed to be a universal stage of human development, its particular manifestation in the child's everyday practice has unique personal, social and cultural dimensions. In her own unique way, each mother shapes her child's personal development. In particular, the way in which a mother attends to the needs of her baby shapes the child's development of confidence and trust in her. At the group level, the mother, father and siblings protect the baby against threats from the outside world, and the particular social dynamics of the nuclear family influence the forms of trust acquired by the child. Finally, the cultural environment shapes the infant's development. Parents transmit certain expectations about the world through culture-bound child-rearing practices, and teach their children whom to trust and whom to mistrust (Erikson, 1951: 221; Caudill and Weinstein, 1972; LeVine, 1988; LeVine *et al.*, 1994: 247–56).

On this three-dimensional foundational trust established within the intimacy of the home, relationships are built with the outer world, with relatives and friends, but also with society at large and its political institutions. Drawing extensively on Erikson, Giddens (1991: 36–40) has argued that this basic trust provides people with a sense of security that allows them to interact with strangers in an unpredictable social environment. Daily routines and social conventions serve to continuously renew their basic trust, because persons cannot feed for the rest of their lives on the trust established in early childhood. Basic trust is thus not an inalienable part of the personal constitution but can disintegrate beyond recovery after undergoing a traumatic experience.

Trust is by definition intersubjective, and the basic trust given needs to be reproduced just as much as the trust received. The protection provided by the mother and the father shapes them as much as their child. Parents will continue to provide this care for the rest of their lives, wanting to protect the child even when he or she has grown into adulthood. It is the impotence at being unable to give this care to one's suffering child that can be so traumatic, as I will continue to demonstrate with an analysis of dirty war disappearances in Argentina between 1976 and 1983.

Inner and outer, home and state

The abduction of political suspects from their homes and the humiliation of their witnessing relatives by the Argentine military violated the basic trust of the victims involved. The home is the place where a person acquires his conception of the world as a social, moral and physical space divided into an inner sanctuary and an outer world (Piaget, 1971: 331). The home exudes trust and safety because these values are given concrete meaning there between parent and child, brother and sister. The forced entry of the home by a military task force is therefore an attack that takes place as much on the physical and psychological as on the social and cultural level. The basic trust of a person is assaulted as much as the integrity of the body and the sanctity of the home, and family relations are as much damaged as the symbolic order of society in a private and a public domain.

Argentine military task forces had a preference for arresting people at home, during the night hours, and with a massive show of force, even when they knew that the suspect was unarmed. 'They detained me at home', so began Rubén Darío Martínez the typical account of his abduction from his apartment:

A group of people, seven or eight persons, entered ... I was asleep. They broke down the door, covered me with a hood, put me against the wall, and began to inspect the entire place. They asked me where the weapons were, turned the mattress over, broke everything, and forced me to the floor. After hitting me at my home, they placed a pistol to my head, and then took me downstairs. (*Diario del Juicio*, 15: 331)

The impact of the physical and psychological violence of the abductions was so intense because the assaults took place in the home. The state intruded violently on the domestic domain, thus transgressing a social, material and symbolic barrier that is so common in all Latin societies, including Argentina.[4] The public sphere is regarded as a dangerous place whose harmful influences must be prevented from polluting the intimate domestic sphere. Thresholds, material demarcations and open spaces are erected to either prevent unwanted citizens from entering or allow those invited into the home to undergo a symbolic transformation as they move from one social sphere to the other (Brown, 1987; Robben, 1989b; Taylor and Brower, 1985; Van Gennep, 1960: 15–25).[5] Thus, a forced entry violates this social, material, symbolic and emotional division between the two domains. Children sense this infraction on the sanctity of the home immediately: when a nightly task force broke into the house of Marta Lifsica de Chester in November 1976 to abduct her husband Jorge, the 12-year-old daughter Zulema woke up and entered the living room. The surprised commanding officer asked her: 'What are you doing here?,' to which the girl responded: 'I am in my house. What are you doing here?' (*Diario del Juicio*, 32: 594).

The assaults were also extended to the objects that gave content and meaning to the lives of the inhabitants (see Csikszentmihalyi and Rochberg-Halton, 1981). Photographs, paintings, porcelain, toys and momentos were often broken and even urinated upon. In one case this aggression against the home went even to the extreme of tearing down walls and modifying the arrangement of the rooms. This happened to Mrs García Candeloro who, together with her husband, had been abducted in June 1977 from their home in the Andean capital of Neuquén. Her husband died under torture. After her release six months later, Mrs García Candeloro decided to move to the coastal town of Mar del Plata. When she arrived at her house in Neuquén to put it up for sale, she discovered to her dismay that a group of policemen were living there:

> my house was completely plundered. They had destroyed the bookcases and even the walls. They had made compartments. The house had four rooms and with those compartments made out of broken bookcases they had created about seven rooms in the dining room. (*Diario del Juicio*, 8: 175)

The conversion of the dining room into provisional bedrooms turned their sociospatial functions and cultural meanings upside down (see Robben, 1989b). The semi-public living room, where guests used to gather, had now become confounded with the most intimate retreat of the house in a disturbing jumble into which refuge was no longer possible.

Forced separation and basic trust

The ways in which Argentine parents responded to such violent break-ins and the subsequent abductions reveal much about the mobilization of parental feelings of trust and protection. The threat of loss makes parents place their children's well-being ahead of their own. Weiss (1993: 274–5) argues that the mother and father seek to be physically close to the child when it is threatened so that it can be reassured of their protection by touching or at least hearing and seeing its parents.

Whenever a task force entered a home during those cruel years between 1976 and 1983, the thoughts of the mother went invariably first to her son or daughter, and only later to her husband and herself. Generally, she would run to the child's bedroom and stay at its side. When Margarita Michelini was ordered to follow her assailants outside, and hand over her baby, 'I told them to kill me right there, but that I was not going to give them the baby' (*Diario del Juicio*, 9: 207). The 12-year-old daughter of Nelida Jauregui was awakened 'with a machine-gun to her head and they wanted to take her away from me, so I embraced her and I told them that this was not going to be possible because she was an infant and I took her to my bedroom' (*ibid.*, 31: 568). The reaction of mothers in such dramatic situations was so unexpected that in a number of cases the infants were not abducted to be given to childless military couples (see Herrera and Tenembaum, 1990; Nosiglia, 1985).

The feelings between mother and child were reciprocal in the sense that the protection went out not just from parent to child, as Weiss (1993: 275) suggests, but also from child to parent. Twelve-year-old Zulema Lifsica de Chester, who had earlier questioned the assailants' presence in her home, protested again when her blind-folded mother was thrown to the floor:

> My daughter saw this and began to scream that they shouldn't push her mommy. Then they asked her: 'Why do you defend your mother?' She told them: 'Would you have liked it if some-one did something to your mother?', to which she did not receive an answer. (*Diario del Juicio*, 32: 594)

The girl was taken to her bedroom and interrogated about the hid-ing place of political pamphlets. The anguished mother heard the men's questions but not her daughter's replies. 'Then I also begin to scream: "Where is my daughter? What is happening with my daughter?", until they finally throw us together in the hall' (*Diario del Juicio*, 32: 594). Mother and daughter were separated once more and interrogated in their respective bedrooms. Zulema declared nine years later in court that her interrogation took between 30 and 45 minutes during which she was beaten and sexually abused. But even under these trying circumstances her attention went out to her par-ents: 'And I ask him where my parents are; so he tells me that I can go and look for my daddy in a ditch. Then I asked him for my mother and again he tells me that my mother is fine, that she is in the other bedroom' (*ibid.*, 32: 595). When Zulema asked to be taken to her mother, the men fetched the mother instead, and tied her back to back to her daughter. They left the house and took the father with them.

The need to protect the children even endured under torture. How can a mother ever betray her children when she raised them with the certainty that they can always rely on her? Melba de Falcone, who had helped her son move to a new house as he had just married, was detained for abetting a subversive and tortured to reveal his location:

> I asked them if they didn't have a mother. I asked them how they could do this to me. I had gone to help a son move, and they

screamed at me that the mother in them had been killed by the guerrilleros…I really didn't know where he had gone, and if I would have known I would have died for my son, because he was my son. (*Diario del Juicio*, 3: 67)

Maria Elisa Hachmann de Lande was tortured for 48 hours to reveal the whereabouts of her son. 'At that time they thought that it would be easier to force the mother to say something, no? Or to say where they were. But if I gave life to my son, would I then bring him death?' (interview, 13 April 1990).

When the torture of parents did not yield the desired information, then the torturers exploited parental feelings by abusing infants and even unborn babies (CONADEP, 1986: 305–10; Suárez-Orozco, 1987). Norberto Liwski was told that he was going to accompany one of his small daughters into the torture chamber. The attending physician, however, warned the torturer that he could only use the electric prod on children that weighed more than 25 kgs. In a psychological torment, Liwski was shown the soiled underpants of his little girls.

This went on and on, this torture of using the children in this way. At various opportunities they told me that they had such control over my daughters that they had films of them on which I could ascertain myself – if I cared to see them – the degree of control they had over them. (*Diario de Juicio*, 30: 549)

The newspaper publisher Jacobo Timerman witnessed the havoc inflicted on the Miralles family as they were being tortured in each other's presence:

The entire affective world, constructed over the years with utmost difficulty, collapses with a kick in the father's genitals, a smack on the mother's face, an obscene insult to the sister, or the sexual violation of a daughter. Suddenly an entire culture based on familial love, devotion, the capacity for mutual sacrifice collapses. (1981: 148)

From his cell, Timerman heard the father trying to get an apple to his children, and the children trying to learn about the fate of their parents. He learned of the father's powerlessness, 'that impotence that arises not from one's failure to do something in defense of one's children but from one's inability to extend a tender gesture' (Timerman, 1981: 148–9).

This impotence was not only felt inside the torture centers but also by the parents of the disappeared. Waiting quietly for the abducted child to reappear was felt as abandonment, while active protest was regarded as life-threatening. This dilemma became magnified during an official media campaign that carried slogans such as: 'How are you raising your child?' 'Do you know what your child is doing at this precise moment?' (Kordon and Edelman, 1988: 34). Officially intended to make parents aware of the education of their children and make them responsible for the company they kept, it produced tremendous guilt among those parents whose children had been abducted. Mothers were indirectly blamed for not raising their children properly and thus for contributing to their involvement with the guerrilla organizations.

As more and more people disappeared, the numbers of those seeking their abducted relatives also grew. In September 1977, a group of mothers of the disappeared decided to stage a weekly protest against the abductions. They became world-famous as the Mothers of the Plaza de Mayo (*Madres de Plaza de Mayo*). This heroic resistance and protest against the military junta was a natural expression of maternal protection, a demonstration of the trust between parent and child.

The military junta was at a loss about how to react to the public protest. They did not think of mothers as political actors:

> Paradoxically … the military in these societies preach traditional family values and valorize motherhood in an attempt to strengthen patriarchal rule in the home. This insistence upon the woman's sacrifice for and obedience to the family and to her children has backfired on the military as women have demanded to know what has happened to their sons and daughters. (Schirmer, 1988: 45; see also Navarro, 1989)

At first, the Madres were ignored, then belittled as 'the crazy women of Plaza de Mayo' (*las locas de Plaza de Mayo*). Later, the weekly protests at the Plaza de Mayo were repressed; many mothers were abducted, tortured or detained, while some leading figures disappeared altogether.

The Madres utilized their role as mothers brilliantly in their resistance strategy. They emphasized that they did not have political motives or feminist objectives, they simply identified themselves as housewives and mothers who wanted to have news about their disappeared children. What was more natural for a mother than to want to know about the whereabouts of her children? What made their demand unusual was that they expressed these maternal feelings in a public domain dominated by a repressive patriarchal state. They transgressed the division between public and domestic in a reverse direction than the one used by the military assault teams which had invaded their homes and abducted their children. In a second transgressive act, they domesticized the public space by introducing symbols of the home. They donned on their heads scarves resembling diapers and displayed photographs of their loved ones (Schirmer, 1994: 203). The maternal feelings of protection and trust were the principal driving forces behind their crusade.

Guilt also played a role in this incessant search. The feeling that one had not done one's utmost to prevent the abductions is a source of strength not to be underestimated. The struggle of the mothers between 1977 and 1983 has been documented extensively and need not be repeated here (see Bousquet, 1984; Fisher, 1989; Guzman Bouvard, 1994; Oria, 1987; Simpson and Bennett, 1985). What is of more concern here is how mothers affiliated with the Madres and other human rights organizations reacted after a government investigative committee concluded in 1984 that the disappeared could be presumed dead. Once again, conflicting maternal feelings of protection and abandonment were stirred up as now the loss had to be mourned, but the final rights of death could not be administered in the absence of a corpse. The Argentine mothers searched for the remains as if these were still their suffering children, while feeling guilty not only about having abandoned them in the hour of death but also about being unable to provide the maternal care of a proper burial.

Exhumations and revolutionary protest

When Raúl Alfonsín assumed the presidency of Argentina in December 1983, he installed the CONADEP, a commission with the mandate to inquire into the fate of the disappeared. This became an almost impossible task because the military junta had gone to great lengths to destroy the bodies of their victims. Corpses were cremated, abandoned at roadsides, thrown in rivers, or interred as unidentified bodies in mass graves at cemeteries near the torture centers.[6] The Navy even went to the extreme of flinging heavily drugged detainees from planes into the sea (García, 1995: 461–70; Verbitsky, 1995).

The first evidence of the existence of mass graves appeared in late October 1982, only months after the military junta was forced to step down after its debâcle of the Falklands/Malvinas War. An estimated 400 unidentified bodies were found at the cemetery of Grand Bourg near Buenos Aires (Cohen Salama, 1992: 60–2; *Somos*, 1982, 319: 11). The effect of the discovery on the Argentine public was shattering. There was disbelief and anger. More mass graves were opened in dozens of places and the perforated skulls exhibited in what the news media called a 'horror show'. The display of piles of bones and bullet-ridden skulls revealed to the stunned Argentines the horrors of the military dictatorship as well as the realization of the chance that they could very well have met the same fate. Nevertheless, despite the gruesomeness of the discoveries, people were hopeful that now they would be able to mourn and bury their dead.

At first, the human rights organizations were strongly in favor of the opening of mass graves. Hebe de Bonafini, the leader of the Madres de Plaza de Mayo, believed in October 1982 that the exhumations would allow the human remains to be identified. At last, the disappeared would be wrested from anonymity and given a proper burial (*Humor*, 1982, 92: 47). However, De Bonafini and many other mothers in her wake began to have misgivings about the continued exhumations when forensic experts failed to identify the victims. She became convinced in January 1984 that 'there is sufficient proof to send a great number of those guilty of this horror to prison', but she expressed doubts about the political will to prosecute them (*Somos*, 1984, 382: 20). The mothers' faith in the justice system declined further when the Alfonsín government decided to try the nine commanders of the three 1976–82 juntas under military instead of criminal law.

A fundamental disagreement had arisen in 1985 among the Argentine human rights organizations between those in favor and those against exhumations. The division corresponded to two different responses to the loss suffered by the disappearances. Both groups were aware of the political dimension of their position, but the proponents wanted to give the exhumed an honorable reburial, while the opponents wanted to vindicate the political ideals of the disappeared.

The Mothers of the Plaza de Mayo were also divided amongst themselves, and this dispute led in 1986 to a tragic split within the organization that had most courageously opposed the military dictatorship. The majority followed Hebe de Bonafini in her condemnation that the exhumations were a sinister scheme by the Alfonsín government to have them accept and psychologically participate in the death of all who disappeared. The Madres demanded that, first, those guilty of the disappearances and subsequent killings had to be identified before any further exhumations were to be carried out (*Madres*, 1984, 1: 2). Reflecting on the intense soul-searching that preceded their position on the controversial exhumations, Hebe de Bonafini said: 'It cost us weeks and weeks of meetings at which there were many tears and much despair, because the profound Catholic formation of our people creates almost a need to have a dead body, a burial, and a Mass' (*Madres*, 1987, 37: 10). Despite the anguish, the De Bonafini group decided to keep their emotional wounds open in order to resist the societal process of forgetting:

> It has been eleven years of suffering, eleven years that have not been relieved in any sense. Many want the wound to dry so that we will forget. We want it to continue bleeding, because this is the only way that one continues to have the strength to fight … But, above all, it is necessary that this wound bleeds so that the assassins will be condemned, as they deserve to be, and that what has happened will not happen again. This is the commitment in the defense of life which the Madres have taken upon themselves. (*Ibid.*, 29: 1)

Continued political protest weighed more heavily than individual relief because anxiety was the hinge of memory and oblivion.

The leading figures of the Madres were of course well-aware of the psychological toll of the enduring uncertainty. They realized that their refusal to allow for more exhumations would prevent relatives from mourning their dead, but they were convinced that the government had not only conspired to have them accept the death of the disappeared but had also tried deliberately to set the mourning process in motion in order to depoliticize the surviving relatives, and in particular the vocal Mothers of the Plaza de Mayo. Mourning would break the solidarity of the Madres and hasten a reconciliatory attitude.

As the years went by, there was a profound identification of the Mothers with their disappeared sons and daughters. Activism helped them cope with their grief (see Maxwell, 1995), and many Mothers began to emulate political ideals which they had opposed when their children had still been alive. They began to regard themselves as the embodiment of their children's ideals and struggles:

> In many respects it was like this: my children had given birth to me … If they are not here, then I have to be them, shout for them, vindicate them with honesty and return if even a small piece of life to them. They are in my rallying cries, in this fatigue that maybe nobody can understand but which always recuperates itself; they are in my head and in my body, in everything I do. I believe that their absence has left me forever pregnant. (Hebe de Bonafini in Sánchez, 1985: 74–5)

By late 1988, the idea took hold that the Mothers had to 'socialize their maternity' (*Madres*, 1988, 48: 17) and embrace the suffering of all victims of political violence in the world. 'When we understood that our children were not going to appear, we socialized motherhood and felt that we are the mothers of everybody, that all are our children' (Hebe de Bonafini, *Madres*, 1989, 53: 17). Pressing social problems in Argentina, such as poverty, poor social and medical services, high unemployment, insufficient benefits for the aged, government corruption, police brutality and the privatization of state companies became a political platform to pursue the revolutionary ideals of their children. Clearly, the Madres wanted to extend the maternal protection they had been unable to offer their own children at the hour of abduction to all victims of repression, and at the same time be unconditionally supportive of their sons and daughters by embracing their political ideas and ideals. Trust and protection were the motives of their radical political position.

Reburial and collective mourning

Most human rights organizations did not share the opposition of the Madres de Plaza de Mayo to the exhumations. They were convinced of the legal, political, psychological and historical importance of forensic investigations. Exhumations supplied evidence for legal prosecution, provided historical testimony of the human rights violations committed by the military, gave forensic proof about the birth of children by pregnant disappeared women, and allowed surviving relatives to begin a process of mourning. Exhumations became a recourse for many relatives, as much for their emotional peace as for the political significance of a funeral in times of a budding democracy. Reburial would reconcile the bereaved with their loss, restore the public honor of the victims, reincorporate them into society as deceased members, and politicize the recovered remains.

The multiple significance of a reburial for the surviving relatives can be read from the reactions of the Morresi family and of Mrs Berta Schuberoff. Norberto Morresi had disappeared in 1977, and was finally identified in 1989. His parents Julio and Irma Morresi decided to rebury him in the same grave as the disappeared person who was exhumed together with him.

> The truth, however hard it may be, will in the end bring tranquility. I am no longer searching in that God-knows-where place ... to see if it's Norberto, or visit a madhouse to see if he is there. I know, unfortunately we have this little heap of bones at the Flores cemetery, no? It is like a ritual that we go there every Sunday to bring him even only one flower. It is completely useless, but it helps spiritually ... We go there, we kiss the photo that is hanging on the niche, and it makes us feel good. (Interview, 29 March 1991)

And Berta Schuberoff said the following about the importance of finding the remains of her son Marcelo in 1989:

> I felt that I was emotional because I found my son. I kissed him again. I kissed all his bones, touched him, caressed him. But the emotion was confounded with the pain, because once I found him, he turned out to be dead. So I cried over the death of my

son, and those thirteen years of search vanished. I can't relate
anymore to this period. (Quoted in Cohen Salama, 1992: 249)

These two responses reveal the social and psychological significance
of reburials and their relation to basic trust. Reburial gives parents
the final opportunity to demonstrate and enact their basic trust to
their deceased children by providing them with a proper resting-
place and observing their departure with a culturally appropriate
funerary ritual. The torn fabric of society is restored by the funeral,
the remains come to share the sacred ground of the cemetery, and
their souls are reconciled in the society of the dead (see Hertz, 1960:
54). These purposes seem to have been served in Argentina for
nearly 200 disappeared who have been reburied. The violent deaths
of the disappeared at the hands of the state give the reburials a distinct political meaning. Reburial implies a reincorporation of the
former disappeared as political victims in Argentina's troubled history. Their disappearance, death, unceremonious burial, and the subsequent exhumation and reburial turn into an enduring reminder of
state repression.

Robert Hertz (1960: 83) has observed that 'It is the action of society on the body that gives full reality to the imagined drama of the
soul'. What a society and, for that matter, a state does with its dead
determines the place of their souls in those social configurations.
The planned disappearance of the bodies of its citizens implies that
the soul can neither pass from the land of the living to the land of the
dead. The wandering spirit continues to haunt the living in the
form of the constant anxiety of relatives who cannot mourn the disappeared and keep demanding a reckoning from society and its
political and military leaders.

The two predominant responses of Argentine mothers have been
either to search for the remains of their children and rebury them,
or to propagate the revolutionary ideals associated with the disappeared in a constant appeal for justice. Both reactions arise from
the same basic trust and unconditional support which the parents
wanted to provide their disappeared children. The public protests
against pressing social problems and the reburial of exhumed remains
seem to have offered the mothers some emotional respite from their
tremendous grief. However, the realization that justice was not
served, and that those responsible for the disappearances were not

convicted, is for many unbearable and makes them distrustful of the Argentine polity. Peace cannot return to a society and the polity cannot operate properly when its members are unable to reconcile themselves with the past. The deliberate obstruction of reburials impedes a return to normality and the repair of the social fabric.

The long-term political consequences of the dirty war are impossible to fathom, but the continued uncertainty about thousands of unrecovered dead and the impunity of their executioners cannot but gnaw at the heart of the nation. The massive trauma of the dirty war has undermined people's trust in the state and its authorities because a society that does not assume responsibility for its dead can never entirely trust the living.

Notes

1. The political violence of the 1970s or, more narrowly, the military rule of Argentina between 1976 and 1983, has been described with a confusing array of names that each betray different imputed causes, conditions and consequences. The military have used terms such as dirty war, antirevolutionary war, fight against subversion, and the Process of National Reorganization. Human rights groups talk about state terror, repression and military dictatorship. Former revolutionary organizations employ terms used by human rights groups, but also talk about civil war, war of liberation, and anti-imperialist struggle. Whether the violence of the 1970s is described with the term antirevolutionary war, civil war or state terror is important because each designation implies a different moral and historical judgment that may turn patriots into oppressors, victims into ideologues, and heroes into subversives. I have chosen to use the term 'dirty war' because of its common association with disappearances and state terror.
2. To be exact, 62 per cent of the people still missing in 1984 were arrested in their homes, 24.6 per cent in the street, 7 per cent at work, and 6 per cent at their place of study (CONADEP, 1986: 11).
3. On 6 October 1975, the Argentine government signed secret decree no. 2772 which authorized the armed forces 'to carry out military and security operations necessary to annihilate the actions of subversive elements in the territory of the entire country'.
4. The roots of this division lie in ancient Greek and Hebrew culture (Arendt, 1958: 22–78). A similar dichotomy can be found in contemporary Islamic and Mediterranean cultures. The opposition between public and private is elaborated in cultural values such as honor and shame, modesty and display, and loyalty and betrayal (see Benn and Gauss, 1983; DaMatta, 1987; Moore, 1984; Peristiany, 1965; Robben, 1989a,b).

5. See Feldman (1991: 88–97) for a Foucaultean analysis of the transgression of the domestic sanctuary by the nightly house arrest of political suspects in Northern Ireland.
6. The military rulers made two official attempts to have the disappeared pronounced dead, even in the absence of a corpse. A law was issued in September 1979 that declared all persons presumed dead who had disappeared between 6 November 1974 and 6 September 1979. They hoped that this decree would end the insistent appeals from human rights organizations. After the 1982 defeat in the Falklands/Malvinas War, the interim government of general Bignone published a final report about the 1976–82 dictatorship and declared once again all disappeared as presumed dead (San Martino de Dromi, 1988: 343, 360; *Somos*, 1983: 346–51).

8
Political Orientations and Factionalism in the Brazilian Armed Forces, 1964–85

Kees Koonings

Introduction

The aim of this chapter is to review the military regime in Brazil (1964–85) from the point of view of the political orientation of the military corporation. This approach takes as a point of departure the proposition that, in order to properly understand the dynamics of institutionalized militarism in South America, we must primarily take into account the role of the armed forces as a 'political actor'. This is especially relevant in the case of Brazil, given the long history of political interventionism of this country's military and also in view of the specific nature of the Brazilian military governments between 1964 and 1985. This specific nature rested on the preservation of considerable elements of the pre-coup political structure, in combination with a high degree of autonomy enjoyed by the military in power. This meant that the military was able to shape, as one would of course expect, the nature of the regime it established, but also that it only succeeded in doing so by elaborating sophisticated political strategies. The result was a complex military–civil 'authoritarian situation' that brought out quite clearly the factors that influence the constitution and evolution of the military as a specific political actor.

In addition, Brazil's long-lasting period of military rule was characterized by the existence of factions within the politically active part of the armed forces. These factions assumed different positions during the period of military rule, which can be broken down into a number of stages, each with its own political dynamics. The changing

political situation, from intervention by the military and consolidation of their 'Revolution', through closure of the regime and repression, to a gradual liberalization and, eventual, redemocratization,
was in part shaped by, and further exacerbated, differences within
the military institution as to the nature and extent of its political
involvement. These kinds of differences are not often highlighted in
the scholarly debates on militarism; often, simple reference is made
to the military as a political actor, as if the armed forces constitute a
monolithic bloc. Internal divisions within the military are important for an assessment of their political role: among other things
they point at possible internal mechanisms of change within
authoritarian regimes dominated by the military.

To analyse the Brazilian case, I will distinguish, in this chapter, a
'moderate' and a 'hard-line' faction within the armed forces. I will
try to relate the position of each of these two factions within the
authoritarian regime for each of three stages of the dictatorship: the
coup d'état and the moderator-style consolidation of the regime
(1964–68); the period of repression and regime closure (1968–74);
and the drawn-out transition 'from above' (1974–85).

The next section of the chapter discusses the theoretical underpin-
nings of the constitution of the military as a political actor. Then, I
give a brief general overview of the period of military governments
in Brazil, to serve as a background to the discussion of the two
rivalling political orientations within the Brazilian military in each
of the three stages mentioned above. The third section of the chapter presents this discussion. In the conclusion, I will try to put the
issue of factionalism within the Brazilian military in a broader perspective of militarism and change in an authoritarian regime.

The military as a political actor

During the 1960s and the 1970s, a number of approaches set out to
explain militarism in Latin America on the basis of broader societal
relations and processes that were seen as giving rise to military rule.
Three perspectives have been quite influential in this debate: the
'modernization' (Lieuwen, 1961; Johnson, 1964), the 'class hegemony' (Nun, 1967) and the 'dependent authoritarianism' (O'Donnell,
1973; Collier, 1979) approaches. They share a common flaw, however, in that they fail to offer an integrated or complete view of the

interaction between the internal dynamics of the military institutions themselves and the wider processes of socioeconomic and political change in Latin American countries.[1] I take as a point of departure that we look at the constitution of the military as a 'political actor' in its own right. To do so, we should take into account the ways in which the general institutional role of the military is transformed into taking on the political and moral task of guarding the national interest, and from there into taking on political power directly.

A key aspect of the constitution of the military as a political actor can be found in the connections between the military institution and the problems of national order and national destiny. Central to this task was the maintenance of the integrity of the state, usually, but not necessarily, in connection with the preservation of the existing social order. In this connection it must be understood that the professionalized Latin American military form, on the one hand a strong corporate entity isolated from civil society and civic culture and with its own specific forms of organization, hierarchy, socialization and loyalties relatively insensitive to values like consensus, equality and democracy, on the other hand sees itself, the armed forces, as closely linked to society and especially the state.

The notion that the 'protection' of the internal integrity of the nation and the state is the primary task of the military is reinforced by the effective absence of an external security threat. Often a sense of superiority is developed *vis-à-vis* civil society with respect to the execution of state power. The military can not only act as protectors and guarantors of the constituted order, but they are perceived as the very founders and the embodiment of national existence itself. As is argued by Hayes, this orientation can take on the form of a veritable 'mystique' which he defines, for the Brazilian case, as '... a complex of semi-mythical beliefs of a generic nature which formed around the army, imbuing it with transcendental and esoteric importance' (Hayes, 1989: 5). This importance is translated into current politics by ascribing to the military the task of pursuing so-called 'permanent national objectives' (Loveman, 1994). Rial (1990: 9) stresses the self-definition of the Latin American armed forces as 'national institutions' which means that their role extends well beyond the prosaic task of defending the national territory against external threats. This assumption gives the military a more or less autonomous and legitimate role in national political life. It is their mission to preserve the national order and to guide the nation to its manifest destiny. To do so, the nation, and particularly the state, must be protected against its domestic foes, among which the 'inept' civil politicians may at times be included.

As such, the military institution can easily present itself as standing above the existing political framework, making its intervention in politics self-legitimizing. These interventions are derived from the overall military ideology in Latin America, which holds that the armed forces are pivotal for the maintenance of national order in its institutional, social and even moral dimensions.[2] Such an orientation does not automatically mean the rejection of the notion of democracy. However, the Latin American military tend to embrace corporatist forms of democracy in which political participation is organized through institutionalized social sectors rather than through individuals constituting an amorphous electorate. Democracy can then be subjected to the overriding priority of stability. In fact, this orientation transfers the internal logic of military organization, strategic planning and hierarchic control and command to politics and public administration.

This process in the Brazilian case has been analysed, in a very illuminating way, by Stepan (1971, 1976), who advances the notion of 'new professionalism', which means that a high level of professional sophistication can lead precisely to what he calls 'military role expansion'. The starting points of this new doctrine are fairly common conceptions of the role of the military in defending the nation. This role presupposes a clear notion of 'threat' and 'enemy', linked to a geopolitically inspired concept of national integrity and security. As Stepan shows for the case of Brazil, military doctrine gradually shifted away from the conventional conception of an external enemy and a geographically defined national integrity to the perception of an internal enemy threatening the sociopolitical and ideological ('moral') integrity of the nation.

Brazil illustrates that this kind of reorientation of the 'national security doctrine' is not necessarily only the result of the subordination of Latin American strategic doctrines to the requirements of the geo-strategic and ideological priorities of the United States. In Brazil, the nationalist character of the security doctrine has remained quite pronounced. This has been one of the underlying determinants of the strong links seen by the Brazilian regime between *segurança* (security) and *desenvolvimento* (development), the post-1964 version of *ordem e progresso*. The project of national economic development, the basic prerequisite for order, stability and security, was not left, as in the posterior cases of the Southern Cone, only to the vicissitudes of the capitalist market, namely, the capitalist class. State capitalism was one distinctive aspect of the Brazilian model based on an integrated security concept of total resource mobilization under state control. Furthermore, a fair degree of autonomy in the overall strategy of the military has inspired the notion of the 'military quasi-party': the military as being organized within political society around a clear economic and political project of its own while elaborating a strategy to attain state power on the basis of a legitimizing ideology (Andrade, 1977). Rouquié (1989: 271) states it as follows: 'The armies that have regularized their participation in this way constitute genuine political forces whose functioning is affected by their nature and manifest purpose'. Their nature is hierarchy, authoritarian command, and strategies against internal enemies; their manifest purpose is to safeguard the state.

This focus upon the constitution of the military as a political actor, or even as a quasi-party, should not overlook the possibility of fissures within the armed forces themselves. The 'political military' does not form a monolithic block; rather, we often deal with 'military politicians', for whom a general adherence to the values and integrity of the armed corporation does not exclude engaging in intra-military factionalism. Classically, the Latin American armed forces were split according to the three branches: the Navy was, as a rule, conservative and aristocratic, the Army tended to be more populist and possibly even reformist, while the Air Force – of more recent origins and working with prestigious equipment – was reputed to be 'technocratic'.[3] However, military factionalism can also stem from differences in political ideology (conservative, populist, or even radical communist), or from different views on the legitimacy and desirability of civilian political supremacy. In the broadest sense, this leads to the distinction between authoritarian 'hard-liners' or 'hawks', institutional loyalists (those who give priority to the corporate status of the armed forces), and 'legalists', that is those supporting the incumbent civilian government or civil democracy in general. In the case of Brazil, the political insertion of the military quasi-party led to complex civil–military alliances in which party politics together with networks of personalized loyalties were always prominent. It is, therefore, useful to give some attention to the issue of factionalism during the 21 years of military rule from 1964 to 1985.

The Brazilian dictatorship: general features and dynamics

The roots of the military regime of 1964–85 can be found in the gradual developing of an interventionist military institution that began as early as 1889. Throughout the twentieth century, the Brazilian military developed into an active player on the national political stage; the armed forces turned into a 'quasi-party' as suggested in the previous section. The aim of this military party was to influence or take part in government on behalf of a project of national development and 'greatness'. After the advent of the Republic in 1889, brought about through a military coup, the army adopted the task of modernizing the nation, often in defiance of the dominant regional oligarchies.[4] With this army-led overthrow of Emperor Pedro II, the military took over, to all intents and purposes, the role of a moderating power (*poder moderador*) that until then had been the role of the Emperor. This role assigned to the military the task of guaranteeing the nation and its constitutional order against all threats, both external and internal, and to intervene for that purpose if necessary.

After 1950, the political orientation of the military gradually acquired a new dimension. Immediately after the Second World War the armed forces seemed to adhere to liberal democratic principles when they forced Getúlio Vargas to step down and to end the *Estado Novo* dictatorship. But the foundation of the Escola Superior de Guerra (ESG) in 1949 and the return of Vargas to the presidency, this time as an elected populist in 1950, pushed the military slowly but steadily towards a more authoritarian orientation. During the 1950s, the concept of national security was further developed into a comprehensive doctrine to guide the internal political strategy of the armed forces. This process has been amply documented (Alves, 1985; Dreifuss, 1981; Stepan, 1971). For the purpose of our discussion, it is important to note the consequences for the sharpening of the political orientation of the military, the core element of which was the fusion of military and political objectives and strategies in relation to internal affairs. The goal of national development and the task of efficient public administration was seen as crucial for national security, since the latter necessarily rested on the full capacity to mobilize national economic, political and 'moral' resources. At the same time, this vital interest was seen as being threatened by increasing radicalization of populist and left-wing sectors. Thus, the concept of the 'internal enemy' was construed not just in the guise of open armed opposition (which was largely absent prior to 1964), but in relation to anybody opposing conservative-capitalist modernization, the stability of the state, and the integrity of its embodiment, the armed forces.

Eventually, this orientation led to the military intervention of March 1964, when the João Goulart presidency was seen as having definitely fallen into the hands of radicals, to the extent that the government itself crossed the boundaries of legality as defined by the military. Under the 1946 constitution this gave the armed forces the right, if not the moral obligation, to intervene. The expectation was that a 'classic' moderator-style coup would open the way for the installation of an anti-populist civil government. However, between 1964 and 1967 the decision of the generals eventually resulted in the installation of long-term military rule, which reformed the state in such a way that both the objectives of national development and the elimination of the internal enemies could be pursued (Alves, 1985).

The sharpening of authoritarianism in the late 1960s followed a short period of relative political opening endorsed by Castelo Branco (the first military president) and his successor Costa e Silva. During 1968, social and political resistance against the military regime grew, however, when students and industrial workers mounted large-scale protest meetings and strikes while opposition politicians tried to set up a broad anti-authoritarian alliance named the Frente Ampla (Broad Front). This alliance united politicians of different persuasions, ranging from conservatives Carlos Lacerda and Magalhães Pinto to former presidents Juscelino Kubitschek and João Goulart and the radial populist Leonel Brizola. The Frente Ampla inspired a more assertive stance adopted by Congress against the arbitrariness displayed by the military power-holders. The regime reacted by persecuting student and union leaders, suspending the rights of opposition politicians, and by outlawing the activities of the Frente Ampla.

These challenges to the military regime led to a further round of militarization of politics. By the end of 1968, the construction of the tutelary system was completed after the promulgation of the fifth institutional act (AI-5). This act gave the executive, hence the military, almost unlimited powers to rule in congress, to suspend political rights, and to prosecute political suspects without *habeas corpus* and under military law. The latter provision was further specified by the National Security Law of 1969 that considerably widened the definition of activities considered crimes against national security. As a result, an elaborate quasi-legal structure was put into place which allowed the military to step up repressive actions against any perceived internal enemies. From 1969 onwards, the military regime entered its most violent phase under the interim junta which replaced Costa e Silva after the latter's illness and under the presidency of General Emílio Médici (1969–74).

The selection of Ernesto Geisel as president for the 1974–79 term brought a new shift in the political strategy of the military regime. Brazilian politics from 1974 onwards can in fact be seen as a drawn-out transition to democracy. Although the process was initiated and regulated by the military itself, it ended in a tumultuous but peaceful period of popular manifestations against military rule that contributed to the rise to power of the civil Democratic Alliance in 1985. The basis for this success was the persistent adherence of the opposition to the electoral agenda, combined with increasing popular mobilization within civil society. After 1982 this led to the construction of a viable political alternative to the military regime.[5] Since Brazilian militarism after 1964 had preserved, at least nominally, some of the institutions of formal democracy, namely elections, parties and legislative bodies, the transition was not only regime-led but also, as has been pointed out by Lamounier (1989), election-driven: the opposition MDB was victorious in the elections of 1974, 1976 and 1978. At the same time, opposition forces gained ground within society. Trade unions, the church, legal organizations (such as the Order of Brazilian Lawyers, OAB), the students movement, and other grass-roots organizations became active in denouncing the military regime: its authoritarianism and arbitrariness, its legacy of social exclusion, and its human rights violations. These so-called new social movements and the new trade unionism that emerged during the second half of the 1970s in turn supported the political advance of the anti-regime forces. In this, the 1982 elections (for Congress, state governors, and state legislatures) were crucial since they registered the further electoral advance of the opposition that threatened the regime's control of the Electoral College for the 1985 presidential succession. The process of social and political mobilization reached its apogee during the massive demonstrations, in 1984, in favor of direct presidential elections (*diretas já*). This movement effectively combined massive dissatisfaction with military rule and political arbitrariness with the prevailing economic situation and the way it was handled.

The regime tended to react to the opposition's gains by regressive initiatives, curbing the political space of the opposition by *ad hoc* exceptional legislation. The implicit aim was to secure control over the executive until at least the end of the term of Figueiredo's successor, to be elected by the Electoral College in 1985. In fact, Figueiredo committed himself formally to the restoration of 'full democracy', provided gradualism was observed and order maintained. In essence, the transition strategy of the Figueiredo administration failed: its objective was to hand over power in 1985 in the usual controlled way to yet another (military) candidate of the regimes party (ARENA, later PDS). However, as one social sector after another rallied behind the opposition banner (including the urban middle classes and the business elites), the January 1985 appointment of the new president by the Electoral College (Congress plus a number of state legislation deputies) showed a majority for PMDB's candidate Tancredo Neves. During the months leading up to the indirect election, the opposition parties PMDB and PFL (a split-off from the PDS) formed the Aliança Democrática (AD) to boost Tancredo's candidacy and to come to an arrangement with the military.

Factionalism, political orientations and regime dynamics

In the foregoing I alluded to the existence of at least two factions within the Brazilian military and to their positioning during the different stages of the dictatorship. In this section I will try to focus more explicitly on this issue. For the sake of simplicity I will adopt the basic distinction between the so-called moderates and the hard-liners within the armed forces.[6] After a brief demarcation of these two factions, I will proceed by linking them to two possible types of political orientation within the military. I will then use statements about the period of military rule made by high-level officers in order to evaluate to what extent military discourse fits with the two hypothetical types of political orientation.[7] I will follow this procedure for each of the three stages of the military dictatorship, mentioned earlier: the coup itself and the period of consolidation of military rule (1964–68); the period of regime closure and repression (1968–74); and the period of 'decompression' and regime-led transition to democracy (1974–85). Each period will be briefly introduced by mentioning (or restating) the principal political events.

The distinction drawn between moderates and hard-liners within the Brazilian military can be traced back to the beginnings of the period of military rule, that is during the months following the coup on 31 March 1964. In fact the formation of the moderate current was linked to the activities of the Escola Superior de Guerra (Superior War College, ESG) where, after its foundation in 1949, the basic tenets of the doctrine of 'security and development' were elaborated. For this reason, the moderates were also often designated as the *sorbonistas*, which referred to the group of military intellectuals formed within the ESG. Another label to be used was *castelistas*, after Marshal Castelo Branco, who became the first military president and was clearly the most prominent of the moderate faction in 1964. The moderates constituted the core of the military quasi-party: they developed the overall military–political doctrine and were inclined to give priority to considerations related to the long-term stabilization of Brazilian politics under military guidance. Eventually, some form of democratic legitimacy had to be established to reach this objective.

The hard-line faction more or less arose with the first campaigns to neutralize opponents of the military intervention and to carry out systematic political cleansing operations in the aftermath of the coup d'état. Within a month, so-called *inquéritos policiais-militares* (military-police investigations, IPM) were started to carry out these operations. At a later stage, especially after 1967, the hard-liners could be found primarily among officers linked to the intelligence community and among troop commanders and second-level officers involved in the counter-insurgency operations of the DOI-squads, especially in São Paulo (where the Second Army was located).[8] The hard-liners displayed intransigence with regard to the threat of communism and the internal enemy. They tended to support outright authoritarianism, with a conservative nationalist tinge, and carte blanche for the counter-insurgency operations. Their logic came close to a strict subordination of politics to military tactics and procedures.

In a way these two factions constituted two poles of attraction that existed throughout the entire period of military rule. Although one or the other enjoyed a relative predominance during the different stages of the dictatorship, neither could be ignored at any single conjuncture between 1964 and 1985 (and even beyond). The permanent intra-regime problem during the period of military governments was how to reconcile the two factions: any failure to do so might have put the stability of the regime, or the unity and integrity of the armed forces, or even both in jeopardy.

The coup and regime consolidation

The military came to power in March 1964, leading a broad coup coalition that included anti-populist right-wing politicians from the UDN, various business interests, and technocrats and lobbyists (Dreifuss, 1981). This coalition enjoyed considerable support from the urban middle classes who feared the prospects of uncertain social reform and political radicalization they expected to be the result of the tactics of President João Goulart. Two weeks after the military take-over, a cleansed Congress voted Marshal Castelo Branco into the 'vacant' presidency to terminate the mandate originally won by Jânio Quadros in the 1960 elections. Castelo was the leader of the group of officers linked to the ESG and hence a prominent *sorbonista*. His appointment to the presidency can be seen as a confirmation of the notion that the coup was the result of a strategy of the military quasi-party and its allies. The goals then would be to restore order, relegitimize the political system, and set in motion a revitalized process of national economic development. In other words, the military, led by the moderates, disposed of a clear 'project' that could now be put into practice.

It is noteworthy that recent statements by high-level officers (who were mostly colonels at the time of the coup) make little mention of the existence of such a premeditated project, even when it concerns observations made by officers supporting the moderate point of view (D'Araujo, Soares and Castro, 1994a). For instance, an officer belonging to the moderate faction explained the initial absence of purpose among the intervening military:

> Because the Revolution [the coup of 1964] did not have a project ... The absence of a reaction of the government, the lack of an ideology and a project left everybody stunned ... The binomial development and security was precisely adopted because a really original ideology was lacking.[9]

Instead, a generalized sense of danger had taken hold of the higher-ranking officers by early 1964. It seems that the threat posed by the increasing influence of 'communist radicals' to the corporate integrity of the armed forces itself was the decisive factor to prompt the military coup. Although references are sometimes made as to the centralized and premeditated nature of the intervention, many military observers of the era felt that the coup could have been avoided if the Goulart government would have taken steps to guarantee the principles of military unity and discipline. Again, General Moraes Rego, who was a junior colonel at the time of the coup, stated that one of the decisive moments was the participation of President Goulart in the mass demonstration for basic reforms, in March 1964 in Rio de Janeiro, in front of the Central do Brasil railway station:

> I stood a hundred meters from the stage where Jango [João Goulart] stood, there in front of the Central. If only he had not appeared ... An anti-communist declaration by Jango, a call in favor of discipline, against subversion and lack of discipline that was already present within the Armed Forces, would have kept him in office longer.[10]

But others were inclined to put the perception of threat in a broader perspective, but not without mentioning the issue of military corporate integrity. General Ivan de Sousa Mendes, who became head of the Intelligence Service SNI under the Sarney administration in 1985, recollected:

> ... it was not only the military hierarchy, no. It was the very republican hierarchy that was at stake. The respect for the vested authorities. All that would have been turned upside down.[11]

For many military officers, the fear of the threat of communism was not primarily inspired by the conservative ideological position prevailing within the armed forces, but rather by the notion that communist radicalization would put the integrity of the armed forces and hence the nation into jeopardy. The memory of the role of the communist military in the 1935 uprising of the communist National Liberating Alliance (ALN) further nurtured these fears. In turn, many civilians, linked to the anti-populist UDN and to the business community, called for an intervention. Their expectation was that a 'classic' moderator-style coup would open the way for the installation of an anti-populist civil government.

Indeed, Castelo always stated that he would 'respect' the existing constitutional order political institutions as much as possible (after having justified the intervention with the first Institutional Act), including the elections for state governors in 1965 and for Congress and the presidency in 1966. But from the outset, Castelo (candidated by the military for ratification as president by Congress in April 1964) had to take the views of the hard-liners into account. The hard-line faction came into being directly after the coup, to take control of the 'Revolution' and to carry out the political purges. Their leading figure became General Artur Costa e Silva, appointed Minister of the Army under the Castelo presidency. After the 1965 elections, in which the opposition parties PSD and PTB were successful, the hard-line pressure grew leading to the promulgation of the AI-2, which included the suspension of direct presidential elections and the restriction of party politics.

From 1966 onwards, the hard-line tendency gradually gained the upper hand. This became manifest through the appointment, within the armed forces, of General Costa e Silva as presidential candidate against the will of the moderates.[12] And although Costa e Silva initially seemed to allow for a certain liberalization (*alívio*) of the regime, the rapidly increasing manifestations of social and political opposition (especially after the beginning of 1968) strengthened the hand of the hard-liners to side-step the legal order and to create the conditions for an authoritarian clampdown. This came with the AI-5, on 13 December 1968.

Closure and repression

After the promulgation of AI-5, events followed rapidly one after the other in an atmosphere of increasing tension and crisis. One ingredient was the intensification of violent opposition actions against the regime (such as the kidnapping of the US ambassador), another was the sudden illness of Costa e Silva in August 1969. While a junta of the three military branch ministers took over – impeding the constitutional succession to the presidency of Costa e Silva's civilian Vice-President Pedro Aleixo, who had previously refused to sign the AI-5 – the military corporation initiated a curious internal electoral process in order to select a new military president. This dispute among 113 three- and four-star generals of the High Command resulted in the candidacy of General Emílio Médici, which was as a matter of course ratified by a 'gagged and bound' Congress.[13]

The Médici government signified the consolidation of the hard-line predominance within the regime. From 1969 to 1974, the political priority of the military was to crush the threat of communist subversion; while at the same time the supervision of the economy was left entirely to a group of ambitious civilian technocrats headed by Finance Minister Antônio Delfim Neto. The logic of warfare began to dominate the political agenda, while the opposition party MDB pondered the decision to dissolve itself in face of the effective closure of the political arena by the regime. At the same time, the groundwork was laid for the growing influence of the intelligence and counter-insurgency entities of the regime, constituting an enduring mainstay of hard-line power throughout the subsequent stage of liberalization.

Already in 1967, the three armed services themselves had started to improve their independent intelligence capacity, complementary to the SNI. The most important was the Centro de Informações do Exército (Center of Army Intelligence, CIE). This new agency was allowed to operate separately from both the SNI and the conventional 'E2' sections of the regular army units, and reported directly to the Minister of the Army in the cabinet. Two years later, in 1969, an operational anti-subversive capacity was built up (under supervision of the regional army commanders and the CIE), first in São Paulo, where the Operação Bandeirantes (OBAN) took over the fight against the (armed) opposition from the regular state police and army forces. It resided directly under the military command of the Second Army, and received funds from the Paulista business community. It was authorized to carry out covert operations, including arrests and interrogation of suspects of subversive activities. In 1970 the counter-insurgency apparatus was consolidated by forming the so-called Destacamentos de Operação de Informações (Operational Intelligence Units, DOI). These units were autonomous and consisted of personnel from all armed forces, the police forces, the fire brigades, and so on. Operational supervision was wielded by Centros de Operações de Defesa Interna (Operational Centers for Internal Defence, CODI), in order to bypass the hierarchy and communication bottlenecks between the different branches of the security apparatus. Formal command of the DOI–CODI system resided with the regional army commanders.

The size and the power of the security apparatus stood in no real relation to the limited significance of the armed opposition, which in Brazil never even remotely attained the scale of its Southern Cone counterparts (especially the Tupamaros in Uruguay and the Montoneros in Argentina), let alone the opposition armies active in Central America in the 1970s and 1980s. The Brazilian armed opposition was small, fragmented and of short duration. In all, probably no more than a few hundred men and women were involved in various efforts to mount armed resistance against the military regime. It was doomed to failure from the outset, not only because of the military superiority of the Brazilian army, but also due to the lack of unity and clarity of purpose within the ranks of the radical opposition itself (Alves, 1984; Archdiocese, 1986; Mir, 1994).

The various efforts at engaging in armed struggle against the military were a reaction to the strengthening of repression after 1968. In turn, such armed activities led to the further expansion of the security apparatus directed against the 'internal enemy'. Especially after the founding of OBAN and the DOI units, covert operations, detentions and torture in clandestine interrogation centers became routine practice. Despite the relatively limited scale of the armed opposition, counter-insurgency violence was heavy-handed and often brutal. Widespread institutional torture occurred, yet at the same time the higher-level commanders could pledge their ignorance and, in some cases, their formal rejection of these coercive methods. The military was convinced that it faced a severe internal security threat posed by an unseen enemy, warranting every type of retaliation. This notion has remained unchallenged among Brazilian military officers until the present day. For instance, in 1992 General Leonidas Pires Gonçalves, operational commander during the 1970s and later the Minister of the Army in the Sarney government (1985–90), observed:

> ...I think the operations of the DOI–CODI were very good. And if they are so badly criticized today, we owe that to the enemies who are within the media, because 95 per cent of the actions of DOI–CODI were to defend this country...That was a fight. That was war.[14]

Médici himself, in a rare interview to *Veja* magazine in 1984, said that he was forced to employ the army in counter-insurgency operations because the police was not up to the task. He recalled saying to his Minister of the Army, General Orlando Geisel (Ernesto Geisel's brother):

> But only our men die? Then when you invade an *aparelho* [an urban guerrilla hideout], you'll have to go in firing machine guns. We are in a war, and we cannot sacrifice our men. Even today [addressing the interviewer] there is no doubt that it was a war, after which it was possible to restore peace to Brazil. I got rid of terrorism in this country. If we had not accepted that it was a war, if we had not acted drastically, we would have had terrorism even today.[15]

The notion of war was one not only employed by the military but also by members of the guerrilla groups. Members of the latter did not hesitate to use violence themselves. The only survivor of the *comandantes* of the ALN, Carlos Eugenio Paz, described in an interview in 1996 his involvement in bank assaults, one of the methods employed to raise money to set up *foco*-type guerrilla operations in the backlands:

> ...often you were firing a machine gun to escape from the surrounding police and you could not know if you had hit anyone, and even less, if you had killed anyone. But when I killed, it was always to survive...The logic in which we lived, at that time, was the logic of violence, of war, and a clean war does not exist.[16]

In addition, not only the (known) perpetrators of armed opposition were targeted; repression was unleashed against a wide range of political and social organizations and to individuals who were considered threats to national security. In effect, the consequences of repression in Brazil in terms of generating an overall climate of arbitrariness and fear went much beyond the actual size of the armed opposition or the amount of violence needed to repress it. At the same time, many Brazilians were either unaware of state terrorism or chose to turn a blind eye. The years of the most brutal operations of the regime coincided with the so-called economic 'miracle'; support, especially among the middle class, for the Médici government was substantial; in addition, the top-brass of the military hierarchy always denied that 'extraordinary' amounts of violence were employed and systematic violations of human rights took place. Excesses were either denied or justified referring to the 'war', or in the best of cases seen as lamentable actions of a few lower-ranking military personnel.

It is noteworthy that in the course of this process the security agencies became increasingly autonomous and arbitrary. As Stepan notes, the pace of repression was even stepped up after 1974 when the military themselves claimed the final victory over armed rural and urban opposition (Stepan, 1988: 28). So despite the relatively small scale of the direct armed confrontation between the military and their opponents, the intense political polarization of the late 1960s and early 1970s led to the subsequent strengthening of the hard-liners within the regime. The latter used the anti-subversive strategy to legitimize the closure of the political system and the abuse of human and civil rights by referring to the 'state of war' Brazil was experiencing at the time. Also, it contributed to the evolution of the security forces into what Stepan called 'the army's relatively autonomous repressive apparatus' (1988: 28). This issue proved to be an important factor in the problems faced by the gradual, regime-led transition to democracy after 1974.

The return to democracy

The drawn-out transition, for a long period regime-led (Smith, 1987), can be subdivided into two distinct phases coinciding with the presidencies of the Generals Ernesto Geisel and João Figueiredo. On the one hand, their governments signified the return to a leading position of the moderate faction. This meant that the problem of repression was replaced by the problem of institutional legitimization of the regime. Ernesto Geisel had always been a prominent officer within the *sorbonista* group; furthermore, he had become an accomplished technocrat in the state-owned oil company Petrobrás. With Geisel came the return to power of General Golbery, the archetype military intellectual and formulator of the strategy of liberalization dubbed *distensão* in his capacity as head of the civil household of Geisel. Figueiredo would prove to be a more ambivalent figure: although posing as an institutionalist groomed in the ESG tradition, he had also been chief of the Casa Militar under Médici and head of the SNI in the Geisel government.

On the other hand, Geisel and Figueiredo had to deal with almost constant pressures emanating from the hard-liners against the scope and pace of the democratization process. These hard-liners were present within the government, for example Minister of the Army, General Frota, in the Geisel government, and the Generals Walter Pires, Army Minister, and Octávio Medeiros, head of the SNI, in the Figueiredo government. But the foundations of the hard-liners had to be found within the labyrinths of the security apparatus. The anti-transition considerations of these sectors were shaped by two elements: the continuation of the perception of threat posed by radical regime opponents (which came to mean anyone not adhering to the authoritarian hard-line position), and fears of *revanchismo* in the event of the rise to power of the civilian opposition to the regime, especially with respect to prosecuting human rights violations committed during the counter-insurgency operations. In addition, a certain taste for power had developed within this faction during the years of the repression.[17]

The continuing weight of the hard-liners markedly influenced the pace of the transition ventured by the regime. Geisel and Golbery stressed the need to return to institutional legitimacy, and to curb the dangerous autonomy of the security apparatus. At the same time, they refused to abolish the legal artifacts of the repression years, such as the AI-5, the National Security Law, and the authoritarian constitutional amendments passed by the junta in 1969 during the illness of Costa e Silva. Geisel merely deactivated these artifacts temporarily, to be reused in times of crisis – meaning undue political headway made by the opposition or 'irresponsible' agitation by popular organizations and leaders (Velasco e Cruz and

Martins, 1983: 45–6). In retrospect, Geisel commented upon this strategy in the following terms:[18]

> It was my idea, really, to avoid the use of the AI-5 whenever pos-
> sible. But then appeared the lack of understanding of the opposi-
> tion. I demonstrated, in speeches and public acts … that I wanted
> to normalize the country's situation, to end press censorship, etc.
> They thought that was weakness and decided to launch an
> attack. So they forced me to react. If I wouldn't have reacted, my
> power clearly would have been weakened and then a series of
> projects that I wanted to realize, including the *abertura*, perhaps
> would have been impossible.

Geisel as well as Figueiredo had to balance stick and carrot: the authoritarian safeguards could only be used if at the same time clear but controlled progress was made at the transition front. Geisel thus adhered to the notion of a *democracia forte* (strong democracy), which meant a limited return to civil liberties granting some political influence to parties and civil society. The military were, however, supposed to act as guardians of order and stability, with a virtual right of veto within the political system. From the moderate mili-
tary faction's point of view, the *distensão* process faced danger from two sides: on the one hand, the possibility that the civil political opposition would try to use the space opened up by the regime to speed up the democratic transition and to go beyond the limits of the *democracia forte*; on the other hand, the resistance likely to be put up by the hard-liners within the regime, principally those linked to the security complex. Geisel phrased this dilemma in the short-
hand characteristic of military discourse: 'I had to fight on two fronts: against the communists and against those who fought the communists.'[19]

Geisel's transition strategy was meant to allow for a greater representation of interests within the political arena in view of increas-
ingly complex economic and social problems, thus enhancing the long-run legitimacy of military rule while controlling the more obscure sides of the authoritarian situation.[20] Under Geisel, this progress could be found in the widening of the scope for electoral politics, an increasing official adherence to civil liberties, some advances in taking disciplinary measures against officers responsible

for human rights violations, and the determination to block the bid for power by the hard-liners through the self-proclaimed presidential candidacy of Army Minister Sílvio Frota (who subsequently was fired by Geisel, a feat without precedent during the military regime). At the very end of his government, with the hand-over of power to Figueiredo secured, Geisel finally felt secure enough to abolish AI-5 and to negotiate an amnesty law with the opposition. Under Figueiredo, a formal commitment to restore full democracy was adopted by the regime, civil liberties were by and large restored, party politics were further liberalized and the scope of elections was widened, leading to major oppositionary gains in the 1982 elections. But both presidents were firmly opposed to allowing the opposition to make a successful bid for governmental power, let alone to restore the principal of 'direct' presidential elections, that is by popular vote. The general reluctance even among the moderate military to abandon the concept of a limited or 'strong' democracy is reflected in an observation made by General Golbery in 1984. Although, as a true *sorbonista*, he was against changing the rules of the game of the presidential succession of 1985, which were escaping the regime's control as the result of the opposition gains in the 1982 elections, the dissidencies within the government party and the pressures from mass mobilization in favor of restoring direct presidential elections, he noted:

> The people certainly want the direct elections. To vote is a strong desire of society, for many reasons: tradition, the natural wish to participate and even the attraction of the civic festival, alongside other interests, some of which are hard to confess. The direct elections offer advantages, but also many drawbacks and risks… The principal risks reside in untruthful demagogy, in reckless opportunism, in irresponsible charisma, and in the exploitation of the good faith and the naïveté of the people.[21]

This type of statement offers a good illustration of moderate military political thinking at the eve of redemocratization. We can observe a certain sensitivity for the issue of popular sovereignty, but also fear for a break of order if irresponsible or opportunistic characters abuse political freedom. Implicitly, military guidance and controlled rules of the game cannot be forfeited.

However, not all the military took recourse to subtlety during the twilight stages of the military dictatorship. During the voting in April 1984 of a constitutional amendment, presented by the opposition representative Dante de Oliveira, to restore the direct election for the presidency, the military sealed off the federal capital Brasília. They feared that announced demonstrations might disturb the propitious climate for the voting, that is, might put congressmen from the government party under pressure to vote for the amendment. The rash hard-line General Newton Cruz, in charge of the Planalto Military Command, put tanks in the streets and personally rode his white horse on the Brasília avenues to batter upon the hoods of the cars that had taken the streets in huge numbers to offer a horn-blowing support to the amendment and against the arrogant military show of force. More covertly, hard-line military personnel made a desperate last attempt to block the imminent victory of the opposition candidate in the indirect elections of January 1985, Tancredo Neves. Generals within the government, notably Pires and Medeiros, supported the idea of a new military intervention, *uma virada de mesa*, justified by the 'crisis' caused by the failure of regime control over the succession. Part of the manoeuvre consisted of spreading false information on links between Tancredo and the Communist Party of Brazil.[22] The political astuteness of Tancredo and his political allies to defuse the crisis, in combination with the resistance to the intended coup put up by legalist forces within the upper echelons of the armed forces, prevented the coup from really happening in September 1984.

Conclusion

The principal purpose of the foregoing discussion of the role of the military as a political actor in the Brazilian case is to develop a more diversified perspective on the issue of militarism, seen as the outcome of political strategies and interests advanced from within the armed forces. I pointed at the elements that make up the military political actor: identification with the nation and the state, the notion that the armed forces hold the historical mission to guarantee the internal order within Latin American societies, so that involvement in politics, particularly the take-over of state power by force, constitutes an integral and legitimate part of the military's self-ascribed mission, not seldomly to defend democracy against itself. Still, this approach – using the concept of the military as a 'quasi-party' – runs the risk of assuming too much a unity of long-term strategic purpose within the military; it also presupposes a basic homogeneity of the military as a political player.

The insights I tried to draw from the Brazilian case help to amend such possible biases: the formulation and implementation of a clear-cut military political project probably wasn't an initial driving force behind the coup of 1964. Rather, more strict corporate considerations – related to the integrity and hierarchy within the armed forces – seem to have ignited the coup and set up the regime. Once in power, a clear project may have come into existence on a trial and error basis, from an *ex post* point of view. Much of the dynamics of the dictatorship was the result of intra-military factionalism, in which the moderates tended to give priority to institutionalization and legitimization, while the hard-liners tended to defend a more repressive brand of military political involvement in view of the perceived threat to internal security. Within the Brazilian regime there was a constant tension between the two poles, but they were also each other's hostage: neither of the two factions dared to stage a rupture, for fear of destroying the ultimate unity of the military corporation. When the opposition was institutionally weak and resorted to armed rebellion, this meant the prevalence of the hard-line and the canonization of the logic of state terror. After the recomposition of civil society and the resurrection of the political opposition, the moderate faction recovered prominence and established new forms of articulation with the civilian political opposition during the democratic transition. This transition, however, remained controversial within the military, right up to the point of handing over power to the civil opposition.

Notes

1. For a more detailed discussion see Koonings (1991, 1996).
2. Rial (1990: 16–18) draws a relevant distinction between the politicized military institutions of Latin America (or developing countries in general) and the organizational 'civil-servant-in-uniform' type of the North Atlantic advanced nations.
3. I am indebted to Dirk Kruijt for this typification.

4. The Old Republic (1889–1930) was marked by the supremacy of regional elites linked to landownership and the local and state-level political machines. These oligarchies tended to distrust the federal army, giving preference to the regional paramilitary forces they controlled. The army, in turn, gradually developed an anti-oligarchic stance, either cloaked in a conservative modernization discourse or in a leftist-reformist one. Cf. Hayes (1989), Quartim de Moraes (1991).

5. See for excellent accounts of the Brazilian transition: Lamounier (1989); Martins (1986); Moisés and Albuquerque (1989); Reis and O'Donnell (1988); Skidmore (1989); Smith (1987).

6. See especially Alves (1984); D'Araujo, Soares and Castro (1994a,b, 1995); Stepan (1988); Velasco e Cruz and Martins (1983). The latter in fact distinguish four factions (moderates, hard-liners, right-wing nationalists and troop commanders) but the first two have been most prominent politically.

7. Fascinating accounts by military officers involved, in various ways, in the 1964–85 regime are collected in D'Araujo, Soares and Castro (1994a,b, 1995), who make the distinction as to regime stages also adopted in this chapter. In addition, I will also use interviews with Generals Golbery do Couto e Silva and Médici in *Veja* (no. 819, 16 May 1984), the extensive statements given by General Ernesto Geisel in D'Araujo and Castro (1997), as well as a number of accounts in *Veja*, *Senhor*, *IstoÉ/Senhor* and *IstoÉ* magazines.

8. The complex and increasingly autonomous intelligence community consisted of the Serviço Nacional de Informações (SNI) (linked directly to the Presidency), the separate intelligence services of the Army, Navy and Air Force (CIE, Cenimar, CISA, respectively), and the operational mixed DOI–CODI units actively involved in counter-insurgency. Especially the CIE (Centro de Informações do Exército) was an influential body residing directly under the Minister of the Army and pivotal for the 'anti-subversive struggle'. See Alves (1984); Archdiocese of São Paulo (1986); D'Araujo, Soares and Castro (1994b); Stepan (1988).

9. General Moraes Rego in D'Araujo *et al.* (1994a: 50). All Portuguese quotations translated by the author.

10. General Moraes Rego in D'Araujo *et al.* (1994a: 40).

11. General Ivan de Souza Mendes in D'Araujo *et al.* (1994a: 143).

12. Costa e Silva was 'elected' by Congress in October 1966 through the votes of the recently established Aliança Renovadoral Nacional (ARENA). The allowed opposition party Movimento Democrático Brasileiro (MDB) abstained.

13. See *IstoÉ* no. 1219, 10 February 1993 ('A guerra dos generais', by Maurício Dias).

14. General Leonidas Pires Gonçalves in D'Araujo *et al.* (1994b: 254).

15. Interview conceded to A.C. Scartezini, *Veja* no. 819, 16 May 1984: 15.

16. Carlos Eugenio Paz in *Veja* no. 1455, 31 July 1996: 8.

17. I am grateful to Celso Castro for this observation.

18. General Ernesto Geisel, in D'Araujo and Castro (1997: 389–90).
19. General Ernesto Geisel, in D'Araujo and Castro (1997: 369).
20. See Stepan (1988), especially chapter 3.
21. General Golbery do Couto e Silva to Elio Gaspari, *Veja* no. 819, 5 May 1984: 9.
22. See reports in *Veja* no. 895, 3 October 1985; *IstoÉ/Senhor* no. 1162, 8 January 1992; see also the statement by General Leonidas Pires Gonçalves in D'Araujo *et al.* (1995).

9
Civil–Military Relations in Post-Authoritarian Chile

Francisco Rojas Aravena

Introduction

Since the late 1980s Chile has been experiencing a protracted and complex process of democratic transition and consolidation. Factors such as the pacted character of the transitional process itself, the inheritance of a non-democratic constitution, and the persistence of a series of 'authoritarian enclaves' mean that Chile today still possesses an imperfect democracy. Since the armed forces constitute a crucial actor for the maintenance of political stability in the country, the democratic governments of Patricio Aylwin, Eduardo Frei and Ricardo Lagos have paid extraordinary attention to the handling of civil–military relations. However, in the case of Chile the nature and quality of civil–military relations are strongly determined by past experiences, particularly by the fresh memories of the military government led by General Augusto Pinochet (1973–90). Nevertheless, the democratic coalition governments have so far succeeded in avoiding a narrow discussion of civil–military matters by focusing instead on a national defense policy. This approach is intended to overcome the polarized vision of civil–military relations linked to the past, in favor of a focus on professional development and perspectives for the future.

Today Chilean society is divided into two large political blocks which express the feelings and aspirations of most of its citizens. The first block represents a corporatist position associated with the former military government. One of its major concerns is the preservation of what is called the 'oeuvre' of the military regime, which includes the preservation of a free-market economy and the constitutional framework left by the military. From an electoral point of view, this sector represents between 35 and 40 per cent of voters. The second block is represented by all sectors – from the moderate right to the moderate left – that since the early 1980s firmly fought for a peaceful democratic transition in the country. Since the 1988 plebiscite, the party coalition which represents this sector has managed to obtain the support of around 55 per cent of the electorate (or even more as was the case during the electoral contest of December 1993 when Eduardo Frei was elected).

But despite the electoral majority held by the Concertación governments and their efforts to eliminate the authoritarian legacy of the past, they have not managed to fully achieve that objective. Particularly the still unresolved human rights issues (such as the question of the 'desaparecidos') have put the civil–military relations under increasing strain. Pinochet's arrest in London in October 1998 exacerbated the existing tensions between the former Frei government and the military institutions, and created new ones within the governmental coalition and within Chilean society at large which is firmly divided in its judgement of General Pinochet.

Civil–military relations in a polarized society

The Chilean political system stands out in the Latin American context for its high level of institutionalization, and democratic development achieved considerable importance and depth from the 1930s until the institutional breakdown in 1973. Civil–military relations during the period 1932–70 have been characterized as being of 'formal constitutionalism', which means subordination of the military to civil authority without an effective commitment from the armed forces to the democratic system. Formal constitutionalism was expressed by the armed forces' separation and isolation from the rest of society (Varas, 1987).

Since the mid-1960s, the Chilean political system has been characterized for its growing polarization. Chile in fact experienced in a very short period of time three political revolutions. In the mid-1960s the Frei Montalva government launched a process of democratic capitalist modernization under the motto 'revolution in liberty'. A few years later, the Unidad Popular government sought to establish a 'socialist revolution *a la chilena*' ('with the flavor of Chilean red wine and *empanadas*', as Allende once put it). And following the coup, the military regime initiated a capitalist counter-revolution which has been called by its followers 'the silent revolution'. Each one of these political projects generated deep changes in the country's economic, social, political and cultural structures.

In the period 1964–70, governmental policies were primarily directed towards the incorporation of marginalized sectors of society into the national economic and political realms. During those years, a significant number of tensions – which until then had been only latent in Chilean society – began to manifest themselves in the sphere of civil–military relations, one important manifestation of which was the quartering in 1969 of Santiago's Tacna regiment when the military's demands were mainly centered on economic and professional matters.

In the early 1970s, Chile experienced profound political and social change following the electoral victory of Salvador Allende and his Unidad Popular coalition. In this period, Allende sought to deeply transform the very nature of the Chilean state. Even before the new government assumed power in November 1970, opposition forces – both local and international – severely opposed Allende's plans, and in the final days of the Unidad Popular experience, both the country's governability and institutional foundations were put in question by all the actors involved. Civil–military relations during the years 1970–73 were extremely complex. As part of a mounting political polarization produced by Allende's victory in September 1970, military insubordination reached critical levels. In an attempted kidnapping, the Commander-in-Chief of the army, General René Schneider, was murdered on 22 October 1970 by a right-wing commando.

During the first period of his government Allende was able to maintain rather good relations with the armed forces' leadership. For instance, he sustained particularly warm relations with the Commander-in-Chief of the Army, General Carlos Prats. As a result of the serious political crisis generated in the country since 1972, the Unidad Popular government invited the armed forces to fulfil important government duties, and by establishing a civil–military cabinet Allende attempted to achieve some degree of political stability and consensus in the country in order to avoid the collapse of the political system. The armed forces reacted in a divided way about this new political role as many saw in this a government manoeuver to use the armed forces' popular prestige for its own political advantage. The growing tensions within the armed forces became visible to public opinion when a hostile group of officers' wives demonstrated in front of General Prats' residence. This and other expressions of institutional disconformity did finally force General Prats to resign from his post as Commander-in-Chief of the Army. A few weeks later, after the House of Deputies had declared the government's actions to be illegal, the newly appointed Commander-in-Chief of the Army, General Augusto Pinochet, launched the coup d'état, representing the most dramatic breakpoint in contemporary Chilean political history (Ruiz-Esquide, 1993).

The collapse of the old Chilean democracy in 1973 was the result of a constellation of national and international factors. Chile's political class was not able to resolve the severe tensions that originated between order and social incorporation, equity and accumulation, participation and governability, resulting in the growing polarization of the political arena. This all culminated in the destruction of the democratic order in Chile. The military takeover marked the end of four decades in which the civil and military authorities had maintained a marked distance between themselves; and during the almost 17 years of military rule, the distance between the military and the civilian world have become even greater.

The authoritarian government led by General Pinochet proclaimed that one of its main objectives was the establishment of a new political order, which was termed 'protected democracy'. In pursuit of that goal, the military government defined its long-term political agenda, starting with the writing of a new constitution which embraced the new authoritarian conception of legal and societal order in which any expression of popular sovereignty was avoided.

In the period 1973–89, the military government radically changed the structure of the Chilean state and economy. These radical transformations were accompanied by high social costs which are still felt today after a decade of democratic restoration. The economic liberalization and the strengthening of the export sector clearly enlarged the country's international economic presence, which helped the regime to maintain the political support from some sectors of Chilean society. Nevertheless, the relation between the military and the civilian world remained as distant as in the previous period.

The 1988 plebiscite and the 'authoritarian enclaves'

Following the coup of 11 September 1973, a military junta was established representing all branches of the armed forces and police. However, power became rapidly personalized in the figure of General Pinochet who eventually managed to concentrate all state executive powers until March 1990 (cf. Arriagada, 1988; Valenzuela, 1995). This was facilitated by the extreme sense of hierarchy and obedience to superiors (the so-called *verticalidad del mando*) existing in the Chilean armed forces. In the end, the armed institutions recognize only one source of authority: the person who fulfills the function of Commander-in-Chief of the armed forces, that is General Augusto Pinochet.

Pinochet decided to provide some kind of legal support to his personal rule in an attempt to legitimize the regime and to lessen foreign criticism. For this purpose, he formed a commission of legal experts who had the task of writing a new constitution to codify all the authoritarian principles defended by his regime and to allow him to extend his regime until the late 1990s. The idea was that after his regime, institutionalization would have to respond to the characteristics of a so-called 'protected democracy', meaning a limited democracy in which there would be no place for left-wing forces. The constitution was written with the purpose of guaranteeing the existence of an authoritarian regime, which would maintain personalized leadership, after the Pinochet era (Garretón, 1989, 1993).

This constitution was finally adopted in 1980, following a referendum which was strongly objected to by the democratic opposition. It established a constitutional time schedule which set the rhythm of the political process, establishing, among other things, that in 1988 a plebiscite should take place in which the Chilean population could vote yes or no for the extension of another eight years of the Pinochet regime. Pinochet's legal and political advisers assured him this was a calculated risk as they were confident that, amidst continuous economic growth, a majority would vote for the yes option. The democratic opposition, however, decided to make use of this instrument to defeat the General on his own terms.

The 1988 plebiscite represented a milestone in the long process towards democratic restoration. Contrary to official expectations, a large majority of the population (55 per cent) rejected Pinochet's plans to remain in power until 1996. This historical result enabled the celebration of general elections in 1989 which were won by the opposition forces, marking the initiation of the democratic restoration. The armed forces accepted the results, which called for their withdrawal from government, and the country's return to an open political system (cf. Drake and Jalsić, 1995).

Between the referendum defeat in October 1988 and the installation of President Patricio Aylwin in March 1990, the military government introduced a series of laws (the so-called 'leyes de amarre') to guarantee the permanence of several authoritarian enclaves in the country's constitution and legal system in general after the restoration of democratic rule. In 1989, they negotiated with the opposition a series of important constitutional reforms which were approved by the population by another plebiscite. Although these reforms eliminated some important authoritarian components of the existing constitution, still many non-democratic elements remained in the Chilean institutional and legal system.

Three central aspects define these authoritarian enclaves:

1. The minority political veto. The establishment of designated senators and a bi-nominal electoral system favors the minority veto and impedes the expression of the majority of the country.
2. Constitutional autonomy of the armed forces. This is expressed not in functional and professional aspects, but rather in the fact that the armed forces remain unregulated by democratic institutional instruments. This has been defined as a '*de facto* power'.
3. The existence of a Constitutional Tribunal which gives it superiority and a certain sense of veto of congressional decisions (Moulian, 1995).

The constitutional framework of 1980 combined popularly elected organs with the presence of '*de facto* power'. This situation perverted the democratic institutions and, in turn, established a tendency towards the participation of the armed forces in the country's political life beyond their institutional scope.

Even before the installation of the democratic government, the constitutional issue became a key component of the country's political debate. The warped constitutional perspective will remain as long as there is no constitutional text that reflects the vast majority of the country.

The 1980 constitution deals with the position of the armed forces in four articles: articles 90, 91, 93 and 94. Chapter XI of the constitution provides for a National Security Council, whose role is defined in articles 95 and 96. The constitutional debate has been mainly centered around the role of the armed forces as the 'institutional guarantor', and their institutional autonomy. Article 90 states that 'The armed forces are composed solely of the Army, the Navy and the Air Force, exist solely for the defense of the homeland, are essential for national security, and guarantee the institutional order of the Republic.' Interpretation of this last part of the paragraph has generated important debates about the role and missions of the armed forces. The armed forces are the institutional guarantors, but this does not imply a free, open and autonomous mandate. Interpretation of this text under democratic legal schemes indicates that as a result of the constitutional reform of 1989, a new meaning distinct from the original was established. The 1989 reform provided democratic legitimacy and forced a reinterpretation of the whole set of norms, in particular the one referred to, from the perspective of a democratic system (García, 1994; García and Montes, 1994).

A second aspect of the constitutional debate refers to the degree of autonomy given the military institutions in defining and delimiting policies. This is related to the functions of the National Security Council and the issue of presidential prerogatives *vis-à-vis* those of the Commanders-in-Chief in relation to nominations, promotions and retirements in the armed forces (Ensalaco, 1995). The inclusion of a National Security Council with the composition and attributes as they appear in the constitution constitutes a complete break with Chile's constitutional tradition, as it places the President of the Republic in a position of subordination to the military power (Arriagada, 1996).

The search for constitutional change

Due to the strong limitation of democratic rule left by the military regime, the first democratic government led by Patricio Aylwin (1990–94) placed the democratization of Chile's political and legal structures, together with the aim of national reconciliation, at the top of its agenda.

President Aylwin presented a project to modify the organic laws of the armed forces and police (Carabineros) in March 1992. He had undertaken a rigorous constitutional analysis of the three central aspects of the debate: the 'independence' of the armed forces and Carabineros; the constitutional duties of the President with respect to the armed forces; and, finally, 'career bureaucrats' of these institutions and their 'nominations, promotions, and retirements'. The President demonstrated that no legal interpretation supports the notion of independence (Aylwin, 1993), and, furthermore, he emphasized that the armed forces are 'essentially obedient and non-deliberative' according to the constitution. It is the President, in agreement with Article 33 of the constitution, who exercises the supreme authority of the state. However, Aylwin's proposal for constitutional reform did not prosper in Congress, and later his successor, President Frei, reiterated the need to establish constitutional reforms.

The Aylwin government however succeeded in normalizing communications with the right-wing opposition and in eliminating some of the authoritarian legacies of the past. While maintaining the market-oriented character of the economy as introduced by the military regime, the Aylwin government forcefully emphasized the need to increase equality in the country by attacking extreme poverty. However, less success was achieved in the field of human rights, as the authoritarian enclaves in the legal system (such as the 1978 amnesty law) and the fierce opposition of the armed forces and their right-wing supporters impeded the achievement of substantial results. The question of human rights clearly complicated relations between the civilian government and the armed forces. Also, the permanence of General Pinochet as Commander-in-Chief of the Army until March 1998 created serious tensions in the civil–military relations as a significant part of the population believed he should retire (cf. Varas and Fuentes, 1994). During the December 1993 presidential elections, Eduardo Frei Ruiz-Tagle obtained 58 per cent of the votes. During his administration (1994–2000) the government's efforts were directed to the modernization of the country (in both social and economic terms), and the consolidation of the Chilean economy in external markets. However, the Frei government proved unable to eliminate a series of authoritarian enclaves, such as the institution of designed senators and Pinochet's senator-ship 'for life', the President's inability to remove the senior military, and the existence of the National Security Council. The representatives of the right-wing opposition in Parliament did successfully block all the executive's actions in that direction and when his presidential term ended in March 2000 none of these goals had been achieved.

In August 1995 President Frei, as part of the initiatives intended to achieve national reconciliation and a stable political system, sent Congress a proposal to modify the Constitutional Organic Law of the Armed Forces. As he put it:

> this is a legal initiative that gathers, summarizes, and synthesizes the legislative debates that were developed during 1992 and 1993 in a similar plan. For that reason, this initiative assumes the original criticisms and accumulates the previous arguments expressed at that time. (Frei, 1995a)

Both texts have similar objectives; the first is to restore the historical powers that the presidents of the Republic have had in the past democratic era; and at the same time, reform should give coherence to the constitutional text so that the President can fulfill his mandate that establishes, among other things, that he can stipulate 'nominations, promotions and retirements of officers in the armed forces and the Carabineros'.

The fundamental difference between the proposals presented by President Aylwin and by President Frei is rooted in President Frei's message which, in consideration of the previous debate, establishes a more restricted level of power, stipulating that retirement be applied to general officers without an intervening proposal from the Commander-in-Chief. In a similar vein, President Frei sent to Parliament two other constitutional reform proposals linked to a global perspective of reconciliation. One project deals with human rights, aiming to uncover the truth with respect to those detained or disappeared, and other human rights cases. The second proposal involved other institutional changes: (i) elimination of the designated senators; (ii) modifications to the composition of the National Security Council to include the President of the House of Deputies and to give the President the deciding vote; and (iii) alteration of the formation of the Constitutional Tribunal (Frei, 1995b). These reforms were essential to achieve full democracy. Transforming the imperfect democratic system by the elimination of authoritarian enclaves was the fundamental purpose of the reform proposal.

The qualified quorum and the form of popular representation in the bi-nominal system, plus the so-called 'designated senators', have prevented the package's approval. The Chilean Senate was established along the guidelines of the 1980 constitution and possesses a dual structure: one part is formed by 38 senators who are chosen by direct vote, but on the other hand the Senate also possesses a group of nine so-called 'designated senators' who represent 20 per cent of the total number of senators. These designated senators are chosen in the following manner: three by the Supreme Court, two by the President of the Republic, and four by the National Security Council, this last group is referred to as the 'military bench' because they are composed of the former Commanders-in-Chief of the armed forces and police. In addition, the 1980 constitution allowed General Pinochet to occupy a seat as a senator for life. Since 1998 the Senate has had only three designated senators whose political tendencies lean towards the Concertación government. This construction has affected many of the structural reforms that have been attempted, with the subsequent effect that almost 15 per cent of those senators who are not members of the Concertación are now aligned with the democratic opposition. This directly influences the quorums necessary to progress with the transformations.

This situation illustrates the paradox of the Chilean political system. On the subject of the mentioned quorums, the 'designated' senators will be decisive with their representation of 20 per cent of all of the senators; with their votes they will determine close to a minority veto depending on what quorums are requested. Within the 1980 constitution the title 'qualified quorums' is granted to all of those in which groups called 'authority enclaves' are clearly established; these groups limit the full expression of Chilean democracy. In this current system, the possibility of reform from the inside seems completely diluted.

Civil–military relations and defense policy 1990–2000

10 March 1998 was the date of a historic change of command from General Pinochet, who had held his position for 25 years, to

Lieutenant General Ricardo Izurieta Caffarena. This marked the beginning of a new era in military–civilian relations, and closed an important chapter in the country's institutional history. The new Commander-in-Chief will continue to advance relations between civilians and the military, by concentrating on institutional aspects, and this should be easier for him since General Izurieta has never been associated with human rights violations.

Given the characteristics of the democratic consolidation process in Chile, tensions in the area of civil–military relations have been expressed in the institutional sphere with respect to legal norms. In some cases, it has been suggested that the limits of legality had been exceeded. From a general point of view, civil–military relations in the period 1990–2000 have differed significantly under the three governments of the Concertación. The period 1990–94 produced two extremely tense situations between the civil authorities and the armed forces, in particular the army. In hindsight, during the first government of the Concertación the use of legal power with respect to leadership and autonomy in the areas of defense and military policy was tested. The use of legal instruments was exercised with a strong symbolic reference to issues of leadership and autonomy. This first period was essential for the definition of the body of law related to civil–military relations. In the second government of the Concertación, having resolved this issue, a policy which focused on essentially professional issues was developed. Similarly, issues of a political and judicial (human rights) nature were transferred to the political and judicial spheres, that is to say to the Ministry of Justice and the corresponding political debates. In this way, it was possible to establish an adequate framework for the principal objective of the period 1994–2000: the establishment of an explicit defense policy.

In the Chilean case, the principal protagonist in the tension has been the army, for two principal reasons. Firstly, the army assumed the most relevant and preponderant role during the military government, especially in the last stage. And secondly, the figure of General Pinochet as Commander-in-Chief of the Army, who had retained power for 17 years, carried great weight. Differences with other branches of the military have had little public relevance. Moments of tension and strong public expression have been focused on issues of the past, in particular issues that affect the highest levels of authority of the army. They tell of the kind of 'protection' enjoyed by the holder of the most important position in the military government, and are linked to situations which directly affect the Commander-in-Chief of the Army. These situations of tension and politico-institutional crisis have been denominated: *ejercicio de enlace* ('liaison exercise') which began on 19 December 1990; the *'boinazo'* of 19 April 1993; and the *'peucazo'* of 22 July 1995.

Table 9.1 synthesizes the characteristics of these three events, allowing a comparison of these unusual and surprising movements led by the army in the context of a redemocratized political system.

Another area which has been a source of tension, both from a political and judicial point of view, has been the issue of human rights. This is a topic on which consensus has not been reached, either in society or among the political elite. In Chile there are two distinct and contradictory historical memories, making it difficult to reach consensus and consequently to interpret and evaluate the dramatic events that occurred in the country in the area of human rights (cf. Silva, 1999). Moreover, despite efforts to achieve national reconciliation, not all actors in the political system have

Table 9.1   *Civil–military tensions and crisis in Chile 1990–95*

	1990	1993	1995
Character of the crisis	Surprise action	Surprise action	Progressive action
Context	Tension	Normality	Tension
Issue that precipitated crisis	Check case Accusation against Pinochet	Check case	Check case Human rights
Action taken by the Army	Quartering (units)	(High Command meets) Quartering	Clear action Progressive action
Government response	Surprise	Surprise Lack of coordination	Surprise Coordination
Support from other branches	(Navy)	Unidentifiable	Navy (FACh)
International repercussion	Low	High Significant	High Very important
Time	Very short	Brief	Prolonged

made gestures significant enough to overcome the profound polarization existing around this subject. The principal national challenge is to achieve national reconciliation, but ten years after the
reestablishment of democracy, Chile has still not achieved full reconciliation. In the area of human rights, this became evident following the pre-sentation in March 1991 of the Report of the Truth and
Reconciliation Commission (the so-called Rettig Report). When confronted with the report, the Army expressed its opposition and reaffirmed its traditional argument that a 'civil war' had existed, thereby
freeing itself of any responsibility in the area of human rights.

During the Aylwin government, human rights occupied a position
of extreme importance, and the achievement of reconciliation was at
the center of the redemocratization efforts. Although the advances
made in this area were not extraordinary, a substantial leap was
made in the discovery of the truth. Similarly, the pursuit of repara-
tions was also greatly advanced. However, achieving 'justice within
the possible' was a limited target. An important event was the judicial
ruling in the Letelier case, which acquired a more general, symbolic
character – the punishment by imprisonment of those responsible
for the planning of the crime. (Orlando Letelier, former minister of
foreign affairs under the Allende government, and an American colleague, Ronni Moffitt, were killed in Washington on 21 September
1976, on their way to work when Chilean intelligence agents deto-
nated a remote control bomb that tore through Letelier's car.)

Under the government of President Frei, the issue of human rights
was dealt with from a judicial perspective. Different initiatives were
taken, designed to resolve the issue in a more permanent way, but a
parliamentary climate favorable to the advancement of the subject
matter was never found. A group of parliament members constitutionally accused General Pinochet, then in retirement, in March of
1998. The group presented an accusatory petition in the House of
Congress which brought about the appointment of a special commission for the investigation of the petition. It was decided that
General Pinochet could be accused of 'having put the stability of
democracy in danger during the government of President Aylwin',
through mechanisms called 'connection exercises' and 'boinazo'.
The declared objective of the accusation was to prevent General
Pinochet from being sworn in as a senator for life, but the accusation was found, 'inconvenient' and 'inconducente' by the government. Nevertheless, the presentation of this petition had produced a

division in the interior of the Christian Democratic party between those in favor of the accusation and those who were not.

The petition was voted on by secret ballot in the House of Congress on 9 April 1998, and was rejected with the following breakdown: 62 votes against, 55 in favor and one abstention. By secret ballot, and in the midst of the incidents in the tribunals, the House of Congress had rejected the constitutional accusation against Pinochet with the help of votes from various members of the Christian Democratic party. Their central argument was that it did not contribute to the success of the 'transition process'. They would only be able to look at the facts after 1990 and that it would not produce effective results. The separation of these issues of the past from definitions of defense and security policy generated a change in the perspective of civil–military relations, orientating discussion towards the achievement of the principal objective in this area – the establishment of an explicit policy of defense and a contribution to the transparency of the international system of security.

Given the distinct historical memories of the two coalitions in the area of civil–military relations, it is essential to examine the perspectives for future national development. The changing of the central theme of civil–military relations towards professional issues can permit a dialogue which looks to the future. But for this to occur it is necessary to overcome in a positive way, with a strong ethical emphasis and without reference to ideology, the issues linked to human rights. The issue of autonomy will be placed in its true context when it refers to professional issues and clearly expresses civil leadership of the defense sector.

Modernization and defense policy

The second government of the Concertación sought to pass from transition to modernization. The political authorities decided that, without abandoning the theme of constitutional duties, the political priority of the government should be the modernization of the country. This implies generating conditions for harmonious development that guarantee equity and at the same time signify a qualitative change in the living standards of the population. The focus of civil–military dialogue on professional issues allowed a basic lack of trust to be overcome, generated space for communication and produced a drastic decrease in the prominence of the military authorities linked to the military regime. The defense policy has come into the central theme, thus forcing the actors who play a part in this area to adapt themselves in both political and technical terms.

The Frei government opted for a strategy which would reevaluate professional aspects and postulate the need to make explicit a non-partisan and consensual defense policy. The government authorities have sought to establish a clear distinction between topics corresponding to the political sphere and those corresponding to the field of defense. The issues of transition previously divided between the diverging visions of 'civilians' and 'military', have begun to be substituted by a technical and professional debate concerning defense policy. Issues referring to the authoritarian enclaves represented the most sensitive political issues on the agenda. Nevertheless, the government authorities have signalled that they will not place the political system under strain while it is still in a period of democratic consolidation. The definition of an explicit defense policy was connected to the general perspective of advancing the modernization of the country, investing in the people, and generating the necessary conditions for sustainable development. The government realized that the consolidation of the democratic process required a clear state policy in this field, and this led to a public debate on the subject, and the publication in September 1998 of the 'Book of National Defense of Chile' as part of this effort. It placed the issue of defense in Chile in a new scenario in which peace, democracy and development are articulated with the support of a wide variety of actors.

In the case of the Ministry of Defense, modernization means making defense policy explicit (Pérez Yoma, 1994). This would make it possible to define goals, determine modernization projects for the sector, and advance civil–military relations (Concertación, 1993). The change in axis signified the distension of government–armed forces relations; however, the conflict over the functional autonomy of the armed forces endures even today, manifesting itself as bureaucratic differences within a formalized state. The question that quickly arose was how civilian constitutional leadership could develop policies in an institutional framework where the armed forces have the autonomy to develop their own specific policies. The reactions and 'demonstrations' of the armed forces have been concerned with situations referring to political issues of the past and not with issues of professional development.

The type of civil–military relations that have developed in Chile have three founding characteristics. First, within the armed forces there exists a tradition of professionalism. In Chile, the armed forces' tradition of disassociation with political partisanship is clear, and facilitates a civil–military relation focused on professional topics. This tradition of institutional professionalism is formed with a certain vision and develops from a long-term strategic perception of the national political direction. The danger of politicization of the armed forces in recent years appeared principally linked to the authoritarian enclaves in the constitution, especially to the role of the designated senators and the political functions of the National Security Council. This is why the democratic sectors have assigned importance to changing these aspects of the constitution, which is ironic since the military sees the Council as a way to avoid the dangers of politicization.

A second element is the military hierarchy with the Commander-in-Chief of the institution at the top of the pyramid. For civilian authorities this has been a guarantee of stability and a key element in the capacity to govern the country. The result of the Letelier case and the respect for its significance, especially for the jail sentence against the highest authorities of the principal repressive entity of the military government, tested the respect of the hierarchy.

Finally, the third characteristic comes from civilians which, especially among partisans of the Concertación, demonstrated a growing interest in addressing the topic of defense in a more systematic manner. The academic world contributed much to the testing of civil–military relations, of defense subjects, and strategic regional and international themes. Despite advances in this field, much remains to be done. As the former Minister of Defense under the Frei administration emphasized,

> In Chile there is not a true community of defense ... Many perceive defense as an exclusive problem for the armed forces – if we review the history of this century, we realize that such a perception tends to be dominant ... The challenge is to combine democratic consensus with an attitude change in the whole of the Chilean people without distinctions. (Pérez Yoma, 1996)

The road to constituting a defense community has been favored by the creation of diverse arenas for the civil–military dialogue. Academic institutions like FLACSO, CED, Universities and the academic institutions of the armed forces have served a very significant role in the construction of such fora and the discussion of corresponding policies. The former Minister of Defense, Pérez Yoma, tried to support the civilian leadership in this matter by making routine the functioning of high-level institutions dedicated to defense issues. Similarly, the Congress, despite limitations, has participated in this process. Notwithstanding the generation of fora and arenas for increasing transparency, we ought to note that distinct visions of the role and particular function of defense endure (see Table 9.2).

The principal debates in the area of defense correspond to professional issues, but nevertheless, there are still topics of the past that remain, such as the definition of the roles of the armed forces in the political system. Likewise, a number of issues linked to human rights are also present. However, the principal area of debate concerns the issue of the modernization of defense, which entails dealing with the character and scope of the military as one of the instruments which the democratic system relies upon when promoting the country's interests. It also involves dealing with issues of leadership and autonomy when civilians and military tackle professional issues and the consequent definitions in this area. Civil leadership and the development of skills are essential from the

Table 9.2   *Civil–military relations under democracy*

Subject	Tension	Determining factors
Role of the armed forces	Subordination vs autonomy	A legal framework favorable to autonomy Civil support for autonomy
Modernization of defense	Civil management vs autonomy	Lack of trust between civilians and the military Autonomous military development Limitations of the Ministry of Defense Legal framework favorable to autonomy Shortage of civilian experts

perspective of democratic consolidation. A professional informed dialogue will contribute in a decisive manner to overcoming the distrust which still exists, even though it will not be possible to reconstruct a common historical memory. As already noted, Chile continues to be an imperfect democracy, largely as a result of authoritarian enclaves. Nonetheless, it cannot be said that Chile is a tutelary system, oriented towards those in uniform. The process of democratic consolidation is still incomplete, especially as to the crucial definitions of the political system, but the subordination of the armed forces to the constitutional system is certainly increasing.

The fundamental idea defining civil–military relations in this period of democratic consolidation are strong military institutions and a high degree of professionalism. These, together with increasing civilian leadership in defense and security matters, make it possible to promote one of the three essential points of agreement on which transition and democratic consolidation are based in Chile. In effect, construction of the new political system has been based on three founding points of agreement: consensus regarding democracy; consensus regarding economic liberalization orientated towards exports and with a perspective of equity; and consensus in the design of a new form of civil–military relations.

At the beginning of the twenty first century, the Chilean political system is characterized by a strong link to the country's democratic trajectory, especially a strong attachment to legal aspects; a pluralist system; and the search for increased participation. The central theme is how to overcome the institutional enclaves that principally affect political dimensions and are expressed in the constitutional arena, undoubtedly affecting the international image of the country. Only the consolidation of democracy will allow Chile to maintain its expectations of economic growth and stability. The outlook is very promising; however, to transform this into facts and actions the democratic governability pact should be permanently reinforced. The establishment of a new form and a new course in defense themes supports this pact and will make possible the consolidation of the trilogy of peace, democracy and development.

Governability will not be assured by an imperfect democracy. The governmental responsibility of Parliament and of the political parties is to construct the consensus necessary for the establishment of effective democracy. This requires looking beyond the present, consolidating the three points of agreement which have made the successful transition possible, and transforming those points of agreement into instruments for Chilean development in the twenty-first century. A new period in the democratic process has been initiated since the departure of General Pinochet from his position as Commander-in-Chief of the Army and his entrance into the Senate in March 1998.

Chile will continue with an imperfect democratic system for an important period, given its institutional structure. What will be required to insure democracy will be important incentives from the democratic government. However, this is not evident in the short term. The challenge for democracy will be to find effective formulas in order to continue with growth, to generate equality, and to strengthen the political and institutional stability by means of securing effective democracy for all Chileans.

Civil–military relations after Pinochet's arrest

The arrest in London of General Pinochet on 16 October 1998, and his prolonged detention in that country, has enormously influenced the further development of the Chilean political process. The British Home Secretary's decision to arrest General Pinochet followed a request for extradition issued by Spain. After a while, similar petitions were issued by France, Italy, Sweden and other European countries. Pinochet's arrest generated a controversial political issue for the western world, with a global impact in the field of international law on matters of human rights far beyond the particular consequences which this event would provoke in Chile. After almost 17 months of passionate legal struggle, the British government finally decided on 2 March 2000 to allow Pinochet to fly back to Chile.

The detention of General Pinochet in London dramatically substantiated one of the main contentions of this chapter: that the democratic transition in Chile represents a complex, lengthy and imperfect process. In addition, there is a structural obstacle within Chile's institutional system due to the veto position the opposition minority enjoys, and which makes any major transformation of the political system almost impossible. For instance, this situation has impeded the adoption of reforms directed to increase the democratic leadership of civilians over the military institutions. The current constitution confers high levels of autonomy on the armed forces, and certainly does not facilitate the way for the establishment of an adequate framework for normal civil–military relations within a context of democratic rule.

The initiation of the legal procedures in London to extradite Pinochet to Spain produced an almost automatic polarization among the leaders of all political sectors in Chile, leading to a dramatic reduction in levels of trust in the political system and among the main political figures in the country. This has clearly complicated the further formulation of long-term national policies (the so-called políticas de Estado). The polarization shows that there are two very different historical memories in Chile about the events which led to the breakdown of Chilean democracy in 1973 and the legacy of the military dictatorship in the period 1973–90. The events in London led to an abrupt change in the national political agenda. From initial worries concerning national stability, attention rapidly moved on to the unfinished debate on the political leadership of the country. The reactions and attitudes adopted by the main political actors around Pinochet's arrest were dominated by their political and electoral calculations around the general elections of 12 December 1999.

Another aspect which should be mentioned here is the general perception within the country that civil–military relations have deteriorated since Pinochet's arrest. There have been many important achievements connected with these relations, particularly on close cooperation between the government and military leaders on political-strategic matters, and on subjects related to the institutional development of the armed forces. The Chilean armed forces chose to adopt an attitude of 'military insulation' and have almost entirely centered their institutional relation with the government around the fate of the old General in London. What is clear from all this is that after a decade in which the restoration of democratic rule took place, Chile needs once again to face the key questions of the democratic transition in order to find permanent solutions and so avoid a situation of recurrent and endemic political crisis which can seriously place the further development of the country at risk.

The British decision also proved the limited power small countries possess in the international system. It is still too early to make an evaluation of the global effects which could follow the possible supremacy of human rights issues above the principle of national sovereignty. However, it can be stated with certainty that it will have significant consequences in the political realm with respect to political negotiations between government and opposition during transitional processes and the possible judgement of crimes against humanity. Since Pinochet's arrest and throughout the 17 months he was forced to remain in Britain, a strong debate emerged in Chile about the transition agreements made in the late 1980s between the military regime and the former opposition (now in government) and its consequences for the current evolution of the political system. So after many years of collective historical amnesia, Chileans began to have an increasing interest in the recent political history of the country in order to try to understand the current political events and the effects of Pinochet's arrest on the country's political system.

If we look back to the three essential consensuses achieved in Chile which I have analysed in this chapter, it can be established that the London events did not change their essence. However, there are already some signs which indicate they could be modified in the near future, depending on the course of events in Chile following the installation of President Ricardo Lagos in March 2000. There is a current consensus in Chile on democracy as being the only valid and legitimate form of government. However, following Pinochet's arrest some voices from the right-wing sectors emerged to argue that the extension of the General's detention in Britain constituted a direct threat to democratic rule in the country. Although no Pinochetista-sector has dared to question the desirability of democratic rule, it has become clear that there are some sectors ready to make some tacit threats of the possible use of force by the military against the established authorities. But in spite of this, national institutional stability is not on trial in Chile today. Nevertheless, the detention of Pinochet in London produced an increase in the relative power of actors such as the military and the economic elite to the detriment of those actors empowered with popular representation within the democratic framework.

With respect to the existing consensus on the current economic policies, no challenges have emerged suggesting a regression towards an inward-oriented economy or towards imposing limitations on Chile's participation in the international economic system.

The further opening up of the Chilean economy, the strengthening of its export-orientation, and the expansion of international economic agreements with other countries and regions continues to be supported by all the relevant actors of the political and economic system. The proposed economic retaliation against British and Spanish products, as demanded by Pinochet's supporters in 1998, indicated the overestimation by this political sector of the real potentialities of using this economic instrument in the international arena by a small country such as Chile.

Today, major difficulties can be found in attempts to generate a new type of civil–military relation. Substantial deterioration has occurred in the discussions between the government and the military about the theoretical and policy framework required to deal with questions such as the further professionalization and modernization of the armed forces, and this became evident in the difficulties in deploying a common national political-strategic perspective on the Pinochet affair. Whereas the current situation shows institutional normality (for instance, the National Security Council has met on several occasions), the discussions around possible changes to the 1980 constitution were considerably dominated during 1998–2000 by the calculations of its effects for General Pinochet in the eventuality of him returning to the country. After a decade, the general context in which these three consensuses were built has changed. On the one hand, the impact of globalization has become more evident for all Chileans. In spite of its segmentation between political, economic and especially financial affairs, its impact on Chile cannot be arbitrarily divided into 'suitable' and 'undesirable' categories. This means that Chile cannot say that economic globalization is convenient and hence it has to be strengthened, while at the same time attempting to avoid the political effects of political globalization such as the support and protection of human rights and the recognition of the increasing authority possessed by international law.

Finally, globalization and modernization processes have also had an impact on young people. Chilean youngsters have obtained an influential voice in the country's public opinion, and many have consciously decided not to enroll in the electoral registers and have actively criticized the deficiencies of Chilean democracy. The University students' movement has also played a pivotal role in recent protests against the costs of higher education and the lack of justice in Chile, and also in demonstrations in support of indigenous groups in Southern Chile and their struggle against logging companies and the construction of a hydroelectrical plant.

Politicians have a highly complex task to achieve in their attempt to accommodate stability and justice. This has become a particularly difficult task as collective trust has been diminished, and the country has become strained and polarized around the two large political coalitions – one promoting democracy and the other promoting a protected order. This situation continues to prevent the establishment of a broad national consensus on the ways Chile should meet the social, economic and political challenges of the coming years.

Pinochet in Chile

When Pinochet returned to Chile on 3 March 2000 he found a quite different country as the one he had left in October 1998. The victory of the Socialist Ricardo Lagos in the second round of the presidential elections held in January 2000 made Pinochet's political future very uncertain. The elected president was during the military regime one of his most fervent opponents. So the joy of the General's supporters following his return to the country was constrained by the real prospects that he should be legally prosecuted in Chile.

Soon after his installation on 12 March 2000, President Lagos stated that the fate of Pinochet would be in the hands of the Chilean judiciary system. By this he firmly rejected the attempts made by some right-wing political leaders to link the pending constitutional reforms to the Pinochet case. They had expressed their readiness to give their parliamentary support to most of the constitutional reforms proposed in the past by the previous Concertación governments in change for 'leaving the old General in peace'. By eliminating the Pinochet affair from the political arena and placing it entirely in the judiciary sphere, Lagos has succeeded so far in maintaining political stability in the country and gradually improving the relations between the new government and the armed forces.

President Lagos has developed a remarkable good personal relationship with the chief of the army, General Ricardo Izurieta. This has generated a favorable climate between the two leaders to discuss in a direct way a scries of pending issues. This direct line of communication has certainly facilitated the historical agreement achieved on 12 June 2000 within the so-called 'mesa de diálogo'. This was a high-level discussion group established in October 1999 by the former Defense Minister, Edmundo Pérez Yoma, in an attempt to bring new life into the difficult process of reconciliation among Chileans. One of the mesa's main objectives has been to find a workable way to recover the bodies of the one thousand political adversaries who disappeared during the military regime. For the very first time since the restoration of democratic rule in 1990, members of the armed forces, legal representatives of human rights organizations, and a group of highly respected 'wise men' from different religious and social backgrounds, have held for many months a series of difficult discussions. Following Pinochet's return to Chile this initiative was almost completely paralysed and many people expected it should soon end in a total failure. However, the rapid improvement in the relations between the Lagos government and the military leadership made this agreement possible. In this historical agreement the Chilean armed forces recognize for the first time since the 1973 coup the human rights abuses committed during the military regime. They also promise to gather and to provide within a period of 6 months all the information available within the armed institutions about the location of the bodies of the *desaparecidos*.

Also in the legal sphere, some unexpected developments have taken place. On 23 May 2000 a Chilean court of justice decided to withdraw Senator Pinochet's parliamentary immunity, so he should have to face the more than 140 legal denounces presented against him by the victims of his regime and their relatives. At the moment of writing (July 2000), the Chilean Supreme Court is still deliberating about the appeal to this sentence presented by Pinochet's attorneys. Most analysts expect that the previous decision to withdraw his parliamentary immunity will be reconfirmed by the Supreme Court. However, it is quite doubtful that in the end Pinochet will ever have to face a trial because of his age and bad health conditions, as certified by British doctors.

Whatever the result of this legal battle, it seems that the Chilean armed forces have initiated a new stage in their institutional development, trying to leave behind the Pinochet era and to normalize their relationship *vis-à-vis* the civilian authorities and Chilean society at large.

10
In Permanent Retreat? The Modest Future Role of the Armed Forces in South America
Paul Cammack

Introduction

This chapter assesses the extent to which space currently exists in Latin America – and in the Southern Cone in particular – for political projects based upon the military. The first section introduces the concept of a 'political project' in the sense in which it is employed here, and briefly explicates the 'new materialist' theoretical framework within which it is set. The second section offers a retrospective analysis of the context of intervention and prolonged military rule in the 1960s and 1970s, and the third examines the contrasting context of the present decade. The fourth then compares these periods, and argues that the circumstances which prompted military intervention and prolonged military rule in the 1960s and 1970s no longer exist. The fifth section identifies a modest scope in the present for conjunctural interventions as a last resort, but argues that there is now no political space for projects which seek to institutionalize military rule. In conclusion, it is argued that to the extent that liberalizing civilian projects come under threat in the region, the response will be to retain the civilian form of government but to circumscribe its democratic content, rather than to opt for military rule as an alternative.

Political projects in a new materialist perspective

Two decades ago, it was common to argue that there was an 'elective affinity' between the crisis of import-substituting industrialization and the establishment of authoritarian political regimes in Latin America. It is just as common today to argue that there is such an affinity between the processes of political democratization and economic liberalization. Both claims are dubious. O'Donnell's (1973) 'bureaucratic-authoritarian regime' thesis not only suggested that a particular economic crisis could give rise to a specific form of political regime, but made the mistake of identifying a local and conjunctural response as the basis for a new regime of an enduring kind. Thus in *Generals in Retreat* I argued that it was a weakness of the model that its scope was 'limited by the initial identification of a particular crisis in the development of delayed and dependent capitalism with the emergence of a single regime type' (Cammack, 1985: 5), and that in any case the model 'derived its internal consistency from the nature of the conjuncture in which the regime emerges, rather than from the identification of the character of the regime in the longer term' (*ibid.*: 8). The most striking feature of the model in retrospect is its extreme determinism: the inevitable emergence of an authoritarian regime of a very particular kind from a specific historical-structural crisis. Such determinism, which was characteristic in different ways of world-system theory and of Anglo-Saxon dependency theory, was of course widespread at the time.

The contemporary literatures on democratization and neoliberalism offer a curious contrast. The process of liberal democratization which has been underway since the late 1970s, and which has now left the region without a military regime, has been celebrated, as much by O'Donnell as by anyone, as a triumph of choice over structural predetermination. But at the same time, the adoption of broadly neoliberal economic policies on a similarly regional scale has been identified, in the literature on 'globalization' in particular, as evidence of the compulsion which faces peripheral states in a world where global competition forces states to compete with each other for shares in the world market. Politics, as it were, has become the realm of choice, while economics has become the realm of necessity.

Neither of these versions of the relationship between the economic and the political is quite satisfactory. The purely ideological celebration of politics as the realm of choice – what we might call the discursive separation of politics from economics – offers a distorted reflection of a fundamental constitutive feature of capitalism which O'Donnell's earlier BA thesis entirely overlooked: the necessary detachment of direct political authority from ownership and economic power. From it follows the 'relative autonomy' of the political sphere, which is an historical product of the transition from feudalism to capitalism and the concentration of the authority to govern in the hands of a specialist class. This development creates conditions in which the needs of different sectors of capital can in principle be reconciled, and the hegemony of capital over labor assured, but at the same time it makes the relationship between the interests of capital and the form of government contingent. This inevitably opens the way to the possibility of divergence and contradiction between the character of the political regime on the one hand, and the interests of the economically dominant class and the prospects for smooth capitalist reproduction (which are, of course, different things) on the other. In other words, the separation of the political from the economic, a constitutive feature of capitalism, is simultaneously *necessary* and *contradictory*.

It follows from this that states and political regimes should be analysed in relation to class and economic interests, but at the same time that they cannot be reduced to or read off from such interests. There is no one form of political regime, or one form of state, which is uniquely appropriate in a capitalist economy. In the first place, there is no reason to suppose that a single political form is required by a capitalist system, however abstractly and formally it might be defined. In addition, from a *spatial* perspective, the fact that capitalist development on a global scale is *combined* and *uneven* means that national capitalisms will vary in type and level of development, giving particular social formations a unique international position and national character; and from a *conjunctural* perspective, the evolution of political and economic systems and the relationship and degree of fit between them should be expected to vary over time. In particular, regime forms should be expected to experience *discontinuous change*, as a consequence of the combined effects of class struggle, the changing demands of capitalist reproduction at the national level, and the tendency (inherent in the separation of politics and economics) for the political system to evolve, within limits, in accordance with a dynamic and an institutional logic of its own. The result of this will be periodic political crises which will precipitate changes, some superficial and some fundamental, in regime form. In sum, there will always be an 'organic connection' between economic and political systems (a connection which bourgeois social science is increasingly pre-programed to render obscure), but the connection will be complex, conjunctural, and subject to variation over time.

In these circumstances, means have to be developed for arriving at an understanding of the simultaneous 'separation and organic connection' between politics and economics. It is wrong to abandon the insight that patterns of regime change over time are fundamentally related to changes in the national and global political economy, but equally wrong to attempt to read off the former from the latter in a mechanical way. I seek to address this point by introducing into the structural context provided by the analysis of political economy the issue of human political agency, and the institutional forms it takes. To this end I offer a spatial and conjunctural analysis which interprets politics in any given environment as consisting of a contest between competing *political projects*, each of which proposes a more or less comprehensive and explicit package of social, economic and cultural policies for a determinate space in the global economy.

Within this broad framework, a *national political project* is a program for the realization of determinate goals through the political process. The particular goals it proposes will arise from an understanding of local, national, regional and/or global conjunctures, and will be pursued by means of a program which may contain social, economic and ideological components. These will be aimed to respond to concrete and identifiable interests, but in a comprehensive project these will be subsumed into a broader vision which takes account of competing interests and constructs a distinctive account of the 'general interest'. Such a project will be pursued by means of a political-institutional strategy which may include the adoption, adaptation or invention of specific practices, the pursuit of alliances, and the utilization, transformation or creation of institutions. If our concern is with the history of military intervention and military rule, and the possibility that it might return, we should explore the specific circumstances in which such projects have taken or might take that institutional form. We should then ask whether the present structural context is one which appears to favor such projects.

Such an analysis could doubtless be conducted from within a number of competing analytical frameworks. Mine is Marxist in inspiration. It privileges, in the interpretation of such projects, their relationship to the logic of class conflict, capitalist competition and development at national, regional and global levels, and it draws upon broader elements of Marxist theory in order to do so. As regards both political-institutional and economic aspects of determinate national projects, it seeks to clarify their *conjunctural*, *temporal*, *spatial* and *relational* logics. In the context of Latin American debates and developments, it seeks to integrate previous debates on authoritarian regimes and current debates on democratization and 'globalization' into a single theoretical framework, overcoming the ideological trick which sees determinism in the one case, and the exercise of free will in the other. In this endeavor, no general or universal significance is attached to the adoption of either authoritarian or liberal democratic political regimes. It is recognized that development of the system as a whole takes place over time. In this connection, the intensification of global exchange and the pressures it brings is seen not as an ultra-modern novelty requiring a new analysis and a new vocabulary, but as the realization of the phase of global competition identified by Marx and Engels as built into the dynamic logic of capitalism when they drafted the *Manifesto of the Communist Party* 150 years ago. It is giving rise to a new and significant phase in the development of capitalism as a global system, but not one which requires new concepts: the same principles of analysis will apply as have applied in the past.

In view of the continuity with classical Marxism in terms of analytical principles, and the new conjuncture to which the analysis is applied, I describe my approach as 'new materialist' in character. The new materialist perspective suggests that capitalist-oriented states seek to preserve and constantly extend *the general conditions for capital accumulation* within their own national space and, to the extent that they have the capacity to do so, within the global system as a whole. It argues that in the current context of the completion of the world market and the universalization of the imperatives of capitalist competition (or what is loosely called globalization), competition between firms and capital accumulation take place on a global scale. As a result, autonomous projects for capitalist accumulation secured at the level of the state – briefly possible in a minority of cases in the past – are generally problematic.

At the level of global economic management, this situation is reflected in the emergence of global regulatory agencies (international organizations) and regional and interregional initiatives sponsored and carried forward by state leaders in an effort to mitigate the difficulties they face in advancing what they take to be their 'national interest'. NAFTA and Mercosur, in the Latin American context, represent examples of this phenomenon (Cammack, 1999). States naturally carry into these global, regional and interregional contexts their need to compete with each other, as well as their need to cooperate, if they can, to establish the general conditions for the global hegemony of capitalism.

In this context, regional, interregional and global regulatory institutions are both supporting frameworks and sites of struggle between competing projects sponsored to different degrees by states, capitalist firms and international agencies themselves. As capitalist competition becomes global in scale and the imperatives it generates become universally binding, such initiatives may variously resist, modify or promote the logic of global capitalist competition. However, the tendency is for the logic of capitalist competition to assert itself on a global scale, and states, firms and international organizations are as much shaped by the process as shaping it.

In this environment of global competition for profit, states are increasingly driven towards making their territories hospitable to capitalist investment and accumulation, whether domestic or foreign. In order to do this, they must adapt themselves to the prevailing international regulatory framework supported by the dominant regional, interregional and global organizations, if they cannot shape it to their own advantage. In the present global context, this subjects the great majority of states in the global system to the logic of the familiar neoliberal agenda which removes obstacles to the free range of capital by privatization and the removal of protection, and cuts the costs of its operation by reducing taxes and promoting 'efficient' systems of targeted welfare. This overall agenda is currently pressed at global level by such regulatory agencies as the IMF, the World Bank, and the World Trade Organization.

At the heart of this process, however, capitalism is still what it always was. Central to it is the exploitation of labor by capital, a process which in turn entails a drive to bring workers directly under its control – the promotion of what Marx called the *real subsumption of labor to capital,* or the creation of circumstances in which the majority are proletarianized, and have no option but to offer themselves for employment in a labor market thoroughly permeated by the logic of capitalist competition. It is a central feature of capitalist development, then, that states engage in domestic, regional, inter-regional and global initiatives in order to secure, maintain or reinforce the domestic hegemony of capital over labor, in order to enhance their ability to promote the hegemony of capital and to 'capture' capital accumulation on their own terrain. It follows, from the new materialist perspective, that one should give pride of place in analysing particular situations to the question of capitalist hegemony – the extent to which the hegemony of capital over labor is realized, and the relationship between this question and the character of the political regime, and the processes of political and regime change. I have elsewhere applied this framework to the 'Asia Crisis' which has been gathering pace since 1997 (Cammack, 1999). Here I apply it to the case of Latin America.

Latin American authoritarianism

The wave of military interventions in Latin America from the 1960s represented a heavily overdetermined conjunctural response to a set of related regime crises. The common roots of these were in a crisis of bourgeois hegemony dating from the breakdown of consensual elite rule in the wake of the ending of the period of successful export-oriented development in 1930. Within this common framework, there were significant differences in class structure, class alliance and class conflict across the region: both broadly between Central and South America (or South America and Mexico), and between individual countries in each group. Herein lies part of the explanation for the variety of regime forms between Argentina, Brazil, Chile and Mexico, say, or between Costa Rica, El Salvador and Nicaragua.

Beyond this, there were contingent institutional dynamics in each case. Hence the need to attend to the forms of institutionalization of successive political regimes. As became apparent, O'Donnell's (1973) bureaucratic-authoritarian approach completely obliterated the *institutional* differences between the authoritarian regimes of Argentina, Brazil and Chile. By the 1960s, however, all the institutional solutions to the deep-seated crisis of bourgeois hegemony in the region (of which 'populism' in its various forms was the most successful of the 'second-best' responses) were beginning to fail. This failure, in my opinion, was more to do with the character of class politics and weakening of dominant-class political control than with some supposedly final crisis of import-substituting industrialization.

In addition, though, the widespread emergence of military regimes in the region was heavily overdetermined by the regional and global conjuncture: the cold war; the regional impact of the Cuban revolution; US support for repression after a brief and contradictory flirtation with progressive reform; and the rapid spread of doctrines of national security. While the logic of military intervention was conjunctural, their accumulation of institutional resources enabled military regimes to remain in power long after the circumstances which provoked their entry had disappeared.

Each long-lived military regime can be seen as representing a particular political project and institutionalizing it in a particular form. Such projects should be examined within the broad framework set out above, and can be compared with each other, and with those pursued by civilian regimes of various kinds. As is now apparent, authoritarian military regimes could either pursue a neoliberal model (as in Chile) or resist it (as in Brazil). Equally, broadly neoliberal economic programs can be pursued by civilian regimes, whether democratic (as in contemporary Brazil), or semi-democratic (as in Mexico). In every case, a comprehensive analysis of the project in its spatial and temporal context and of the particular manner in which it was institutionalized is essential to its interpretation.

Latin American democratization

Comparison of authoritarian and democratic regimes should begin by conceptualizing Latin American projects for political democratization and economic liberalization as national projects. There is no implication in this that they are the projects of sovereign states immune from pressure from their external environment. On the contrary, they are explicable only in the context of powerful global dynamics and constraints. But it is very misleading to present this as a novelty. One of the strengths of Anglo-Saxon dependency and world-systems theories, which outweighed their weaknesses, was precisely their insistence on the extent to which successive national projects in the modern era have been subject to such dynamics and constraints. To think otherwise is to confuse political sovereignty with economic autonomy.

These national projects have been reinforced by the support offered by global regulatory institutions and by emerging subregional and regional projects for economic integration made possible by the changed policy of the United States. Despite the different and in some ways competitive origins of NAFTA and *Mercosur*, for example, they tend to open the way to an enlarged free trade area, as promoted by the United States in the form of the Enterprise for the Americas initiative launched by President Bush in 1990. Such regional initiatives do not represent the imposition upon Latin American states of imperialist or global capitalist projects over national reluctance or resistance. They represent auxiliary means by which ruling political elites can reinforce and perpetuate bourgeois hegemony and the general conditions for capitalist reproduction in the national context. In other words, they are part of, rather than apart from, the various state projects in the region.

In comparative regional terms, even so, Latin America has been and continues to be highly incorporated into the modern capitalist world system, and weakly resistant to its global dynamics. It was incorporated at a very early stage into the emerging Atlantic world system, at a moment when fragile political sovereignty combined with extreme economic backwardness. The national projects arising in these circumstances, built around export-oriented development, reflected this situation. Successive national projects (state-led development in the postwar period, and the authoritarian military projects discussed above) have been precipitated by changes in global circumstances and dynamics, and have been adapted to rather than resistant to such changes. Where they have promised to make a more fundamental break with the global system (as with socialist experiments in Chile, Cuba and Nicaragua) they have been isolated or defeated. This broad historical characteristic is reflected in the fact that enduring national projects have relied heavily and still rely, in every case, on external capital, technology, and markets. This applies as much to state-led development projects, whether populist or military-authoritarian, as it does to earlier episodes of export-oriented development, and is in sharp contrast with other regions – especially the Pacific region generally and East Asia in particular.

Projects for political democratization and economic liberalization in Latin America should therefore be understood in terms of a heavily overdetermined regional conjuncture, in which global, regional and national dynamics have come together. This has its origins in the relationships between the outcomes of the class conflicts which spread across the region from the 1960s onwards, the regional implications of the collapse of the postwar Bretton Woods regime and the phase of intensified global competition which ensued, and the reorientation of the US position on global and regional issues in the wake of the ending of the bipolar conflict of the cold war.

The starting-point here was a series of national class struggles in the 1970s and 1980s which ended in the defeat of radical alternatives in state after state in the region. These had their origins in the breakdown of the populist-developmentalist projects which dominated, in various forms, in the leading states of the region in the postwar period. The clearest case of conclusive class struggle is that of Chile, where the imposition of a neoliberal economic regime followed upon an unequivocal defeat of the organized working class and a ruthlessly authoritarian restructuring of domestic capital. In every case (Chile included) where an authoritarian regime proved conjuncturally necessary, that regime equally proved unable to guarantee the conditions for renewed capitalist accumulation in the longer term.

Against this background, the latest manifestation of external dependence, the 'debt-crisis' of the early 1980s, put an end to the capacity of states in the region to resist alignment with the prevailing trends in the global economy. This brought conclusive evidence of the fragile and contradictory basis of 'state-led' development. States in the region were no longer able to act as privileged agents mediating between external and national capitals, and lost the ability to exert any autonomy from domestic capital other than that afforded by the *internalization of the logic of global competition*. This became their national project. Paradoxically, though, the disappearance of the conditions for state-led development resolved the crisis of bourgeois hegemony. This is not as paradoxical as it seems – it simply introduced a degree of economic compulsion which simultaneously forced the state to accede to the global pressures exerted by capital, and undermined the ability of workers to resist the reimposition of dominant class hegemony.

We are once again, then, in a heavily overdetermined conjuncture – but this time one which favors the adoption of liberal democratic regimes. The local defeat of radical alternatives is reinforced on the one hand by the global dominance of capital and the powerful dynamic of global capitalist competition, and on the other by the political circumstances arising from the reincorporation of the countries of the Soviet bloc into the capitalist economy. One central feature of this conjuncture is that US governments are no longer supportive of military regimes in Latin America, now that the conjunctural reasons for which they previously supported them have disappeared.

The complex, conjunctural relationship between politics and economics is nevertheless perfectly exemplified by the variations in the individual and institutional bearers of projects of economic liberalization from case to case. These range from the sequence of personal dictatorship and competitive liberal democracy in Chile to the combination of continued institutionalized civilian authoritarian rule in Mexico, and reformed Peronist populism in Argentina. Most strikingly of all, the project of economic liberalization is carried forward in Brazil, where it has proved difficult to find an appropriate form of political institutionalization, by Fernando Henrique Cardoso, the leading exponent of Latin American dependency theory, at the head of a still weakly institutionalized center–right coalition.

Against this background, the adoption of liberal democratic political systems should be seen in regional and conjunctural rather than universal and deterministic terms. It reflects long incorporation into the economic, social and culture space of the modern 'Atlantic' world order and the exhaustion of the ability of repressive and authoritarian regimes to contain class conflict and direct successful capitalist reproduction as much as any presumed affinity between economic liberalization and liberal democratization.

Contrasting conjunctures: the 1960s–1970s and the 1990s

The 1960s and 1970s witnessed a protracted crisis in the postwar global political economy structured at the international level by the

Bretton Woods institutions and characterized, despite the broad global hegemony exercised by the United States, by the existence of a number of competing models of accumulation and development. The postwar prestige of the Soviet Union and its capacity to extend its hegemony over Eastern Europe meant that its pattern of state-command socialist development was available as an alternative to capitalist models, while in the capitalist world liberal, social democratic and developmentalist options existed side by side. This rendered the construction and maintenance of bourgeois hegemony particularly problematic. Given the existence of what appeared a real socialist alternative, pure liberal doctrines were on the defensive, and in the 'developing world' interventionist models gained ascendancy, with an equal emphasis upon state intervention in production, and the provision of welfare again through the agency of the state.

In this context, some limited space existed in Latin America for models of developmentalism which endorsed state intervention, challenged the existing balance of class forces, and sought to construct new alliances linking the state to sectors of the working class and an emerging national bourgeoisie. The populist regimes which emerged, in Argentina and Brazil in particular, are best understood in this context. However, the conditions which prompted their emergence were already in the process of disappearing by the early 1960s, because of both the dynamic of class conflict to which they gave rise, and the changing pattern of capitalist accumulation at a global level, which rendered inoperable the project of accumulation on the basis of the national market. In sum, the military regimes which arose in the period came into being in the context of a combined crisis of global and domestic patterns of accumulation, and of the political regimes which had been created in order to pursue projects of *national development.* Once the developmentalist options failed, it was not possible to restore bourgeois hegemony through electoral means because of the weakness of conservative and liberal alternatives. Military intervention was the consequence (Cammack, 1997).

The situation in the 1990s is different. The protracted crisis in the postwar global political economy has been resolved by means of a neoliberal revolution which has brought about the reconstruction of the Bretton Woods institutions and the system of global economic regulation. The World Trade Organization (WTO) first envisaged in the 1940s has been brought into being alongside the IMF and the World Bank; and the IMF, supported in particular by the governments of the UK and the United States, has set about defining an explicitly neoliberal system of global economic governance. Competing models of accumulation and development have fallen away, with the crisis of the welfare state and social democracy, the collapse of the Soviet Union and its Eastern European allies, and the protracted crisis of developmental states, first in Latin America itself and latterly in East and Southeast Asia. The space that once existed in Latin America for national developmentalism has been compressed to the point of disappearance, and newly invigorated projects have appeared which have proved able to combine acceptance of the new conditions of 'globalization' and neoliberal global regulation with a commitment to democratic politics and an ability to defeat more radical alternatives at the polls. This is not to say that the new democracies in Latin America are invulnerable; it is to draw attention to a fundamental feature which differentiates the current situation from that of the 1960s and 1970s. Current democratic governments around Latin America are committed to projects which are broadly consistent with the current global hegemony of neoliberalism, and are working within the regulatory frameworks and understandings laid down by leading states in the system, and by the institutions of global economic governance they have developed and supported. Those governments and institutions are wary of military and authoritarian regimes, not least because of the difficulties provoked by military regimes in Latin America in the closing years of their presence in power. As a consequence, to the extent that elected regimes in Latin America pursuing projects consistent with the framework of global neoliberalism find themselves in crisis, regional and global mechanisms will be operated in order to repair and strengthen the hegemony of those regimes rather than to replace them. And in view of the extreme instability of global markets, military intervention will appear the least attractive option. Far from it now being necessary to oust regimes which persist in the pursuit of national developmentalism, with its destabilizing consequences for class relations, the need now, from the perspective of dominant forces in local and global capitalism, is to shore up regimes which persist in the implementation of neoliberal projects and commit themselves as a consequence to the restructuring of class relations in ways which strengthen the ability of capital to assert its hegemony over labor.

The limited space for military projects

Projects for economic liberalization in Latin America reflect the general pressure on states throughout the now genuinely global capitalist world economy to adapt themselves, on pain of extinction, to the imperatives of global competition. They also reflect, at a regional level, the legacy of the manner in which the region was incorporated over centuries into the emerging world capitalist economy. Latin American states, in comparative terms, have historically had and continue to have relatively little ability to resist the forces generated within the international political economy. This is not a matter of historical destiny or of predestination, but the fact remains that successive regional conjunctures have tended to reinforce this characteristic. Ever since political independence (and 'sovereignty') came to the greater part of the region in the early nineteenth century, national projects have been framed in these circumstances, and the current crop of projects share the character of their predecessors. The specific form they take is the overdetermined outcome of overlaid national, regional and global dynamics, which happen for the moment to combine to produce a pattern of broad similarity.

While national projects oriented towards economic liberalization may continue to gain prominence in Latin America, there is no reason to assume that there is any tendency for political regimes to evolve uniformly. First, the struggle over outcomes is not resolved. There is no certainty that neoliberal economic projects will prevail in every case. Second, Latin American capitalism remains combined and uneven, and different national societies remain more or less hospitable to democratic political regime forms. It is possible to differentiate significantly between current projects: neoliberal and liberal democratic in the Chilean case, neoliberal and suspended between authoritarianism and liberal democracy in the Mexican case, and neoliberal and personalist in the Argentine case (reflecting the current absence of an institutional framework capable of carrying the project forward). The most interesting case is that of Brazil, where there is no doubting the commitment of the Cardoso regime to the internalization in Brazil of the disciplines of global neoliberalism, but the associated political project remains reformist in character and inspiration.

Despite this level of institutional variation, however, it is evident that there is at present very little conjunctural space for military intervention. There is no reason to expect a general return to interventions of the kind which proliferated after 1960. While it is impossible to rule out further brief interventions, it is possible to say that there is limited structural space for projects based upon military rule. It is perfectly possible, though increasingly unlikely, that *inertial interventions* could take place here or there: interventions, in other words, made possible by the previous accumulation of institutional resources. The analogy is with the 'inertial' theory of inflation, which argued (whether rightly or wrongly is immaterial in this context) that the underlying conditions which generated inflation had disappeared, but that it persisted because it had been institutionalized. Such interventions may equally be described as anachronistic or quixotic, and in my terms can be described as lacking connections with any credible political project. Examples of attempted interventions which have failed in recent years readily come to mind, and the danger of such perverse inertial interventions explains the emphasis placed by the architects of the consolidation of democracy on the institutional reforms which extend civilian authority over the military.

Secondly, civilian rulers may disrupt the constitutional order with institutional backing from the military. Here the paradigmatic case is Fujimori in Peru, and the crucial point is that the initiative comes from the civilian rather than the military side. The creation of the *Estado Novo* in Brazil in 1937 is an interesting parallel. Equally, there is an interesting reverse symmetry between the early 1960s, when the military intervened but ruled through civilian proxies, as with the Peruvian and Argentinian interventions which produced the Belaunde government and the Guido interregnum respectively, and the Fujimori case, where a civilian ruler broke with the constitution and relied upon military support. On the analogy with populism as a 'second-best' solution to the previous crisis of bourgeois hegemony, this might be seen as a 'last-best' means to the restoration of bourgeois hegemony. Here the military does not act as an autonomous force, but rather as an *executive agent*. The central question is whether the executive is advancing a coherent political project (as Fujimori unquestionably was), and whether the institutional means were appropriate to the end (which they probably were). In Serrano's case in Guatemala, the reverse was true.

Thirdly, sectors of the military may side with opponents of neoliberal reform, and seek to effect an *oppositionist* intervention. The failure of such initiatives in Venezuela suggest that this is a difficult undertaking, and in the immediate future at least one of steadily diminishing likelihood.

These possibilities each relate to the conjuncture of *transition*. As regards the future, the fact that Latin America entered this new phase in the development of the global capitalist economy in the wake of significant class confrontations and significant defeats for the varying projects put forward in opposition to liberal capitalism, and in a specific conjuncture that favored the adoption of liberal democracy, may have lasting consequences for the balance of class power and the character of political regimes in the region. But the various national capitalisms in the region will continue to differ in content, as the protagonists of capitalist development will continue to differ in their ability to formulate and implement political projects by which their plans can be driven forward. There is no reason to suppose that all will prove equally capable of pursuing capitalist development while maintaining and consolidating liberal democratic political regimes. However, it is far more likely that the democratic content of civilian regimes will be systematically reduced if bourgeois hegemony comes under threat than that military intervention will occur.

Conclusion: military rule or state-managed democracy

I have argued recently (Cammack, 1998), from which the following paragraphs are adapted, that the main characteristic of the environment of globalization is the pressure on all states in the global system to restructure their economies and societies in order to survive in a competitive global capitalist economy in which production and exchange is increasingly organized along liberal lines. This has far-reaching consequences for the relationship between capitalism and liberal democracy. In the recent past its ideal-typical form (never remotely realized outside a few core capitalist states) combined management of both economic development and social provision by the state with a political system arising out of civil society and remaining largely autonomous (a liberal polity, in other words, in a socioeconomic framework managed by the state). In a future structured by globalization, the ideal-typical pattern will be the reverse: an economic and social system shaped by liberal economic forces operating at a global level which states have limited capacity to resist, and a political system managed by the state in order to mitigate the consequences of global economic liberalism (a liberal economy, in other words, in a political framework managed by the state). States will take a more direct role in the management of their citizens, in order to compensate for their decreasing inability to manage the broader social and political environment. If the new democracies around the world survive in such circumstances, they are likely to take the form of 'less-than-liberal' democracies – characterized by the predominance of the executive, pervasive official clientelism, and the consequent domination of electoral politics by 'parties of the state'. They will be 'partial democracies' rather than 'liberal democracies' – distinct from monolithic totalitarian or authoritarian regimes, but characterized by somewhat *limited* government accountability, relatively *unfree and unfair* competitive elections, partially *curtailed* rights to freedom of expression, and more or less *compromised* forms of associational autonomy (Potter, 1997: 5). And if such regimes do proliferate, the outcome is likely to be that changes of government will be relatively infrequent, and will lead to the recreation of regimes heavily biased in favor of incumbents, rather than to their replacement by more participatory and representative systems.

In this context, an institutional capacity to bias political competition in favor of incumbent governments through various forms of executive predominance and state or official clientelism is an effective weapon where elites committed to installing and consolidating competitive market economies face populations unwilling to accept the short-term disruption and the long-term costs. Practices which are portrayed as subverting liberal democratic institutions, and which are fairly prevalent in much of Latin America, represent highly efficient mechanisms through which to reconcile the demand for participation through competitive regimes on the one hand with the disciplines and imperatives of global capitalist competition on the other.

Again, in this context, there is considerable interest in O'Donnell's argument that many new democracies are electoral rather than liberal, and *informally* institutionalized on lines that are simply different to those characteristic of liberal democracy in the West (O'Donnell, 1996). Electoral democracies, according to Diamond (1996: 21–2), may ignore

> the degree to which multi-party elections, even if genuinely competitive, may effectively deny significant sections of the population the opportunity to contest for power or advance and defend their interests, or may leave significant arenas of decision-making power beyond the reach or control of elected officials.

O'Donnell contends, however, that such democracies 'have two extremely important institutions. One is highly formalized, but intermittent: elections. The other is informal, permanent, and pervasive: particularism (or clientelism, broadly defined).' By clientelism and particularism, he means 'various sorts of nonuniversalistic relationships, ranging from hierarchical particularistic exchanges, patronage, nepotism, and favours to actions that, under the formal rules of the institutional package of polyarchy, would be considered corrupt' (O'Donnell, 1996: 35, 40). The form they take is all too often that of 'delegative democracy,' characterized by 'a caesaristic, plebiscitarian executive that once elected sees itself as empowered to govern the country as it sees fit', and other state institutions – congress, the judiciary, and other agencies of control – condemned to a marginal role which prompts the intensification of particularism and corruption (*ibid.*: 44).

If a global market economy does not run smoothly, but is subject to frequent crises of adjustment at both global and national levels, and if, in such circumstances, its ability to run at all smoothly is maximized if states have the capacity to impose the social and economic costs on their own citizens, this may be an 'ideal' form of government for states in a globalized capitalist economy. In a globalizing world in which states are losing control of some of the traditional levers of policy-making, and are less able than they once were to secure popular approval by policy outcomes, those able to bolster their domestic support through electoral and clientelist regimes will enjoy a comparative advantage over states lacking this capacity. In these circumstances, executive predominance, state-orchestrated clientelism and 'parties of the state' are positive assets.

In a future of global capitalist competition under neoliberal principles, then, 'state-managed' democracies will enjoy an advantage over 'liberal' democracies. They will be characterized by the infrequency of opposition victories, the successive incorporation of opposition groups into the regime, and the tendency to bring about changes of chief executive by internally managed succession. Where a clear change of government does take place, it may well be brought about by a negotiated transition in which the combination of the second and third of these means is followed by an election which ratifies the new government in power. And where a ruling system breaks down and is replaced by a genuine opposition, it is likely that the opposition will take over and reconstruct the systems of executive predominance and official clientelism, creating a new 'party of the state' to maintain its hold on power. In such a polity, civilian executives might occasionally have recourse to overt military support, but this would be a worst-case resort, indicative of a breakdown of the means at the disposal of the state to ensure its political ascendancy over a society disciplined by the imperatives of neoliberal capitalism.

References

Alves, M.H.M. (1984) *Estado e Oposição no Brasil, 1964–1984* (Petrópolis: Vozes).

Amsden, A. (1989) *Asia's Next Giant: South Korea and Late Industrialization* (New York: Oxford University Press).

Andrade, R. de Castro (1977) 'Brazil: The Military in Politics', *Bulletin of the Society for Latin American Studies*, vol. 26: 63–82.

Annino, A. (1995) 'Some Reflections on Spanish American Constitutional and Political History', *Itinerario, European Journal of Overseas History*, vol. 19(3): 26–47.

Arceneaux, C.L. (1997) 'Institutional Design, Military Rule and Regime Transition in Argentina (1976–1983): An Extension of the Remmer Thesis', *Bulletin of Latin American Research*, vol. 16(3): 327–50.

Arquidiocese de São Paulo (1985) *Brasil: Nunca Mais* (Petrópolis: Vozes).

— (1986) *Torture in Brazil* (New York: Vintage Books).

Arendt, H. (1958) *The Human Condition* (Chicago: University of Chicago Press).

Arriagada, G. (1986) *El pensamiento político de los militares: Estudios sobre Chile, Argentina, Brasil y Uruguay* (Santiago: Editorial Aconcagua).

— (1988) *Pinochet: The Politics of Power* (Boston: Unwin Hyman).

— (1996) Speech before the Special session of the Senate, no. 47, on 9 April 1996. Official version – 332nd Legislature.

Aylwin, P. (1993) 'Consideraciones al proyecto de ley que modifica las Leyes Orgánicas Constitucionales de las Fuerzas Armadas y de Carabineros de Chile', Secretaría General de Gobierno, Santiago (26 April).

Barros, R.S.M. de (1959) *A ilustração brasileira e a idéia de universidade* (São Paulo: FFCL/USP).

Benn, S.I. and G.F. Gaus (1983) 'The Public and the Private: Concepts and Action', in S.I. Benn and G.F. Gaus (eds), *Public and Private in Social Life* (London: Croon Helm): 3–27.

Best, F. (1960) *Historia de las guerras argentinas: De la independencia, internacionales, civiles y con el indio*, 2 vols (Buenos Aires: Ediciones Peuser).

Bousquet, J.-P. (1984) [1980] *Las Locas de la Plaza de Mayo* (Córdoba: Fundación para la Democracia en Argentina).

Brown, B. (1987) 'Territoriality', in D. Stokes and I. Altman (eds), *Handbook of Environmental Psychology*, vol. 1 (New York: John Wiley): 505–31.

Camp, R. (1985) 'The Political Technocrat in Mexico and the Survival of the Political System', *Latin American Research Review*, vol. 20(1): 97–118.

— (1992) *Generals in the Palacio: The Military in Modern Mexico* (New York: Oxford University Press).

Cammack, P. (1985) 'The Political Economy of Contemporary Military Regimes in Latin America: From bureaucratic Authoritarianism to Restructuring', in P. O'Brien and P. Cammack (eds), *Generals in Retreat: The Crisis of Military Rule* (Manchester: Manchester University Press): 1–36.

——(1997) 'Dictatorship and Democracy in Latin America, 1930–1980', in D. Potter *et al.* (eds), *Democratization* (Cambridge: Polity/Open University Press): 152–73.

——(1998) 'Globalization and the Death of Liberal Democracy', *European Review*, vol. 6(2): 255–69.

——(1999) 'Mercosur: From Domestic Concerns to Regional Influence', in G. Hook and I. Kearns (eds), *Subregionalism and World Order* (London: Routledge): 95–115.

——(1999) 'Interpreting ASEM: Inter-Regionalism and the New Materialism', *Journal of Asia Pacific Economy*, vol. 4(1): 13–32.

Campbell, L.G. (1978) *The Military and Society in Colonial Peru, 1750–1810* (Philadelphia: American Philosophical Society).

Cardini, F. (1995) *Quella antica festa crudele: Guerra e cultura della guerra dal medioevo alla Rivoluzione francese* (Milan: A. Mondori).

Carvalho, J.M. de (1978) 'As Forças Armadas na Primeira República: O poder desestabilizador', *História Geral da Civilização Brasileira*, vol. 9: 180–234.

Castro, C. (1990) *O espírito militar: um estudo de antropologia social na Academia Militar das Agulhas Negras* (Rio de Janeiro: Jorge Zahar Editor).

——(1994) 'Inventando tradições no Exército brasileiro: José Pessoa e a reforma da Escola Militar', *Estudos Históricos*, vol. 14: 231–40.

——(1995) *Os militares e a República: Um estudo sobre cultura e ação política* (Rio de Janeiro: Jorge Zahar Editor).

——(1997a) 'O fim da juventude militar', in H. Vianna (ed.), *Galeras cariocas* (Rio de Janeiro: Ed. UFRJ): 161–80.

——(1997b) 'Os militares e a introdução da educação física no Brasil', *Antropolítica*, vol. 2: 61–78.

Caudill, W. and H. Weinstein (1972) 'Maternal Care and Infant Behavior in Japan and America', in C. Stendler Lavatelli and F. Stendler (eds), *Readings in Child Behavior and Development* (New York: Harcourt Brace Jovanovich): 78–87.

Centeno, M.A. (1993) 'The new Leviathan: The Dynamics and Limits of Technocracy', *Theory and Society*, vol. 22: 307–35.

——(1994) *Democracy within Reason: Technocratic Revolution in Mexico* (University Park: Pennsylvania University Press).

——and P. Silva (eds) (1998) *The Politics of Expertise in Latin America* (Basingstoke: Macmillan).

Charle, C. (1987) *Les élites de la République (1880–1900)* (Paris: Fayard).

Clark, L.L. (1984) *Social Darwinism in France* (Alabama: The University of Alabama Press).

Cohen Salama, M. (1992) *Tumbas Anónimas* (Buenos Aires: Catálogos).

Collier, D. (ed.) (1979) *The New Authoritarianism in Latin America* (Princeton: Princeton University Press).

CONADEP [Comisión Nacional sobre la Desaparición de Personas] (1986) *Nunca Más: The Report of the Argentine Commission on the Disappeared* (New York: Farrar, Straus, Giroux).

Concertación [Concertación de Partidos por la Democracia] (1993) *Un Gobierno para los Nuevos Tiempos: Bases programáticas para el Segundo Gobierno de la Concertación*. Santiago.

Correa, L. (1962) *El presidente Ibáñez, la política y los políticos: Apuntes para la historia* (Santiago: Editorial del Pacífico).

Correa, R. and E. Subercaseaux (1989) *Ego sum Pinochet* (Santiago: Zig-Zag).

Cowley, R. and G. Parker (eds) (1996) *Reader's Companion to Military History* (Boston: Houghton Mifflin).

Crowther, W. (1973) 'Technological Chance as Political Choice: The Civil Engineers and the Modernization of the Chilean State Railways', unpublished PhD thesis, University of California at Berkeley.

Csikszentmihalyi, M. and E. Rochberg-Halton (1981) *The Meaning of Things: Domestic Symbols and the Self* (Cambridge: Cambridge University Press).

Cunha, E. da (1966) *Obra completa* (Rio de Janeiro: Aguilar).

—(1984) *Euclides da Cunha*, Org. Walnice Nogueira Galvão, 2 vols (São Paulo: Ática).

DaMatta, R. (1987) *A Casa e a Rua: Espaço, Cidadania, Mulher e Morte no Brasil* (Rio de Janeiro: Editora Guanabara).

D'Araujo, M.C., G.A.D. Soares and C. Castro (eds) (1994a) *Visões do Golpe: A Memória Militar sobre 1964* (Rio de Janeiro: Relume Dumará).

—(eds) (1994b) *Os Anos de Chumbo: A Memória Militar sobre a Repressão* (Rio de Janeiro: Relume Dumará).

—(eds) (1995) *A Volta aos Quartéis: A Memória Militar sobre a Abertura* (Rio de Janeiro: Relume Dumará).

D'Araujo, M.C. and C. Castro (eds) (1997) *Ernesto Geisel* (Rio de Janeiro: Fundação Getúlio Vargas).

Deutsch, K. (1966) *Nationalism and Social Communication: An Inquiry into the Foundations of Nationality* (Cambridge, Mass.: Massachusetts Institute of Technology).

Devoti, F. (1885) *Considérations médicales sur le Rio de la Plata* (Paris: doctoral dissertation, University of Paris).

Diamond, L. (1996) 'Is the Third Wave Over?', *Journal of Democracy*, vol. 7(3): 20–37.

Domínguez, J. (1993) 'The Power, the Pirates, and "Civilized Conduct" in the American Mediterranean', Paper presented at a conference on 'Security and the Military in South America after the Cold War'), University of California, San Diego, June 1993.

Drake, P.W. (1989) *The Money Doctor in the Andes: The Kemmerer Missions, 1923–1933* (Durham: Duke University Press).

Drake, P. and I. Jalsić (eds) (1995) [1991] *The Struggle for Democracy in Chile* (Lincoln: Nebraska University Press).

Dreifuss, R. (1981) *1964, A conquista do estado: Ação política, poder e golpe de classe* (Petrópolis: Vozes).

Edwards, A. (1952) [1924] *La fronda aristocrática: Historia política de Chile* (Santiago: Editorial del Pacífico).

Encina, F. (1981) [1911] *Nuestra inferioridad económica* (Santiago: Editorial Universitaria).

Ensalaco, M. 'Military Prerogatives and the Stalemate of Chilean Civil–Military Relations', *Armed Forces and Society*, vol. 21(2): 255–70.

Erikson, E.H. (1951) *Childhood and Society* (London: Imago Publishing Co.).

Etchepareborda, R. (1984) *Historiografía militar argentina* (Buenos Aires: Círculo Militar).

Evans, P. (1995) *Embedded Autonomy: States and Industrial Transformation* (Princeton: Princeton University Press).

Fagen, P.W. (1992) 'Repression and State Security', in J.E. Corradi, P.W. Fagen and M.A. Garretón (eds), *In Fear at the Edge: State Terror and Resistance in Latin America* (Berkeley: University of California Press): 39–71.

Farias, O.C. de (1981) *Meio século de combate* (Rio de Janeiro: Nova Fronteira).

Feldman, A. (1991) *Formations of Violence: The Narrative of the Body and Political Terror in Northern Ireland* (Chicago: University of Chicago Press).

Fisher, J. (1989) *Mothers of the Disappeared* (Boston: South End Press).

Fitch, J.S. (1998) *The Armed Forces and Democracy in Latin America* (Baltimore: Johns Hopkins University Press).

Frei, E. (1995a) Message to the Senate, Project to Reform Law 18.948, Santiago, 22 August 1995.

—(1995b) Speech on National Reconciliation. Presidential Press Office, Santiago, 21 August 1995.

Freyre, G. (1974) *Ordem e progresso*, 3rd edn, 2 vols (Rio de Janeiro: J. Olympio).

Frieden, M. (1991) *Debt, Development and Democracy: Modern Political Economy and Latin America 1965–85* (Princeton: Princeton University Press).

Gárate Córdoba, J.M. (1986) 'Las ordenanzas de Carlos III: Estructura social de los ejércitos', in M.H. Sánchez-Barba and M.A. Baquer (eds), *Historia social de las fuerzas armadas españolas* (Madrid: Alhambra).

García, G. (1994) 'Una interpretación de las normas militares de la Constitución de 1980', *Fuerzas Armadas y Sociedad*, vol. 8(1): 45–55.

—and J.E. Montes (1994) *Subordinación democrática de los militares* (Santiago: CED).

García, P. (1995) *El Drama de la Autonomía Militar: Argentina Bajo las Juntas Militares* (Madrid: Alianza Editores).

Garretón, M.A. (1989) [1983] *Chilean Political Process* (Boulder: Westview).

—(1993) 'Las proyecciones del período 1982–1990', in P.W. Drake and I. Jaksić (eds), *El difícil camino hacia democracia en Chile 1982–1990* (Santiago: FLACSO. Preface to the Spanish edition of *The Struggle for Democracy in Chile*): 15–21.

Giddens, A. (1991) *Modernity and Self-Identity: Self and Society in the Late Modern Age* (Stanford: Stanford University Press).

Goltz, C. v.d. (1989) [1883] *Das Volk in Waffen* (Berlin: R. v. Decker's Verlag).

Góngora, M. (1988) [1981] *Ensayo histórico sobre la noción de Estado en Chile en los siglos XIX y XX* (Santiago: Editorial Universitaria).

Goodman, L.W., J.S.R. Mendelson, and J. Rial (1990) (eds) *The Military and Democracy: The Future of Civil–Military Relations in Latin America* (Massachusetts: Lexington Books).

Green, L. (1995) 'Living in a State of Fear', in C. Nordstrom and A.C.G.M. Robben (eds), *Fieldwork under Fire: Contemporary Studies of Violence and Survival* (Berkeley: University of California Press): 105–27.

Grindle, M.S. (1977) 'Power, Expertise, and the "Técnico": Suggestions from a Mexican Case Study', *Journal of Politics* (May), vol. 39: 402.

Guzman Bouvard, M. (1994) *Revolutionizing Motherhood: The Mothers of the Plaza de Mayo* (Wilmington: Scholarly Resources).

Gwynne, R.N. (1986) 'The Deindustrialization of Chile, 1974–1984', *Bulletin of Latin American Research*, vol. 5(1): 1–23.

Halperín Donghi, T. (1968) 'Revolutionary Militarisation in Buenos Aires 1806–1815', *Past & Present*, vol. 40: 86–107.

Hayes, R.A. (1989) *The Armed Nation: The Brazilian Corporate Mystique* (Temple: Center for Latin American Studies, Arizona State University).

Herrera, M. and E. Tenembaum (1990) *Identidad: Despojo y Restitución* (Buenos Aires: Editorial Contrapunto).

Hertz, R. (1960) *Death and The Right Hand* (Aberdeen: Cohen & West).

Holmes, R. (1986) *Firing Line* (Harmondsworth: Penguin).

Huntington, S.P. (1957) *The Soldier and the State* (Harvard, Mass.: Belknap Press).

— (1968) *Political Order in Changing Societies* (New Haven: Yale University Press).

Ibáñez Santa María, A. (1983) 'Los ingenieros, el Estado y la política en Chile: Del Ministerio de Fomento a la Corporación de Fomento, 1927–1939', *Historia*, vol. 18: 45–102.

Imaz, J.L. de (1964) *Los Que Mandan* (Buenos Aires: Editorial Universitaria de Buenos Aires).

Janowitz, M. (1960) *The Professional Soldier* (New York: Free Press).

Jara, A. (1971) *Guerra y sociedad en Chile: La transformación de la Guerra de Arauco y la esclavitud de los indios* (Santiago: Editorial Universitaria).

Johnson, J.J. (1964) *The Military and Society in Latin America* (Stanford: Stanford University Press).

Jorrín, M. and J.D. Martz (1970) *Latin-American Political Thought and Ideology* (Chapel Hill: The University of North Carolina Press).

Kaufman, R.R. (1979) 'Industrial Change and Authoritarian Rule in Latin America: A Concrete Review of the Bureaucratic-Authoritarian Model', in D. Collier (ed.), *The New Authoritarianism in Latin America* (Princeton: Princeton University Press): 165–253.

Keegan, J. (1976) *The Face of Battle* (New York: Viking Press).

— (1993) *A History of Warfare* (London: Hutchinson).

Koonings, K. (1991) 'La sociología de la intervención militar en la política latinoamericana', in D. Kruijt and E. Torres-Rivas (eds), *América Latina: Militares y Sociedad*, vol. 1 (San José: FLACSO): 19–61.

— (1996) 'Onder het zwaard van Damocles: militairen en politiek sinds 1930', in K. Koonings and D. Kruijt (eds), *Democratie en dictatuur in Latijns-Amerika* (Amsterdam: Thela): 59–77.

Kordon, D. and L.I. Edelman (1988) 'Observations on the Psychopathological Effects of Social Silencing Concerning the Existence of Missing People', in D. Kordon *et al.* (eds), *Psychological Effects of Political Repression* (Buenos Aires: Sudamericana/Planeta): 27–39.

Lamounier, B. (1989) '*Authoritarian Brazil Revisited: The Impact of Elections on the Abertura*', in A. Stepan (ed.), *Democratizing Brazil: Problems of Transition and Consolidation* (Oxford: Oxford University Press): 43–79.

Lecuna, V. (1960) *Crónica razonada de las guerras de Bolívar* 2nd edn, 3 vols (New York: The Colonial Books).

Marchena Fernández, J. (1983) *Oficiales y soldados en el ejército de América* (Sevilla: Escuela de Estudios Hispano-Americanos).

LeVine, R.A. (1988) 'Human Parental Care: Universal Goals, Cultural Strategies, Individual Behavior', in R.A. LeVine, P.M. Miller, and M. Maxwell West (eds), *Parental Behavior in Diverse Societies* (San Francisco: Jossey-Bass): 3–12.

—and S. Dixon *et al.* (1994) *Child Care and Culture: Lessons from Africa* (Cambridge: Cambridge University Press).

Lieuwen, E. (1961) *Arms and Politics in Latin America* (New York: Praeger).

—(1968) *Mexican Militarism: The Political Rise and Fall of the Mexican Army* (Albuquerque: University of New Mexico Press).

—(1984) 'Depoliticization of the Mexican Revolutionary Army', in D. Ronfeldt (ed.), *The Modern Mexican Army: A Reassessment* (La Jolla: Center for U.S.–Mexican Studies, University of California) 51–61.

Lind, W.S. (1992) 'Tailhook: The Larger Issue', *Marine Corps Gazette* (November): 38.

Loveman, B. (1979) *Chile: The Legacy of Spanish Capitalism* (New York: Oxford University Press).

—(1993) *The Constitution of Tyranny: Regimes of Exception, the Armed Forces, and Politics in Spanish America* (Pittsburgh: University of Pittsburgh Press).

—(1994) 'Protected Democracies and Military Guardianship: Political Transitions in Latin America, 1978–1993', *Journal of Interamerican Studies and World Affairs*, vol. 36(2): 105–90.

—and T.M. Davies (1989) '*The United States and Military Politics in Latin America*' in B. Loveman and T.M. Davies (eds), *The Politics of Antipolitics: The Military in Latin America* (Lincoln: University of Nebraska Press): 163–5.

—and T.M. Davies (eds) (1997) *The Politics of Antipolitics: The Military in Latin America*, 2nd edn (Wilmington, Del.: Scholarly Resources).

Maxwell, C.J. (1995) 'Coping with Bereavement through Activism: Real Grief, Imagined Death, and Pseudo-Mourning among Pro-Life Direct Activists', *Ethos*, vol. 23(4): 437–52.

Martins, L. (1986) 'The "Liberalization" of Authoritarian Rule in Brazil', in G. O'Donnell, P.C. Schmitter and L. Whitehead (eds) *Transitions from Authoritarian Rule: Latin America* (Baltimore: The Johns Hopkins University Press): 72–94.

Millet, R.L. and M. Gold-Biss (eds) (1996) *Beyond Praetorianism: The Latin American Military in Transition* (Coral Gables: North–South Center Press, University of Miami).

Mir, L. (1994) *A Revolução Impossível: A esquerda e a luta armada no Brasil* (São Paulo: Editora Best Seller).

Moisés, J.Á. and J.A. Guilhon Albuquerque (eds) (1989) *Dilemas da consoli-dação da democracia* (São Paulo: Paz e Terra).

Molina, S. (1972) *El proceso de cambio en Chile: La experiencia 1965–1970* (Santiago: Editorial Universitaria).

Montecuccoli (1735) *Mémoires de Montecuculi Generalissime des Troupes de l'Empereur ou principes de l'art militaire en général* (Strasbourg: J.R. Doulssecker le Pere).

Montero, R. (1938) *Ibáñez: Un hombre, un mandatario, 1926–1931.* (Santiago: Impresa Cóndor).

—(1952) *La verdad sobre Ibáñez* (Santiago: Zig-Zag).

Moore, B. (1967) *Social Origins of Dictatorship and Democracy: Lord and Peasant in the Modern World* (London: Allen Lane, Penguin).

—(1984) *Privacy: Studies in Social and Cultural History* (Armonk, NY: M.E. Sharpe).

Moulian, T. (1995) 'Chile: Las condiciones de la democracia', *Nueva Sociedad*, vol. 140: 4–10.

Mouzelis, N. (1986) *Politics in the Semi-Periphery: Early Parliamentarism and Late Industrialization in the Balkans and Latin America* (Basingstoke: Macmillan).

Navarro, M. (1989) 'The Personal Is Political: Las Madres de Plaza de Mayo', in S. Eckstein (ed.), *Power and Popular Protest: Latin American Social Movements* (Berkeley: University of California Press): 241–58.

Nosiglia, J.E. (1985) *Botín de Guerra* (Buenos Aires: Cooperativa Tierra Fertil).

Nun, J. (1967) 'The Middle Class Military Coup', in C. Véliz (ed.), *The Politics of Conformity in Latin America* (New York: Oxford University Press): 66–118.

Nunn, F.M. (1963) *Civil–Military Relations in Chile, 1891–1938* (Albuquerque: University of New Mexico Press).

—(1970a) 'Emil Körner and the Prussianization of the Chilean Army: Origins, Process and Consequences, 1885–1920', *Hispanic American Historical Review* (May): 300–22.

—(1970b) *Chilean Politics, 1920–1931: The Honorable Mission of the Armed Forces* (Albuquerque: University of New Mexico Press).

—(1972) 'Military Professionalism and Professional Militarism in Brazil, 1870–1970: Historical Perspectives and Political Implications', *Journal of Latin American Studies* (May): 29–54.

—(1975a) 'The Origins and Nature of Professional Militarism in Argentina, Brazil, Chile, and Peru, 1890–1940', *Military Affairs* (February): 1–7.

—(1975b) 'New Thoughts on Military Intervention in Latin American Politics: The Chilean Case, 1973', *Journal of Latin American Studies* (November): 271–304.

—(1976) *The Military in Chilean History: Essays on Civil–Military Relations, 1810–1973* (Albuquerque: University of Mexico Press).

—(1979a) 'Professional Militarism in Twentieth-Century Peru: Historical and Theoretical Background to the *Golpe de Estado* of 1968', *Hispanic American Historical Review* (August): 391–417.

Nunn, F.M. (1979b) 'Latin American Military Lore: An Introduction and a Case Study', *The Americas* (April): 429–71.

— (1983) *Yesterday's Soldiers: European Military Professionalism in South America, 1890–1940* (Lincoln: University of Nebraska Press).

— (1984) 'On the Role of the Military in Twentieth-Century Latin America: The Mexican Case', in D. Ronfeldt (ed.), *The Modern Mexican Army: A Reassessment* (La Jolla: Center for U.S.–Mexican Studies, University of California): 33–49.

— (1992) *The Time of the Generals: Latin American Professional Militarism in World Perspective* (Lincoln: University of Nebraska Press).

— (1994) '*Latino-americanidad* from *Encuentro* to Quincentennial: The "New Novel as Revisionist History"', *InterAmerican Review of Bibliography*, vol. 2: 219–35.

— (1995a) 'The South American Military and (Re)Democratization: Professional Thought and Self-Perception', *Journal of Interamerican Studies and World Affairs* (Summer): 1–56.

— (1995b) 'The Roles of Civilian Experts in the International Strategic Community and Military Professionalism in the New World Order', in E. Gilman and D.E. Harold (eds), *Democratic and Civil Control over Military Forces: Case Studies and Perspectives* (Rome: Nato Defense College monograph series no. 3): 143–56.

— (1997) 'Latin American Military–Civilian Relations Before and After the Cold War: Some Thoughts, Questions, and Hypotheses', *UNISA Latin American Report*, vol. 13(1): 1–15 (South Africa).

O'Brien, P. (1981) 'The New Leviathan: The Chicago Boys and the Chilean Regime 1973–1980', *IDS Bulletin*, vol. 13(1): 38–50.

O'Donnell, G. (1973) *Modernization and Bureaucratic-Authoritarianism: Studies in South American Politics* (Berkeley: Center for International Studies, University of California).

— (1981) 'Las fuerzas armadas y el Estado autoritario del Cono Sur de América Latina', in N. Lechner (ed.), *Estado y política en América Latina* (Mexico City: Siglo XXI): 199–235.

— (1996) 'Illusions about Consolidation', *Journal of Democracy*, vol. 7(2): 34–51.

—, P. Schmitter and L. Whitehead (eds) (1986) *Transitions from Authoritarian Rule* (Baltimore: The Johns Hopkins University Press).

Oria, P.P. (1987) *De la Casa a la Plaza* (Buenos Aires: Editorial Nueva América).

Ouweneel, A. (1995–96) 'The Germination of Politics within the *Directorio* of the Institute of Chilean Engineers, 1910–1927', *Historia*, vol. 29: 357–90.

Paul, H.W. (1985) *From Knowledge to Power* (Cambridge: Cambridge University Press).

Pérez Yoma, E. (1994) 'Planteamientos programáticos del gobierno en el área de la Defensa Nacional', in *Política y Estrategia*, vol. 63 (May–August): 7–14 (Santiago).

— (1996) 'Una visión militar y civil: La defensa nacional no es materia sólo de las fuerzas armadas', in *El Mercurio*, Santiago, 24 March 1996. Speech given on the occasion of the inauguration of the academic year at the Armed Forces' War Academy.

Peristiany, J.G. (ed.) (1965) *Honor and Shame: The Values of Mediterranean Society* (London: Weidenfeld & Nicolson).

Piaget, J. (1971) *La construction du réel chez l'enfant* (Neuchatel: Delachaux et Niestlé).

Pieri, P. (1963) 'Sur les dimensions de l'histoire militaire', *Annales Économies, Sociétés Civilisations*, vol. 18(4): 625-38.

Pinto, A. (1985) 'Estado y gran empresa: de la precrisis hasta el gobierno de Jorge Alessandri', *Colección Estudios Cieplan*, vol. 16: 5–40.

Politzer, P. (1989) [1985] *Fear in Chile: Lives under Pinochet* (New York: Pantheon).

Potash, R.A. (1996) *The Army and Politics in Argentina 1962–73. From Frondizi's Fall to the Peronist Restoration* (Stanford: University of Stanford).

Potter, D. (1997) 'Explaining Democratization', in D. Potter *et al.* (eds), *Democratization* (Cambridge: Polity Press/Open University): 1–40.

Puryear, J.M. (1994) *Thinking Politics: Intellectuals and Democracy in Chile, 1973–1988* (Baltimore: The Johns Hopkins University Press).

Putnam, R.D. (1977) 'Elite Transformation in Advanced Industrial Societies: An Empirical Assessment of the Theory of Technocracy', *Comparative Political Studies*, vol. 10(3): 383–412.

Quartim de Moraes, J. (1991) *A Esquerda Militar no Brasil*, vol. 1, *da conspiração republicana à guerilla dos tenentes* (São Paulo: Siciliano).

Ralston, D.B. (1990) *Importing the European Army* (Chicago: The University of Chicago Press).

Reis, F.W. and G. O'Donnell (eds) (1988) *A democracia no Brasil: dilemas e perspectivas* (São Paulo: Vertice).

Remmer, K. (1991) *Military Rule in Latin America* (Boulder: Westview Press).

Rial, J. (1990) 'The Armed Forces and the Question of Democracy in Latin America', in L.W. Goodman, J.S.R. Mendelson and J. Rial (eds), *The Military and Democracy: The Future of Civil–Military Relations in Latin America* (Lexington, Mass.: Lexington Books): 3–21.

Rizzo de Oliveira, E. (1987) 'O aparelho militar: papel tutelar na Nova República', in J. Quartim de Moraes, W.P. Costa and E. Rizzo de Oliveira, *A Tutela Militar* (São Paulo: Vertice): 54–81.

Robben, A.C.G.M. (1989a) *Sons of the Sea Goddess: Economic Practice and Discursive Conflict in Brazil* (New York: Columbia University Press).

— (1989b) 'Habits of the Home: Spatial Hegemony and the Structuration of House and Society in Brazil', *American Anthropologist*, vol. 91(3): 570–88.

Rouquié, A. (1989) *The Military and the State in Latin America* (Berkeley: University of California Press).

Rueschemeyer, D. *et al.* (1992) *Capitalist Development and Democracy* (Cambridge: Polity Press).

Ruiz-Esquide, A. (1993) 'Las fuerzas armadas durante los gobiernos de Eduardo Frei y Salvador Allende', *Cuadernos del CED*, no. 22 (Santiago: CED).

Sánchez, M. (1985) *Histórias de Vida: Hebe de Bonafini* (Buenos Aires: Fraterna/Del Nuevo Extremo).

San Martino de Dromi, M.L. (1988) *Historia política argentina (1955–1988)* (Buenos Aires: Editorial Astrea de Alfredo y Ricardo Depalma).

Schirmer, J. (1988) '"Those Who Die for Life Cannot Be Called Dead": Women and Human Rights Protest in Latin America', *Harvard Human Rights Yearbook*, vol. 1: 41–76.

—(1994) 'The Claiming of Space and the Body Politic within National-Security States: The Plaza de Mayo Madres and the Greenham Common Women', in J. Boyarin (ed.), *Remapping Memory: The Politics of Timespace* (Minneapolis: University of Minnesota Press): 185–220.

Schneider, B.R. (1998) 'The Material Bases of Technocracy: Investor Confidence and Neoliberalism in Latin America', in M.A. Centeno and P. Silva (eds), *The Politics of Expertise in Latin America* (Basingstoke: Macmillan): 77–95.

Silva, P. (1991) 'Technocrats and Politics in Chile: From The Chicago Boys to the CIEPLAN Monks', *Journal of Latin American Studies*, vol. 23(2): 385–410.

—(1994) 'State, Public Technocracy and Politics in Chile, 1927–1941', *Bulletin of Latin American Research*, vol. 13(3): 281–97.

—(1997) 'Neoliberalismo, democratización y ascenso tecnocrático', in M. Vellinga (ed.), *El cambio del papel del Estado en América Latina* (Mexico City: Siglo Veintiuno Editores): 103–28.

—(1998) 'Pablo Ramírez, A Technocrat Avant-La-Lettre', in M.A. Centeno and P. Silva (eds), *The Politics of Expertise in Latin America* (Basingstoke: Macmillan): 52–76.

—(1999) 'Collective Memories, Fears and Consensus: The Political Psychology of the Chilean Democratic Transition' in K. Koonings and D. Kruijt (eds), *Societies of Fear: The Legacy of Civil War, Violence and Terror in Latin America* (London: Zed Books): 171–96.

Simpson, J. and J. Bennett (1985) *The Disappeared and the Mothers of the Plaza: The Story of the 11,000 Argentinians Who Vanished* (New York: St Martin's Press).

Skidmore, T.E. (1989) 'Brazil's Slow Road to Democratization: 1974–1985', in A. Stepan (ed.), *Democratizing Brazil: Problems of Transition and Consolidation* (New York: Oxford University Press): 5–42.

Smith, P.H. (1979) *Labyrinths of Power: Political Recruitment in Twentieth-Century Mexico* (Princeton: Princeton University Press).

Smith, W.C. (1987) 'The Political Transition in Brazil: From Authoritarian Liberalization and Elite Conciliation to Democratization', in E. Baloyra (ed.), *Comparing New Democracies: Transition and Consolidation in Mediterranean Europe and the Southern Cone* (Boulder: Westview): 170–240.

Sodré, L. (1896) *Palavras e atos*. Belém.

Stallings, B. (1992) 'International Influence on Economic Policy: Debt, Stabilization, and Structural Reform', in S.S. Haggard and R.R. Kaufman (eds), *The Politics of Economic Adjustment* (Princeton: Princeton University Press): 41–88.

Stepan, A. (1971) *The Military in Politics: Changing Patterns in Brazil* (Princeton: Princeton University Press).

—(1976) 'The New Professionalism of Internal Warfare and Military Role Expansion', in A.F. Lowenthal (ed.), *Armies and Politics in Latin America* (New York and London: Holmes & Meier): 244–60.

—(1988) *Rethinking Military Politics: Brazil and the Southern Cone* (Princeton: Princeton University Press).

Stepan, A. (1989) *Democratizing Brazil: Problems of Transition and Consolidation* (New York: Oxford University Press).

Suárez, S.G. (1984) *Las milicias: Instituciones militares hispanoamericanas* (Caracas: Biblioteca de la Academia Nacional de la Historia).

Suárez-Orozco, M. (1987) 'The Treatment of Children in the "Dirty War": Ideology, State Terrorism and the Abuse of Children in Argentina', in N. Scheper-Hughes (ed.), *Child Survival: Anthropological Perspectives on the Treatment and Maltreatment of Children* (Dordrecht, The Netherlands: D. Reidel Publishing Company): 227–56.

Taylor, R.B. and S. Brower (1985) 'Home and Near-Home Territories', in I. Altman and C.M. Werner (eds), *Human Behavior and Environment, Advances in Theory and Research*, vol. 8, *Home Environments* (New York: Plenum Press): 183–212.

Timerman, J. (1981) *Prisoner Without a Name, Cell Without a Number* (New York: Alfred A. Knopf).

Urzúa, G. and A. García (1971) *Diagnóstico de la Burocracia Chilena (1818–1969)* (Santiago: Editorial Jurídica de Chile).

Valenzuela, A. (1995) [1991] 'The Military in Power: The Consolidation of One-Man Rule', in P. Drake and I. Jalsić (eds), *The Struggle for Democracy in Chile* (Lincoln: Nebraska University Press): 21–72.

Van Gennep, A. (1960) *The Rites of Passage* (Chicago: University of Chicago Press).

Vanhanen, T. (1997) *Prospects for Democracy: A Study of 172 Countries* (London: Routledge).

Varas, A. (1987) *Los militares en el poder: Régimen y gobierno militar en Chile, 1973–1986* (Santiago: Pehuén/Flacso).

— (ed.) (1988) *La autonomía militar en América Latina* (Caracas: Editorial Nueva Sociedad).

— and C. Fuentes (1994) *Defensa Nacional: Chile 1990–1994* (Santiago: FLACSO).

Valdés, J.G. (1995) *Pinochet's Economists: The Chicago School in Chile* (Cambridge: Cambridge University Press).

Velasco e Cruz, S.C. and C.E. Martins (1984) 'De Castello a Figueiredo: uma incursão na pré-história da "abertura"', in B. Sorj and M.H. Tavares de Almeida (eds), *Sociedade e Política no Brasil pós-1964* (São Paulo: Brasiliense): 13–61.

Verbitsky, H. (1995) *El Vuelo* (Buenos Aires: Planeta).

Vergara, P. (1985) *Auge y caída del neoliberalismo en Chile* (Santiago: FLACSO).

Wade, R. (1990) *Governing the Market: Economic Theory and the Role of Government in East Asia* (Princeton: Princeton University Press).

Weiss, R.S. (1993) 'Loss and Recovery', in M.S. Stroebe, W. Stroebe and R.O. Hansson (eds), *Handbook of Bereavement: Theory, Research, and Intervention* (Cambridge: Cambridge University Press): 271–84.

Wiarda, H. (1990) *The Democratic Revolution in Latin America: History, Politics, and U.S. Policy* (New York: Holmes & Meier).

Zea, L. (1976) [1965] *El pensamiento latinoamericano* (Mexico City: Editorial Ariel Seix Barral).

Index